GPS For Dummies

W9-BMG-287

Cheat Sheet

Recommended GPS Receiver Features

Activity	Useful Features
Hiking, mountain biking, cross country skiing	Altimeter/barometer
	Electronic compass
	Sunrise/sunset table
	Uploadable topographic maps
Geocaching	Electronic compass
	Uploadable topographic maps
Hunting	Hunting and fishing calendar
	Sunrise/sunset table
	Uploadable topographic maps
Fishing	Fishing calendar
	Floats
	Saltwater tide table
	Sunrise/sunset table
	Waterproof
Boating (inland & offshore)	External power supply
	Floats
	NMEA output (for autopilots)
	Saltwater tide table
	Sunrise/sunset table
	Uploadable nautical charts
	Waterproof
Canoeing, kayaking (inland & coastal)	Floats
	Saltwater tide table
	Sunrise/sunset table
	Uploadable nautical and topographic maps
	Waterproof
4x4ing, motorcycling, ATVing	Electronic compass
	External power supply
	Uploadable topographic maps
Flying	External power supply
	Jeppesen database
	WAAS
Mapping, data collection	Area calculation
	Differential GPS
	External antenna
	Helix versus patch antenna
	Large number of waypoints and tracks
	WAAS
Caving, scuba diving, visiting art museums	Sorry, you're out of luck! You need a clear view of the sky for a GPS receiver to work.

GPS For Dummies®

Cheat Sheet

GPS Accuracy

GPS Mode	Distance in Feet	Distance in Meters
GPS without SA	49	15
GPS with DGPS	10 to 16	3 to 5
GPS with WAAS	10	3

Popular PDA Mapping Programs

Program	Pocket PC	Palm	Web site
DeLorme Street Atlas USA Handheld	X	X	www.delorme.com
Destinator	X		www.destinator1.com
Intellinav	X		www.intellinav.com
Mapopolis Navigator	X	X	www.mapopolis.com
Microsoft Pocket Streets	X		www.microsoft.com
Quo Vadis		X	www.marcosoft.com
TeleType	X		www.teletype.com
TomTom Navigator	X		www.tomtom.com

For Dummies: Bestselling Book Series for Beginners

GPS

FOR

DUMMIES®

GPS FOR DUMMIES®

by Joel McNamara

WILEY

Wiley Publishing, Inc.

GPS For Dummies®

Published by
Wiley Publishing, Inc.
111 River Street
Hoboken, NJ 07030-5774

Copyright © 2004 by Wiley Publishing, Inc., Indianapolis, Indiana

Published by Wiley Publishing, Inc., Indianapolis, Indiana

Published simultaneously in Canada

For general information on our other products and services or to obtain technical support, please contact our Customer Care Department within the U.S. at 800-762-2974, outside the U.S. at 317-572-3993, or fax 317-572-4002.

Wiley also publishes its books in a variety of electronic formats. Some content that appears in print may not be available in electronic books.

Library of Congress Control Number: 2004102594

ISBN: 0-7645-6933-3

Manufactured in the United States of America

10 9 8 7 6 5 4

1B/SV/QY/QU/IN

WILEY

About the Author

Joel McNamara first got involved with digital maps in the early 1980's. At the time he was studying archeology and instead of going out and playing Indiana Jones, he found himself in front of a computer monitor trying to predict where archeological sites were located based on LANDSAT satellite data.

The lure of computers ultimately led to his defection from academia to the software industry, where he worked as a programmer, technical writer, and manager; eventually ending up at a rather large software company based in Redmond, Washington. Joel now writes and consults on technology he finds interesting, such as GPS and digital maps.

Over the years he's had practical experience using GPS and maps for wild-land firefighting, search and rescue, and disaster response and planning. He's also an avid user of the great outdoors (which means there's way too much gear in his garage), competes in adventure races and other endurance sports, and so far has always found his way back home. In his spare time he volunteers for a federal Disaster Medical Assistance Team.

This is his second book. The first was *Secrets of Computer Espionage: Tactics & Countermeasures* (also published by Wiley), a reference guide for computer security practitioners and anyone interested in stopping sneaky spies.

Author's Acknowledgments

First off, thanks to my wife, Darcy, for her support during my work on this book, especially for putting up with all of the maps, CD-ROMs, cables, manuals, and GPS receivers scattered all over the house during the duration.

Next on the list are the folks at Wiley, including Katie Feltman, my acquisitions editor and Pat O'Brien, my project editor. And a special note of appreciation to GPS and map guru Gavin Hoban, who diligently served as my technical editor.

I'd also like to thank the following manufacturers for supplying review copies of their products to write about: DeLorme (Caleb Mason), Endless Pursuit (Jack Robson), Lowrance (Steve Wegrzyn and Luke Morris), Magellan (Angela Linsey-Jackson), Maptech (Martin Fox), Microsoft, National Geographic, and TopoFusion (Scott Morris). I especially appreciate the help from the folks named in the parentheses who went above and beyond the call of duty in answering questions and providing assistance.

Finally, I'd like to express thanks to the following people for giving me feedback on various parts of the book: Bob Daley, Jan Daley, Cynthia Engel, Jeff Madden, Doug McNamara, and Judy McNamara.

Publisher's Acknowledgments

We're proud of this book; please send us your comments through our online registration form located at www.dummies.com/register/.

Some of the people who helped bring this book to market include the following:

Acquisitions, Editorial, and Media Development

Project Editor: Pat O'Brien

Acquisitions Editor: Katie Feltman

Senior Copy Editor: Teresa Artman

Technical Editor: Gavin Hoban

Editorial Manager: Kevin Kirschner

Media Development Manager: Laura VanWinkle

Media Development Supervisor: Richard Graves

Editorial Assistant: Amanda Foxworth

Cartoons: Rich Tennant (www.the5thwave.com)

Composition

Project Coordinator: Adrienne Martinez

Layout and Graphics: Amanda Carter, Andrea Dahl, Lauren Goddard, Lynsey Osborn, Heather Ryan

Proofreaders: Laura Albert, Brian H. Walls, TECHBOOKS Production Services

Indexer: TECHBOOKS Production Services

Publishing and Editorial for Technology Dummies

> **Richard Swadley,** Vice President and Executive Group Publisher

> **Andy Cummings,** Vice President and Publisher

> **Mary C. Corder,** Editorial Director

Publishing for Consumer Dummies

> **Diane Graves Steele,** Vice President and Publisher

> **Joyce Pepple,** Acquisitions Director

Composition Services

> **Gerry Fahey,** Vice President of Production Services

> **Debbie Stailey,** Director of Composition Services

Contents at a Glance

Table of Contents

Introduction

● ●

*A*s you may have guessed from the title, this book is about GPS (the satellite-based Global Positioning System) and maps; digital maps to be exact.

I remember back in 1989 when Magellan introduced the first handheld GPS receiver, the NAV 1000. (Don't worry. This isn't going to be one of those "I used to walk 20 miles to school in the snow when I was your age," stories.) The NAV 1000 was the size of a brick, and weighed a little less than two pounds. It was single channel receiver, could only track four satellites, and just supported latitude and longitude coordinates. It could save 100 way-points and you could have a single route with up to 10 waypoints. It cost $2,500.

Fast forward to the present. Now I can go down to my neighborhood sporting goods store and buy a GPS receiver smaller than a small cell phone. It weighs a couple of ounces, can track up to 12 satellites, and on a good day tells me exactly where I'm located to within about 10 feet; and in several different coordinate systems by the way. It supports 500 waypoints and 20 routes, with 125 waypoints apiece. Best of all it costs around $100.

Maps have followed the same evolutionary path. Paper maps have turned digital and now you can visit a Web site and print out a map with driving directions to just about anywhere for free. For under $100 you can buy map-ping software that has a collection of CD-ROMs with detailed topographic maps that fully cover any state in the United States. Aerial photographs are readily available over the Internet, and stunning three-dimensional maps can be created with a few mouse clicks. Once the exclusive domain of profes-sional cartographers and GIS (Geographic Information System) specialists, the average computer user can create and use digital maps with relative ease. There are a number of free and inexpensive programs that make *desktop mapping* a reality for the rest of us.

So, does all this mean we're entering the dawn of a new era where no matter where you are it's going to be hard to get lost? Well, yes and no.

Over the past several years, GPS receivers have become extremely popular and affordable. Lots of people who venture away from urban areas are carrying them. Cars come installed with GPS navigation systems for negotiating city streets and highways. Cell phones are even starting to show up with tiny GPS receivers embedded inside. And even if you don't have a GPS receiver you can always go out on the Web and print a map of where you want to go. But, there are a few hitches in this perfect, always found world:

- ✔ GPS receivers tend to boast so many features it's easy to get lost trying to figure them all out. Plus, most GPS receiver owners typically only use a small subset of the available features (and sometimes don't even know how to use these features well enough to avoid getting lost).

- ✔ GPS receivers have capabilities and limitations that many owners (or potential owners) really don't understand. This leads to frustration or not being able to use the devices to their full potential.

- ✔ While many people have a general knowledge of how to read a map, at least the simple road variety, most don't know how to really maximize using a map.

- ✔ And finally, the average computer user isn't aware of the wealth of easy-to-use, free or inexpensive mapping resources he or she could be using to stay found.

The purpose of this book is to help you better understand and use GPS receivers and open your eyes to the world of digital mapping. And hopefully put you on the path of always staying found or finding what you're looking for.

Who This Book Is For

If you're browsing through this book at your favorite bookstore right now, and are wondering whether this book is for you, ask yourself these questions:

- ✔ Are you considering purchasing a GPS receiver?
- ✔ Have you recently purchased a GPS receiver?
- ✔ Have you owned a GPS receiver for a while, but want to get more out of it?
- ✔ Are you interested in using digital maps for your profession or hobby?

If you answered yes to any of these questions, then stop reading and immediately proceed to the cash register, because this book will make your life easier (if you're still not convinced, feel free to continue flipping through the pages to see what I mean).

Getting a bit more specific, people in the following groups should find this book especially useful:

- *Recreation* – Hikers, hunters, fishers, mountain bikers, trail runners, cross country skiers, snowshoers, snowmobilers, ATV and 4 x 4 drivers, prospectors, pilots, paddlers, geocachers, and anyone else who ventures outdoors away from cities and streets (with or without a GPS receiver).

- *Commercial* – Land developers and real estate agents who are interested in the competitive advantage maps can bring them for planning or marketing purposes.

- *Government* – Emergency response agencies (search and rescue, fire, law enforcement, disaster relief) and urban planners who use maps as part of their planning and response activities.

- *Environmental* – Conservation agencies, organizations, consultants and scientists (biologists, botanists, and other *ists*) who use maps for resource management and research.

- *Technology* – Anyone who likes to play with cool technology.

You may have noticed I didn't mention people like surveyors or GIS professionals. If your job primarily focuses on GPS and/or maps, you'll probably discover a few things in the following pages, but just remember that this book is for the average computer user and GPS receiver owner who doesn't have your level of technical experience, proficiency, and skills. Please don't expect to find the nuts and bolts and details of using GIS software or precision surveying electronics.

Setting Some GPS Expectations

Before getting started, I'd like to set a few expectations about the content you'll be reading about that relates to GPS receivers, just so we're all on the same page:

- This book focuses on handheld, consumer GPS receivers typically used for land navigation. In addition to these types of GPS receivers there are larger and less portable consumer and commercial models that are used in airplanes, boats, and vehicles. There are also restricted-use GPS units used by the U.S. government and military, and expensive receivers used for surveying. While some of these GPS receivers are discussed briefly, don't expect to find out as much about them as about the portable, consumer models.

✔ While most GPS receivers have the same functionality, there are a lot of differences in manufacturer and model user interfaces. In a way it's like sitting someone down in front of three personal computers, one running Microsoft Windows XP, one running Linux (with the KDE or Gnome interface), and the other a Macintosh, and asking a computer novice volunteer to perform an identical set of tasks on each of the computers. Good luck! Because of this, you're not going to find detailed instructions on how to use specific GPS receiver models. What you will find is information on how to use most any GPS receiver, with some kindly suggestions tossed in when it's appropriate to consult your user's guide for details.

✔ Finally, don't expect me to tell you what's the best GPS receiver. Like any consumer electronics product, GPS receiver models are constantly changing and being updated. Instead of recommending that you buy a certain brand or model (that could possibly be replaced by something cheaper and better over the course of a few months), I'll tell you what questions to ask when selecting a GPS receiver and give you some hints on which features are best for different activities. You'll be able to apply these questions and selection criteria to pretty much any GPS receiver (no matter how much the marketplace changes), to pick the right model for you.

Take comfort in the fact that it's pretty hard to go wrong when you purchase a GPS receiver from one of the *Big Three* manufacturers (Garmin, Magellan, and Lowrance). All these companies make excellent products, and you can expect to get a number of years use out of them. (The good news is that GPS technology and product features haven't changed as rapidly as personal computers. I can go out and happily use a GPS receiver from 1998, whereas the same vintage personal computer would have been recycled a long time ago.)

How This Book Is Organized

This book is conveniently divided into several different parts. The content in each part tends to be related, but by all means, feel free to skip around and read about what interests you the most.

Part I: All About Digital Maps

This part of the book introduces you to digital maps; actually it presents some important universal concepts that apply to both paper and digital maps such as coordinate systems, datums, and how to read and use maps. The focus is primarily on land maps but there are a few brief mentions of nautical and aeronautical charts. In this part you'll find out about different types of digital maps that are available, especially the free ones you can get from the Internet and about some of the software you can use for digital mapping.

Part II: All About GPS

This is the part of the book devoted to demystifying GPS and GPS receivers. You'll find out about the technology behind GPS (including its capabilities and limitations), basic GPS concepts such as waypoints, routes, tracks, and coordinate systems, how to select and use a GPS receiver, how to use GPS with PDAs (like Pocket PCs and Palms), and all about the popular GPS sport of geocaching.

Part III: Digital Mapping on Your Computer

In this part we'll take some of the theoretical information on digital maps from Part I, and get practical. This section discusses computer requirements needed for basic digital mapping and reviews a number of different software packages you can use to work with aerial photos and topographic and road maps. Many of these programs support uploading and downloading data to and from GPS receivers, so we'll also spend some time talking about how to interface a GPS receiver to a personal computer.

Part IV: Using Web-Hosted Mapping Services

Even if you don't have a GPS receiver or mapping software installed on your computer, with an Internet connection and a Web browser you can still do a remarkable amount of digital mapping with free and subscription Web services. This section discusses how to access and use online street maps, topographic maps, aerial photos, and some slick U.S. government-produced maps. You'll also discover how to save and edit these Web-based maps.

Part V: The Part of Tens

All Dummies books have a part called The Part of Tens, and this one is no exception. In this section you'll find lists of what I consider the best GPS and digital map Web sites on the Internet, where to find free digital maps, tips and hints on printing maps, and if you're a competitive or recreational athlete, how to use a GPS receiver in your outdoor workouts.

Icons Used in This Book

Maps use symbols to quickly convey information, and this book does the same by using icons to help you navigate your way around. They include:

Just a gentle little reminder about something of importance, and because I can't be there to mention it in person and give you a friendly but stern look while wagging my finger, this icon will have to do.

I've tried to keep the real geeky, nerdy things to a bare minimum, but because this is a book about cool electronic gadgets and computer mapping, sometimes the technical stuff does creep in. I'll either give you a plain-English explanation or point you off to a Web site where you can get additional details.

This is good stuff designed to make your life easier; usually gained from practical experience and typically never found in manufacturer user guides and product documentation; or if it is there, it's buried in some obscure paragraph.

The little bomb icon looks like it should signify some pretty bad juju, but in reality it could represent something as minor as *potentially causes a hangnail.* The key here is to pay attention, because there might be something lurking that causes mental, physical, emotional, or monetary suffering of some degree. Who would have thought reading GPS and Maps for Dummies could be an extreme sport?

Some Opening Thoughts

Before you jump into the exciting world of GPS and digital maps, and I know you can't wait, there are a couple final things I'd like to mention:

✔ There are lots of references to Web sites in this book. Unfortunately Web sites change just about as fast as street maps in a city experiencing a lot of growth. If for some reason a link doesn't work, you should have enough information to find what you're looking for by using a search engine such as Google.

✔ You're not going to find every GPS and map software title in existence mentioned in the book. I've tried to list and describe many of the more popular programs, but the realities of page count constraints prevents this book from turning into an encyclopedia. So please don't get upset if I didn't mention a program you use or you feel slighted because I ended up talking about one program more than another.

✔ On some occasions while you're reading this book you're probably going to think I'm starting to sound like a broken record on one point I feel is very important. If you venture out away from civilization with your GPS receiver, please bring a compass and a paper map with you, and know how to use all of them. That means really knowing how to use them, not just kidding yourself that you do. From many years of doing search and rescue work and finding lost people, I've discovered the following truths:

- GPS receiver batteries die at the most inopportune time; especially when you didn't bring spare batteries with you.

- If a GPS receiver breaks or gets lost, it will be at the worst possible moment.

- GPS receivers are not *Star Trek* teleporters that will instantly transport you out of the wilderness and trouble (this is also true when it comes to cell phones).

✔ All the information in this book should set you on your way to becoming an expert with a GPS receiver and maps. That is, if you go out and practice! If you want to have guru status you need to be out there applying what you discover in this book. Even if you don't aspire to becoming one with GPS and a master of maps, in order to get the most use out of your navigation tools you need to become both comfortable and confident with them. Discover, experiment, and have fun!

Part I
All About Digital Maps

The 5th Wave   By Rich Tennant

"Of course your current GPS receiver downloads coordinates, prints maps, and has a built-in compass. But does it shoot silly string?"

In this part . . .

*W*hile digital maps are made up of bits and bytes, they share a number of things in common with their paper and ink cousins — like datums, coordinates systems, scales, legends, and compass roses. In fact if you get some of these concepts down, which hopefully you will after reading this part, you'll be at home with just about any map you encounter, whether it's displayed on your PC's monitor or laying on the front seat of your car.

Paper maps have a certain old school charm, but digital maps are infinitely cooler. That's because you can associate data with a digital map and make it interactive and smart. This part sets the stage for other chapters in the book. We're going to be talking about all sorts of PC, Web-based, and GPS maps, and it's important that you understand the basics of how digital maps work and what types of digital maps are out there; especially the free ones available on the Internet.

Chapter 1

Getting Started with Digital Maps

• •

• •

*T*his chapter introduces you to the fundamentals of digital maps. You find out what a digital map is, the differences between static and smart digital maps, and the different types of programs available for using digital maps.

What Is a Digital Map?

Any *map* is a picture of where things are, generally associated with our planet and its geographic or man-made features. Road maps, hiking maps, maps to Hollywood stars, and all sorts of other maps provide a sense of place and often help you get from one place to another.

Most maps are printed on paper. That's pretty convenient. They can be folded into a lightweight, compact bundle (if you've had a little practice). *Digital maps* (maps made on a computer or meant to be used with a computer) serve the same purpose as their paper cousins. It's just more difficult to fold a CD.

Digital mapmaking is a significant leap forward from traditional paper maps.

 ✔ **Maps can be made faster, cheaper, and more accurately.**

   This is important because of how quickly new roads, subdivisions, and development projects pop up in fast-growing urban areas. An old street map isn't much help in a new subdivision with a couple of hundred homes. The same problem affects political maps; an example is the change in national names and borders after the end of the Soviet Union.

 ✔ **Digital map data can be used with mapping software to make digital maps on your personal computer.**

Making maps

Cartography is the art and science of making maps. Until the 1960s, maps were made the time-honored, traditional way:

1. Draw an original map by hand, based on land survey measurements and other information.

2. Print as many copies as you need.

That changed with the advent of computers, satellite imagery, and Global Positioning System (GPS), which made making maps much easier. Most paper maps now are generated or produced on a computer.

Read on to discover the many types of digital maps.

Static map

A *static map* is the simplest form of digital map. Often it's a paper map that's been scanned and turned into a BMP (bitmap) or JPG (graphic) file. Aside from displaying it, printing it, and perhaps making a few edits, what you can do with the map is limited.

Static maps used to be the only type; often, a static map is all you need.

Smart map

Smart digital maps (as shown in Figure 1-1) may look like static maps, but data is associated with map locations. The data can be as basic as the latitude and longitude of a point, or as detailed about vegetation, soil type, and slope.

Spatial or *geospatial* data is associated with a place. The place can be smaller than a meter or as large as a country. Spatial data can be stored two ways:

 ✔ Embedded in a map graphic file

 ✔ Separate files with references to the locations

TIFF (Tagged Image File Format) is a popular format for storing graphics files. The *GeoTIFF* extension embeds geographic tags into map images. If you view a GeoTIFF file with a standard graphics program, it looks like an ordinary map. A program that uses the data tags can access the spatial data associated with each pixel in the image.

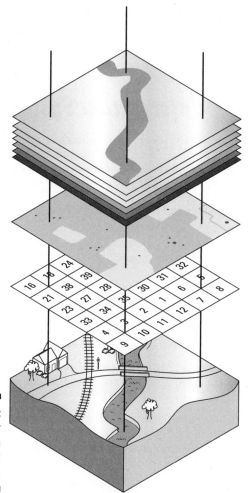

Figure 1-1:
A *smart map* has associated data.

Mapping Programs

Although many different kinds of mapping programs are available, you can classify map programs in two types: consumer programs and Geographic Information System (GIS) software. Here is a quick look at each type.

Consumer programs

A *consumer* mapping program is software that displays street maps, topographic maps, marine charts, or aeronautical charts. Such mapping programs are easier to use (and much less expensive) than their professional counterparts, meeting most computer users' mapping needs.

This book focuses on mapping programs available to consumers.

GIS (Geographic Information System)

A *Geographic Information System* (GIS) is an information system that analyzes, inputs, manipulates, outputs, retrieves, and stores spatial data. GIS is mostly used by governments; large corporations; and engineering and GIS consulting firms for land, natural resources, transportation, environmental, and urban planning and management.

Some people use the terms *digital map* and *GIS* interchangeably. This really isn't correct. GIS isn't just about making maps. GIS involves using computers and special software to help people make decisions by using spatial data.

Distinguishing between consumer mapping programs and GIS programs is important:

- ✔ **GIS software,** which is sold primarily to governments, corporations, and consulting firms, is flexible, powerful, and relatively expensive.

- ✔ **Consumer mapping programs** target the needs of average computer users. These programs are much more limited in scope and functionality — and a lot less expensive — than GIS programs.

  GIS software typically has a steep learning curve; you can earn advanced degrees in GIS. Consumer mapping programs can mostly be used right out of the box and can be mastered in a relatively short period of time.

A typical consumer mapping program is a road map program that costs about $30 and provides exact routing directions to get from one location to another. This isn't a static map because it has underlying data (such as street names, distances, and gas stations), which can lead you to think it's a GIS program. Not so. A true GIS program has built-in precision tools that can (for example) let you input data about traffic flow and vehicle speeds, and then display every street where traffic volume exceeds 500 cars per hour and vehicle speeds are .5 miles an hour over the speed limit. The price tag for such a GIS program would be at least $1,000, not to mention the costs of training people to use it and gathering all the traffic data to input into the system.

Of course, if you have a burning need for high-end precision and complexity, it's still possible to get into GIS on the cheap. A growing community is developing open source and free GIS programs. Although many of these programs lack the polish of a commercial product, they do get the job done. The http://opensourcegis.org and www.freegis.org Web sites are two excellent resources for finding out more about free GIS programs.

Using Digital Maps

There's an old song that goes, "Anything you can do, I can do better." If digital maps could sing that tune to their paper counterparts, they'd be right (for the most part). Digital mapping software offers all sorts of enhancements over paper maps, including these capabilities:

- ✔ Finding street addresses quickly
- ✔ Interfacing with GPS receivers to see where you are or where you were
- ✔ Showing driving directions to just about anywhere
- ✔ Displaying terrain three-dimensionally
- ✔ Annotating maps with pop-up information
- ✔ Creating custom maps
- ✔ Printing a hard copy map (which is sometimes the most important)

Digital maps do have a few drawbacks, including these:

- ✔ **You need a computer.**

  If you have a laptop or personal digital assistant (PDA), you can take mapping software on the road with you.

- ✔ **You need software.**

  This book helps you select and use software packages, particularly mapping programs in the free–$100 price range.

- ✔ **You have to spend time mastering the software.**

  Most mapping software is readily usable, but all programs have nuances that sometimes make their features and user interfaces a little tricky.

Mapping Software: The Essentials

The first step for digital mapping is to understand the available types of mapping programs and their capabilities and limitations; that's what this part of the book is all about.

After you know what software is available, you can match it to your needs. An invitation to a birthday party may consist only of displaying a screen capture of a street map on a Web site, editing and saving the map in Paint, and then e-mailing it to friends. A week-long backpacking expedition would require a *topographic* mapping program (showing land features) to plan your route, view elevation profiles, and upload location data to your GPS receiver.

Before you can select the right tool for the right job, you need a general handle on the options that you can include in your digital-mapping tool chest. This section of the book organizes mapping programs into three categories:

- ✔ Standalone programs
- ✔ Programs bundled with maps
- ✔ Web-hosted mapping services

Standalone programs

A *standalone program* is a program that can open and use digital maps. These programs typically don't come with map data, and you'll need to download or purchase the maps you're interested in using.

Like with a word processor or a spreadsheet, a mapping program needs someone to input data before it can be useful. In this case, the data is bits and bytes that describe how a map should be displayed. Fortunately, an amazing amount of map data is freely available on the Internet, most of it already collected by the government and in the public domain.

A big market exists for commercial map data. People buy data to use with their mapping programs because

- ✔ Free data may not be available for an area or a specific need.
- ✔ Commercial data may be enhanced with information unavailable in the free versions.
- ✔ Firing up a CD filled with data is more convenient than searching for free data and then downloading it.

Many standalone mapping programs aren't tied to one data type. (Chapter 2 shows which types of digital map data are commonly used.) Figure 1-2 shows a three-dimensional map of Mount St. Helens created with 3DEM from free U.S. Geological Survey (USGS) digital elevation map (DEM) data. (Mount St. Helens, an active volcano in Washington State, erupted in 1980.) The elevation map shows the crater and how the volcano blew out its side.

Map programs are viewers, editors, or both:

- ✔ **Viewers** show only maps.
- ✔ **Editors** can make changes.

   Usually you can't change a base map you've opened from a data file, but you can add text and draw shapes on top of the map.

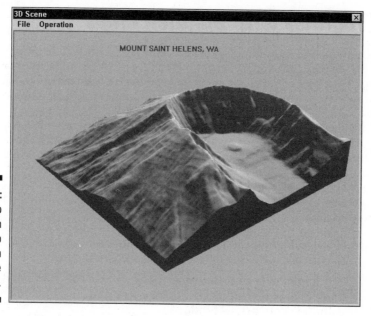

MOUNT SAINT HELENS, WA

Figure 1-2:
A 3-D map
created with
a free map
program
and free
map data.

Many standalone programs are either free or shareware. Two aspects of such programs are especially worth noting:

- Some manufacturers offer free (or cheap) limited-feature versions of their products that are otherwise available as pricy commercial software.
- Standalone mapping programs are mostly suited to a user who has intermediate to advanced computer skills and experience.

Examples of standalone mapping programs include OziExplorer (www. oziexplorer.com), USAPhotoMaps (http://jdmcox.com), and 3DEM (www.visualizationsoftware.com/3dem.html). Don't forget that you can also make maps with Paint or any other general-purpose graphics program. This book shows how to use these programs and others.

Some free, noncommercial mapping programs have advanced features that are normally more suited to professional users. Don't be intimidated by every feature and option. You can use some commands and features to make maps for your needs. And you can master those other features if you ever need to.

One big disadvantage to standalone mapping programs is that you need to search the Internet for the data you need, find and download it, and then open it with the map program. This process sometimes involves *registering* a map so that the coordinates all line up. Also, even with a high-speed Internet connection, downloading can still be a hassle. And after all that, you still have to find the map data for an area that you want to view, and then successfully load all that stuff into the mapping program.

Programs with bundled maps

Mapping companies bundle software with digital maps. The program comes with the map data and is distributed on CDs or DVDs; static or smart maps that have a lot of detail can be quite large in size. You install the mapping program, and you're immediately ready to start using the data on the CD.

Data files bundled with software are often in a proprietary file format, which can be read and used only with the software that comes with the product. The same usually holds true for maps that you can upload to a GPS receiver; only maps from the manufacturer can be used.

Sometimes you don't have much choice between using a standalone program or one bundled with maps.

 ✔ Topographic map data of the United States is widely available for free. You can use a number of free or shareware programs to view maps.

 ✔ Only outdated Census Bureau map data is available for United States streets and roads. Most free or shareware programs don't match the features in commercial products.

Software that comes with bundled maps has gotten incredibly cheap over the years. With discounts and rebates, you can often find road atlas software for around $20 that covers the entire United States. For a little under $100, you can buy programs that come with a full set of detailed digital topographic maps for an entire state. Considering that a single paper USGS 1:24,000 map costs around $7 — and there can easily be over a thousand maps per state — that's a pretty decent value. Figure 1-3 shows a map made by Terrain Navigator (`www.maptech.com/land/TerrainNavigator`), which is a topographic mapping program that comes bundled with map data.

Manufacturers that sell bundled map programs (particularly those with street and road data) usually come out with a new release of their product every year or so. In addition to enhancements in the software, the map data contains new roads and updated services information (such as gas stations, restaurants, and hotels, called *POIs*, or *Points of Interest*). Whether you buy an updated copy of the software every year depends on your circumstances. If you usually travel on major roads, or in areas that haven't experienced much development and growth, you probably don't need to update every year. On the other hand, road atlas software is fairly inexpensive, so if you travel a lot and rely on the program, it can be a cheap investment.

If you have beginning to intermediate computer skills and experience, you can come up to speed quickly with bundled map programs. The user interfaces are generally simpler than those found in feature-rich, standalone programs.

Examples of programs that come bundled with maps are DeLorme's Street Atlas USA (`www.delorme.com`), National Geographic's TOPO! (`http://`

`maps.nationalgeographic.com/topo`), and mapping software from GPS manufacturers that interfaces with their receivers. These programs and others like them are discussed in following chapters.

Figure 1-3:
A 1:100,000 scale topographic map displayed with Maptech's Terrain Navigator.

Web-hosted mapping services

A *Web-hosted mapping service* is a Web site that displays a map. You just need Internet access and a browser to view street maps, topographic maps, aerial maps, satellite imagery, and many other types of maps. This eliminates purchasing and installing specialized programs and map data on your hard drive, swapping CDs to access new map data, and mastering a new program. (Figure 1-4 is a detailed street map of downtown Port Townsend, Washington, using `www.mapquest.com`, a Web-hosted mapping service.)

If a map isn't displayed, check your browser's Java settings first. A number of Web-hosted mapping services, in particular the U.S. government sites that all share the same mapping engine, require Java and/or JavaScript enabled in your browser before maps can be correctly displayed.

Most Web-hosted mapping services are extremely easy to use. Anyone who can use an Internet browser should be navigating through maps in no time.

Examples of Web-hosted mapping services include MapQuest (`www.mapquest.com`), TerraServer-USA (`http://terraserver-usa.com`), and TopoZone (`www.topozone.com`). You discover how to use these mapping Web sites and others in other chapters of this book.

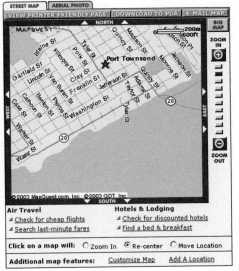

Figure 1-4:
A detailed street map, using a Web-hosted mapping service.

Although most of these free Web sites don't have all the features of a map program that you install on your hard drive, they offer a surprising amount of capability, especially considering their cost. (Some mapping sites on the Web charge for advanced services, such as color aerial photographs, larger map sizes, and enhanced searching.)

A few words on commercial GIS software

This book doesn't dwell overmuch on commercial GIS software packages. If your mapping needs get complex enough to require GIS (or you just want to find out more about these high-end mapping systems), check out the Web sites of the top three GIS companies:

✔ **ESRI:** Environmental Systems Research Institute is the largest GIS company in the marketplace. Its Arc products (such as ArcInfo and ArcView) are standards in the GIS field. For more information about ESRI, go to www.esri.com.

✔ **MapInfo:** MapInfo develops and sells a wide array of GIS products. For more information on the company and its products, see www.mapinfo.com.

✔ **Autodesk:** Autodesk is the developer of AutoCAD, a widely used computer-aided design program. Autodesk add-ons and standalone GIS programs are used throughout the world. You can find out about the Autodesk mapping applications at www.autodesk.com.

The GIS Lounge is a great Web resource that isn't tied to a specific manufacturer. This site provides information on all aspects of GIS, and has informative and educational content for novices to professionals. For more information, go to www.gislounge.com.

Chapter 2

Dissecting Maps

Maps are everywhere. They tell us how to get places we want to go and give us a better understanding of our surroundings.

Some people think that they can pick up a map and immediately start using it. If you don't have a lot of experience using different types of maps, that's a little like thinking just because you can read, you can sit down and understand a book that's written in French, German, or Spanish even if you've never had a foreign language class in your life. Yes, you may make a little sense of the book by picking out a few words you recognize or by looking at the pictures, but in the process, you're missing out on some important information.

Discovering the Types of Maps

Maps have their own language and a number of dialects depending on the type of map. To use paper or digital maps effectively, you need at least a tourist's understanding of their language. The more you know, the better off you are.

That's what this chapter is all about — different types of maps, basic map concepts and principles, and the various kinds of digital maps that you can access on a computer. By the end of the chapter, you'll have a handy enough grasp of conversational map-speak that you can ask the right questions to avoid getting lost.

Anatomy of a map

Most maps have elements in common. Here are some, along with the terms that *cartographers* (mapmakers) use to describe them:

Citation: This is information about data sources used in making the map and when the map was made.

Collar: This is the white space that surrounds the neatline (see the upcoming definition) and the mapped area.

Compass rose: A map has either a simple arrow that shows north or a full *compass rose* (an image that indicates all four directions) so the user can correctly orient the map to a compass.

Coordinates: Maps usually have either letters and numbers or coordinates (such as latitude and longitude values) marked along the borders so users can locate positions on the map.

Legend: This is a box that shows an explanation of symbols used on the map. Some maps show all the symbols; others rely on a separate symbol guide.

Mapped area: This is the main part of the map, displaying the geographic area.

Neatline: This is the line that surrounds the mapped area.

Scale: This distance-equivalence information (such as "one inch = one mile") helps you estimate distances on a map and is typically found at the bottom.

Title: This is usually the name of the map, but it also tells you which area it's mapping.

Begin by looking at the basic types of maps that you can use to navigate and better understand your surroundings. (Although there are maps for traveling under the ocean, visiting the moon, or zooming around in space, it's unlikely that you'll need these anytime soon.)

An important point to consider is that no one universal map type does it all. Different map types display the different features and details that are suited for a particular use — or user. A skilled map user always selects a map that meets his or her specific needs.

Maps are almost always oriented so the top of the map is facing north. If a map doesn't follow this convention, a good mapmaker places an arrow on the map that points north.

Land

Because we spend most of our time with our feet or tires on the ground, land maps are pretty important to know how to use. In general, the two types of land maps are topographic and planimetric.

Topographic maps

Topographic maps show natural land features such as lakes, rivers, and mountain peaks as well as man-made features such as roads, railroad tracks, and canals. These maps also have contour lines that trace the outline of the terrain and show elevation. *Contour lines* suggest what the land looks like in three dimensions.

A *contour interval* is the distance between contour lines. For example, if a contour interval is 20 feet, every time you go up one contour line, the elevation increases by 20 feet. Conversely, every time you go down a contour line, the elevation decreases by 20 feet. When the contour lines are close together, the terrain is steep. When they're spread apart, the terrain is closer to flat. Different maps have different contour intervals and the distance is usually noted in the map legend.

The most popular topographic maps for use within the U.S. are made by the United States Geological Survey (USGS). These maps cover different sizes of area; the smaller the area, the greater the detail. Topographic maps are often called *topo maps*. The topo maps that show the most detail are sometimes called *quad sheets* or *7.5 minute maps* because they map just one *quadrangle* (geographer-speak for rectangular shaped piece of land) that covers 7.5 minutes of longitude and latitude. Figure 2-1, for example, is a topographic map of The Dalles, Oregon.

A compass uses degrees to tell direction. North is 0 or 360 degrees, west is 90 degrees, south is 180 degrees, and east is 270 degrees.

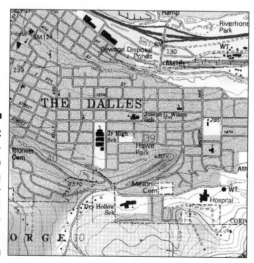

Figure 2-1: A topographic map showing contour lines and other features.

Most topographic maps show *magnetic declination.* Compass needles point to magnetic north, but most maps are oriented to true north. Because the earth's magnetic field varies from place to place, magnetic north usually isn't the same as true north; in the continental United States, the difference can be as much as 20 degrees. If you don't account for the magnetic declination, you can get far off-course trying to navigate someplace with a compass. The *declination* tells you how many degrees you need to adjust your compass: If the declination is west, you subtract the degrees from 360 to get true north; if it's east, you add the degrees.

Magnetic declination changes over time, and older USGS maps can have incorrect declination information printed on them. Using the wrong declination can cause all sorts of navigation problems, so check the current declination for your area at the following Web site: `www.ngdc.noaa.gov/cgi-bin/seg/gmag/declination1.pl`.

If your job or hobby takes you off the beaten path, you definitely need a topographic map. If you're staying in your car, driving on paved roads, you probably don't need a topographic map.

Planimetric maps

Planimetric maps don't provide much information about the terrain. Lakes, rivers, and mountain pass elevations may be shown, but there isn't any detailed land information. A classic example of a planimetric map is a state highway map or a road atlas. Planimetric maps are perfect in cities or on highways, but they're not suited for backcountry use. Figure 2-2 is a planimetric map of The Dalles, Oregon, area.

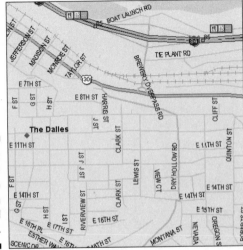

Figure 2-2:
A plani-
metric map
lacks terrain
features and
contours.

When using planimetric maps, you'll often encounter these terms:

✔ **Atlas:** An *atlas* is a collection of maps, usually in a book.

✔ **Gazetteer:** A *gazetteer* is a geographical dictionary or a book that gives the names and descriptions of places.

Marine

Marine charts are maps for inland, coastal, and deep-water navigation. Charts from the National Oceanic and Atmospheric Administration (NOAA) are commonly used for boating. They provide such important information as water depth, buoy locations, channel markers, and shipping lanes. See `www.noaa.gov/charts.html` for more on NOAA charts.

Marine charts aren't available for all bodies of water. If you're boating on a lake or a river, you'll probably use a topographic map for navigation.

This book focuses on land maps, so there isn't much detail about marine charts. Part of a marine chart of San Francisco Bay, California, is shown in Figure 2-3.

If you're more of a sailor than a landlubber, check out Marine Navigator at `www.maptech.com`. This commercial marine-navigation program displays NOAA charts, aerial photographs, 3-D ocean-bottom contours, and tide and current tables.

Figure 2-3:
A NOAA nautical chart, showing important features for mariners.

Aeronautical

Maps designed for aviation use are *charts* (a term that can also refer to their marine counterparts). These maps provide pilots with navigation information including topographic features, major roads, railroads, cities, airports, visual and radio aids to navigation, and other flight-related data.

You can find such aeronautical chart types as

- ✔ VFR (Visual Flight Rules)
- ✔ IFR (Instrument Flight Rules) Enroute
- ✔ Terminal Area Charts

You can find more about aeronautical charts by visiting the Federal Aviation Administration (FAA) National Aeronautical Charting Office (NACO) at www. naco.faa.gov.

Figure 2-4 shows a pilot's-eye view of the Seattle area.

FAA aviation charts aren't freely available for download. The FAA offers a monthly service that provides all charts and updates on DVDs for a year, but the cost is over $300. A number of companies such as Jeppesen (www.jeppesen.com) and Maptech (www.maptech.com) make commercial flight-planning software packages that include digital charts, or you can try the www.aeroplanner.com, a Web service that provides digital charts and other services to pilots. Another noncommercial source of FAA sectional charts is http://aviationtoolbox.org/raw_data/FAA_sectionals.

Figure 2-4:
A sectional aeronautical chart for the Seattle area.

Figuring Out Map Projections

Making a map is quite a bit more challenging than you may think. A cartographer's first challenge is taking something that's round like the earth (technically it's an ellipsoid that bulges in the middle and is flat at the top and bottom) and transforming it into something that's flat, like a map.

Cartographers use a *projection* to reproduce all or part of a round body on a flat sheet. This is impossible without some distortion, so a cartographer decides which characteristic (area, direction, distance, scale, or shape) is shown accurately and which will be distorted.

Although my high-school geography teacher may smack me on the head with a globe for saying this, the average map user doesn't need to know what kind of projection was used to make a map. There are some exceptions if you're a cartographer or surveyor, but usually you won't get in trouble if you don't know the projection. So don't panic if you can't immediately tell a Lambert conformal from a Mercator or Miller projection. Just keep in mind what a projection is and that there are different types of map projections.

Map Datums

A *map datum* is a mathematical model that describes the shape of an ellipsoid — in this case, the earth. Because the shape of the earth isn't uniform, over 100 datums for different parts of the earth are based on different measurements.

Some serious math is involved here for getting into the nuts and bolts of map datums. If you're the scholarly type, these Web sites provide lots of details on projections and datums:

✔ Datums and Projections: A Brief Guide

   `http://biology.usgs.gov/geotech/documents/datum.html`

✔ Peter Dana's excellent Geographer's Craft site

   `www.colorado.edu/geography/gcraft/notes/notes.html`

Datums all have names, but they aren't stuffy sounding. Datums often have exotic, Indiana Jones-style names such as the Kerguelen Island, Djakarta, Hu-Tzu-Shan, or Qornoq datums. (The United States uses such boring datums as NAD 27 and WGS 84.)

You only need to be concerned with datums under a few circumstances, such as these:

🖙 A location is plotted on two different maps.

🖙 A map and a Global Positioning System (GPS) receiver are being used.

🖙 Two different GPS receivers are being used.

In these instances, all the maps and GPS receivers must use the same datum. If the datums are different, the location ends up in two different physical places even though the map coordinates are exactly the same.

This is a common mistake: GPS receivers use the WGS 84 datum by default, and USGS topographic maps use the NAD 27 datum. If you mix the datums, your location can be off by up to 200 meters (roughly 200 yards, if you're metrically challenged).

Utilities can convert coordinates from one datum to another (some are described in Chapter 11) but it's easier just to get all the datums on the same map.

Working with Map Coordinate Systems

A *coordinate system* is a way to locate places on a map, usually some type of grid laid over the map. Grid systems are a whole lot easier to use and more accurate than "take the old dirt road by the oak tree for two miles, then turn left at the rusted tractor, and you'll be there when the road stops getting bumpy."

A simple coordinate system can consist of a vertical row of letters (A, B, C) on the left side of the map and a horizontal row of numbers (1, 2, 3) at the bottom of the map. If you want to tell someone where the town of Biggs Junction is (for example), you put your finger on the city and then move it in a straight line to the left until you hit the row of letters. Then put your finger on the city again, but this time move down until you reach the row of numbers. You now can say confidently that Biggs Junction is located at A12.

I call this the *Battleship Grid System* because it reminds me of the game where you call out coordinates to find your opponent's hidden aircraft carriers, submarines, and destroyers. "B-3. You sank my battleship!"

A grid may be printed on the map or provide *tick marks* (representing the grid boundaries) at the map's margins. Often maps have multiple coordinate systems so you can pick one that meets your needs or that you're comfortable using. For example, USGS topographic maps have latitude and longitude, Universal Transverse Mercator (UTM), and township and range marks.

Most coordinate systems are based on x and y; where *x* is a horizontal value, and *y* is a vertical value. A location's coordinates are expressed by drawing a straight line down to x and across to y. Mathematician René Descartes devised this system in the 1600s.

Letter-and-number coordinate systems are fine for highway maps, road atlases, and other simple maps where precise locations aren't needed. However, if you want to focus on a precise location on a map, you need a more sophisticated grid system. That's where coordinate systems such as latitude and longitude and UTM come in.

When you're figuring out a location's coordinates on a paper map, you have a fair amount of work to do, aligning the location with primary tick marks and then adding and subtracting to get the exact coordinate. With digital maps on a computer, that's usually just a matter of moving the cursor over a location and watching with relief as the coordinates automatically appear. If you're using a paper map, you can make life easier with free overlay grids and rulers from www.maptools.com. With these, you can print grids and rulers for different coordinate systems on clear transparency sheets.

Latitude/longitude

Latitude and longitude is the oldest map-coordinate system for plotting locations on the earth. The Roman scholar Ptolemy devised it almost 2,000 years ago. Ptolemy wrote about the difficulties of accurately representing the earth on a flat piece of paper and created latitude and longitude as a way of solving the problem. That's pretty impressive for a time way before computers and satellites.

Latitude and longitude are based on a little math, but they're not really complicated. Angles are measured in degrees, and they're used for measuring circles and spheres. Spheres can be divided into 360 degrees; because the earth is basically a sphere, it can also be measured in degrees. This is the basis of latitude and longitude, which use imaginary degree lines to divide the surface of the earth (see Figure 2-5).

The *equator* is an imaginary circle around the earth; the circles are an equal distance from the north and south poles and perpendicular to the earth's axis of rotation. The equator divides the earth into the *Northern Hemisphere* (everything north of the equator) and the *Southern Hemisphere* (everything south of the equator).

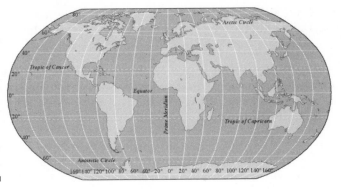

Figure 2-5:
Latitude and
longitude
are imag-
inary lines
that provide
a location
reference.

Latitude

Latitude is the angular distance measured north and south of the equator
(which represents 0 degrees of latitude).

- ✔ As you go north from the equator, the *north latitude* increases to 90
  degrees when you arrive at the North Pole.

- ✔ As you go south of the equator, the *south latitude* increases to 90 degrees
  at the South Pole.

In the Northern Hemisphere, the latitude is always given in *degrees north;* in
the southern hemisphere, it's given in *degrees south.*

Longitude

Longitude works the same way as latitude, but the angular distances are measured east and west of the prime meridian (which marks the 0-degrees longitude
line that passes through Greenwich, England, without even disturbing traffic).

- ✔ When you travel east from the prime meridian, the longitude increases
  to 180 degrees.

- ✔ As you go west from the prime meridian, longitude also increases to 180
  degrees. (The place where the two 180-degree longitudes meet is known
  as the *International Date Line.*)

- ✔ In the Eastern Hemisphere (which is east of the prime meridian to 180
  degrees east), the longitude is given in degrees east.

- ✔ In the Western Hemisphere (which is west of the prime meridian to 180
  degrees west), longitude is expressed in degrees west.

One degree is actually a pretty big unit of measure. One degree of latitude or
longitude is roughly equal to 70 miles.

Degrees are composed of smaller, fractional amounts that sound like you're
telling time.

✔ **Degree:** A *degree* comprises 60 minutes.

One *minute* is about 1.2 miles.

✔ **Minute:** A *minute* is composed of 60 seconds.

One *second* is around .02 miles.

These measurement units are abbreviated with the following symbols:

✔ **Degree:** °

✔ **Minute:** '

✔ **Second:** "

If you use minutes and seconds in conjunction with degrees, you can describe a very accurate location.

These distances are measured at the equator. At higher latitudes, the distance between longitude units decreases. The distance between latitude degrees is the same everywhere.

If you are using latitude and longitude to locate Dillon Falls on a map of the Deschutes River in Oregon, its coordinates are

43° 57' 29.79" N 121° 24' 34.73" W

Too much latitude

Latitude and longitude are pretty straightforward and logical if you think about it. Unfortunately, over the years, people have muddied things a bit by inventing different ways to represent latitude and longitude coordinates.

Latitude and longitude coordinates can be written as

✔ **Degrees, minutes, and seconds:** This is the traditional way, with my example of Dillon Falls expressed as 43° 57' 29.79" N 121° 24' 34.73" W.

✔ **Degrees and decimal minutes:** Seconds are dropped, and the decimal version of minutes is used along with degrees, so now the falls are at 43° 57.4965' N 121° 24.5788' W.

✔ **Decimal degrees:** Minutes and seconds are both dropped, and only the decimal representation of degrees is used, which puts the falls at 43.9582750° N 121.4096490° W.

Remember: Although they look different, all these coordinate notations still point to the same location. The math is pretty straightforward if you want to convert the coordinates from one format to another. If you want to save time, point your Web browser to http://nris.state.mt.us/wis/location/latlong.asp where the friendly people at the Montana State Library have a handy conversion calculator online.

That means that Dillon Falls is

- 41 degrees, 57 minutes, and 29.76 seconds north of the equator
- 121 degrees, 24 minutes, 34.73 seconds west of the prime meridian

Universal Transverse Mercator (UTM)

Universal Transverse Mercator is a modern coordinate system developed in the 1940s. It's similar to latitude and longitude, but it uses meters instead of degrees, minutes, and seconds. UTM coordinates are very accurate, and the system is pretty easy to use and understand.

Although the United States hasn't moved to the metric system, the system is widely used by GPS receivers. UTM coordinates are much easier than latitude and longitude to plot on maps. The two key values to convert metric measurements are

- **1 meter = 3.28 feet = 1.09 yards.**

  For ballpark measurements, a *meter* is a bit over a yard.

- **1 kilometer = 1,000 meters = 3,280 feet = 1,094 yards = 0.62 miles.**

  For ballpark measurements, a *kilometer* is a bit more than half a mile.

Specialized coordinate systems

Here are a few other coordinate systems so you know what they are:

MGRS (Military Grid Reference System): A coordinate system used by the U.S. and NATO military forces. It's an extension of the UTM system. It further divides the UTM zones into 100-kilometer squares labeled with the letters A–Z.

State Plane Coordinate System: A coordinate system used in the United States. Each state is divided into at least one *State Plane zone.* Similar to the UTM system, it uses feet instead of meters.

Proprietary grids: Anyone can invent a coordinate system for finding locations on a map.

Examples of proprietary systems are ZIP code, the *Maidenhead Locator System* (a grid system for amateur radio operators) and *Thomas Brothers street guides* (that match a location with a page number and grid).

Most coordinate systems try to make navigation and surveying more accurate and simpler.

GPS is sending less-used coordinate systems the way of the dinosaur because you can quickly and easily get precise location positions in either UTM coordinates or latitude and longitude with an inexpensive GPS receiver.

The UTM system is based on the simple A, B, C/1, 2, 3 coordinate system. The world is divided into *zones:*

- **Sixty primary zones run north and south.**

  Numbers identify the zones that run north and south.

- **Twenty optional zones run east to west.**

  These zones indicate whether a coordinate is in the Northern or Southern Hemisphere.

  Letters designate the east/west zones.

Often the letter is dropped from a UTM coordinate, and only the zone is used to make things simpler. For example, because most of Florida is in Zone 17 R, if you were plotting locations in that state, you could just use Zone 17 in your UTM coordinates. Figure 2-6 shows its UTM zone map.

To provide a precise location, UTM uses two units:

- **Easting:** The distance in meters to the east from the start of a UTM zone line

  The letter *E* follows Easting values.

- **Northing:** The distance in meters from the equator

  The letter *N* follows Northing values.

There's no such thing as a Southing. *Northing* is used in the Southern Hemisphere to describe the distance away from the equator, even though a location is south of the Equator. (Is that weird, or what?)

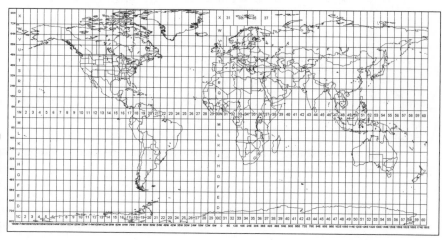

Figure 2-6:
The UTM
zone map
for the
world.

Continuing with my example of Dillon Falls, if you use UTM to locate the falls, the coordinates look like this:

10T 0627598E 4868251N

That means that the falls are in Zone 10T, which is 4,868,251 meters north of the equator and 627,598 meters east of where the zone line starts. (For those of you without a calculator in front of you, that's about 3,025 miles north of the equator, and about 390 miles east of where the number 10 Zone line starts out in the Pacific Ocean.)

Township and Range

The Township and Range coordinate system has been used since the 1790s to survey public lands in the United States. Technically, the official name of this system is the Public Land Rectangular Survey (PLS), but in practical use, most people call it Township and Range.

This coordinate system was developed after the American Revolution as a way to survey and grant title to land that was newly acquired following the country's independence. Thomas Jefferson helped develop the system, which was enacted under the Northwest Land Ordinance of 1785. Township and Range isn't used in the eastern United States (or in a few other states) because land surveys in those states had been completed.

The system is based on the following components, which are shown in Figure 2-7:

✓ **Meridians and baselines.** These lines are the foundation of the Township and Range system:

- *Meridians* are imaginary lines that run north to south.

- *Baselines* are lines that run east to west.

- An *initial point* is where a meridian and a baseline meet.

The California Bureau of Land Management has a nice online map of all the meridians and baselines at www.ca.blm.gov/pa/cadastral/meridian.html.

✓ **Townships:** *Townships* are the horizontal part of the coordinate system.

- Each township is six square miles in size.

- Townships are identified by whole numbers starting with 1.

- The first township at the intersection of a meridian and baseline is 1, the next township is 2, and so on.

- If a township is north of the baseline, it's identified with an N; if it's south of the baseline, it's designated with an S. For example, the fifth township north of a meridian and baseline is T. 5 N.

✔ **Ranges:** *Ranges* are the vertical part of the grid scale.

- Ranges are six miles wide.

- Ranges are numbered starting at the intersection of the meridian and the baseline.

- In addition to a number, a range is identified as being east or west of a meridian. For example, the third range west of the meridian and baseline is R. 3 W.

The intersection of a township and range (a 36-square mile parcel of land) also is also called a township. This bit of semantics shouldn't have an effect on you using the coordinate system, but watch out for someone else doing this.

Like other coordinate systems, Township and Range uses smaller measurement units to identify a precise location. These units include

✔ **Sections:** A 36-square-mile township is further divided into 36 one-mile squares called *sections*.

Sections are numbered 1–36. Number 1 starts in the top, right of the township, and the numbers sequentially snake back and forth across the section, ending at number 36 in the bottom-right corner.

✔ **Quarters:** Sections are divided even further by slicing them into *quarters*.

- Quarters are identified by the part of the section they occupy, such as northwest, northeast, southwest, or southeast.

- You can further narrow the location with *quarter quarters* or *quarter quarter-quarters*.

Figure 2-7:
Elements
that make
up the
Township
and Range
system.

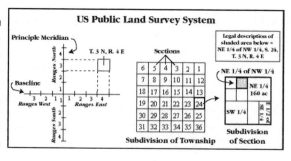

Township and Range coordinates are a hodgepodge of abbreviations and numbers that lack the mathematical precision of latitude and longitude or UTM. For example, the Township and Range coordinates of Dillon Falls are

SE 1/4 of SW 1/4 of NE 1/4, Sect. 4, T. 19 S, R. 11 E, Willamette Meridian

To describe a location with this coordinate system, you start from the smallest chunk of land and then work your way up to larger chunks. Some people ignore this convention and reverse the order, skip the meridian, or use both halves and quarters. (Hey, it keeps life interesting. . . .)

Although scanned paper maps (such as USGS topographic maps) often show township and range information, most digital mapping software and GPS receivers don't support township and range. This is good news because latitude and longitude and UTM are much easier to use.

Township and range information usually is omitted from digital maps because

- ✔ The coordinate system is difficult to mathematically model.
- ✔ Townships and sections may be oddly shaped because of previously granted lands, surveying errors, and adjustments for the curvature of the earth.

Peter Dana's comprehensive Geographer's Craft Web site has lots of good technical information on coordinate systems:

```
www.colorado.edu/geography/gcraft/notes/coordsys/coordsys.html
```

Measuring Map Scales

Most maps have a *scale* — the ratio of the horizontal distance on the map to the corresponding horizontal distance on the ground. For example, one inch on a map can represent one mile on the ground.

The map scale is usually shown at the bottom of the map in the legend. Often, rulers with the scale mark specific distances for you. A scale from a USGS topographic map is shown in Figure 2-8.

Many maps use a *representative fraction* to describe scale. This is the ratio of the map distance to the ground distance in the same units of measure. For example, a map that's 1:24,000 scale means that one inch measured on the map is equivalent to 24,000 inches on the ground. The number can be inches, feet, millimeters, centimeters, or some other unit of measure.

The units on the top and bottom of the representative fraction must be the same. You can't mix measurement units.

Figure 2-8:
Scale information in the legend of a USGS 7.5 minute topographic map.

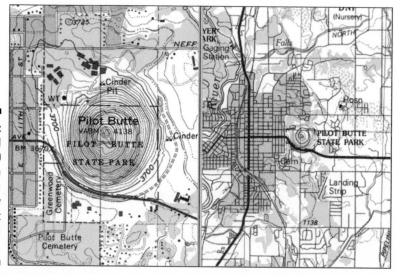

When you're dealing with scale, keep these guidelines in mind:

✔ **The smaller the number to the right of the 1, the more detail the map has.**

A 1:24,000 map has much more detail than a 1:100,000 scale map. A 1:24,000 map is a large-scale map, showing a small area.

✔ **The smaller the number to the right of the 1, the smaller the area the map displays.**

In Figure 2-9, the 1:100,000 scale map shows a much larger area than the 1:24,000 scale map. A 1:100,000 map is a small-scale map, showing a large area.

All sorts of rulers and measurement tools are calibrated to scale for measuring distance on paper maps. Mapping software makes distances easier and quicker to determine by offering tools that draw a line between two points and show an exact distance.

Figure 2-9:
1:24,000 and 1:100,000 scale topographic maps show different details and areas.

Looking at Map Symbols

Symbols — icons, lines, and colored shading, as well as circles, squares, and other shapes — are important parts of a map's language. They give the map a more detailed meaning without cluttering up the picture with too many words. They represent roads, rivers, railroads, buildings, cities, and just about any natural or man-made feature you can think of. Symbols are either shown on the map or are compiled in a separate map symbol guide. Some common symbols found on USGS topographic maps are shown in Figure 2-10.

BUILDINGS AND RELATED FEATURES	
Building	■ □ ▨ ▨
School; church	⚐ ⚐
Built-up Area	
Racetrack	◯ ◯
Airport	✕ ✈
Landing strip	⊏ ⁝ ⁝ ⁝ ⊐
Well (other than water); windmill	○ ⚐
Tanks	● ⊘
Covered reservoir	⊘ ▨
Gaging station	⚐
Landmark object (feature as labeled)	○
Campground; picnic area	⚐ ⚐
Cemetery: small; large	⊡ Cem

Figure 2-10: Selected USGS topographic map symbols.

Whether you're using a paper or a digital map, always familiarize yourself with its symbols. The more symbols you know, the better decisions you make when you're relying on a map for navigation.

Map symbols aren't universal. A symbol can have different meanings on different maps. For example, the symbol for a secondary highway on a USGS topographic map is a railroad on a Swiss map.

These Web sites show what symbols for different types of maps mean:

- ✔ Topographic maps

  `http://mac.usgs.gov/mac/isb/pubs/booklets/symbols`

- ✔ Aeronautical charts

  `www.naco.faa.gov/index.asp?xml=naco/online/aero_guide`

- ✔ Marine charts

  `http://chartmaker.ncd.noaa.gov/mcd/chart1/chart1hr.htm`

Digital Map Data

Here I concentrate on digital map data that the U.S. government makes available for free. You can make your own maps with this data by using freeware and shareware mapping programs discussed in other chapters of this book.

Although other countries use the same or similar data formats as the U.S. government for producing digital maps, trying to obtain detailed international map data can be difficult. In some parts of the world, maps and map data are tightly controlled by the government because they're are considered a key part of a country's national security. Chapter 22 lists a number of Internet resources where you can get maps and map data for areas outside the United States.

TIGER

The U.S. Census Bureau produces Topologically Integrated Geographic Encoding and Referencing (TIGER) data for compiling maps with demographic information. This vector data is a primary source for creating digital road maps of the United States. Figure 2-11 shows a map of downtown San Francisco created from Census Bureau TIGER data.

Figure 2-11:
TIGER data
viewed from
the Census
Bureau's
Web-based
map viewer.

TIGER data is free (check out the Census Bureau Web site at `www.census.gov/geo/www/tiger/index.html`) but in some areas isn't very accurate; roads don't appear on the map and addresses aren't in the right locations. The government is improving the accuracy of the dataset, and plans to provide better data in the future. You're better off using some of the free and commercial street map programs and Web sites discussed in Chapters 12 and 18.

Mapmaker, mapmaker, make me a map

Data for digital maps comes from government sources and commercial mapmaking companies, which license their maps to other companies. These entities get data from satellites, aerial photographs, existing maps, or sometimes from folks driving and walking around with a GPS receiver, using a laptop to record data. As an example, here are the main providers of digital map data for the United States. (Most countries will have a similar collection of government agencies and commercial sources that produce map data.)

✔ **USGS:** The United States Geological Survey (USGS) has been making United States land maps since 1879.

   mapping.usgs.gov

✔ **Census Bureau:** The Census Bureau is in the map-making business because the data it collects is directly tied to location. Its Web site has information on its TIGER data.

   tiger.census.gov

✔ **NOAA:** The National Oceanic and Atmospheric Administration creates and maintains nautical charts and other essential data for marine use.

   www.noaa.com/charts.html

✔ **FAA:** The Federal Aviation Administration National Aeronautical Charting Office (NACO) provides aviation charts and data for the United States.

   www.naco.faa.gov

✔ **NGA:** The National Geospatial-Intelligence Agency (formerly the National Imagery and Mapping Agency) is the Department of Defense agency for producing maps and charts of areas outside the United States.

   www.nga.mil

✔ **States, counties, and cities:** States, counties, and larger cities have Geographic Information System (GIS) divisions that produce maps. This data is often available to the public for free or a small cost. To find whether digital map data is available for your area, search Google for your state, county, or city and *GIS*.

✔ **NAVTECH:** Navigation Technologies is one of the largest commercial suppliers of street and road data. UPS, General Motors, Ford, DaimlerChrysler, and AAA use NAVTECH.

   www.navtech.com

✔ **GDT:** Geographic Data Technology is a commercial supplier of digital map data. GDT licenses its maps to ESRI, MapInfo, MapQuest, and Expedia.

   www.geographic.com/home/
      index.cfm

✔ **TeleAtlas:** TeleAtlas is a European mapmaking company with a United States presence. TeleAtlas licenses its maps to Lowrance, Microsoft, OnStar, and Rand McNally.

   www.na.teleatlas.com

Digital Line Graph (DLG)

Digital Line Graph (DLG) data from the USGS is used to create vector maps. The data includes transportation networks, *hydrography* (measuring surface waters), boundaries, elevation contours, and man-made features. The format is similar to TIGER data but generally has more accurate roads and other features.

Raster and vector maps

These two terms describe the underlying format of a digital map:

Raster maps are composed of a series of pixels (picture elements) aligned in a grid. Each pixel (or bit) contains information about the color to be displayed or printed. Because bitmap images can be very large, graphics formats such as GIF (Graphic Interchange Format) and TIFF (Tag Image File Format) use compression to make images smaller. An example of a raster map is a paper map that's been scanned and saved as graphic file.

Raster maps tend to show more detail than vector maps and don't look as computer-generated. Figure 2-1 is a raster map.

Vector maps are composed of many individual objects. The objects are mathematically based. They can be points, lines, and shapes. Each object has properties that define its appearance and attributes, such as color, thickness, and style. If you've used such graphics software as Adobe Illustrator or CorelDRAW (called *object-oriented* drawing programs), you've used a vector graphics program. A map can contain thousands of these objects, but vector maps tend to be smaller than raster maps because it's more efficient to mathematically describe an object than draw it as a bitmap. Vector maps are scalable, which means you can resize a vector map without distorting the map's information. Vector maps appear to be created with lines and shapes and are linear looking. Figure 2-2 is a vector map.

Figure 2-12 shows a map of the Atlanta Olympics Savannah Yachting Venue, created with USGS DLG data.

DLG data has basic information such as road types, bridges, and highway route numbers, but only GIS software can easily access these attributes.

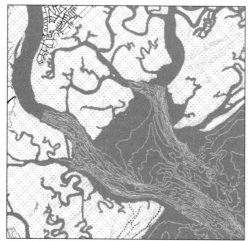

Figure 2-12:
A map created with DLG data.

Elevation data

You're likeliest to run into one of these two main data formats used to represent elevation:

- ✓ **Digital Elevation Model (DEM):** The USGS uses this raster data format to record elevation information (based on topographic maps) and create three-dimensional representations of the terrain. Figure 2-13 shows a map of Mt. Bachelor, Oregon, generated from Digital Elevation Model data with the 3DEM mapping program.

- ✓ **National Elevation Dataset (NED):** This format shows digital elevation data in shaded relief. It's designed for seamless coverage of the United States in large raster files.

Figure 2-13:
A map created with DEM data.

Digital Raster Graphics (DRG)

Digital Raster Graphics (DRG) data is a scanned image of a USGS topographic map. These digital maps are available for free on the Internet or are sold commercially in collections on CDs or DVDs. Figure 2-14 shows a DRG map from the TerraServer-USA Web server. This map is a digital version of a 1:24,000 scale topographic map.

These digital maps are scanned at 250 dpi (dots per inch) and stored in a TIFF file format, using embedded GeoTIFF (geographic information) tags for location data.

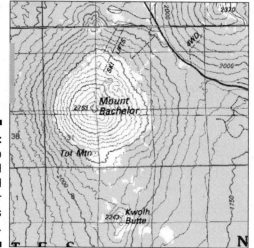

Figure 2-14:
A map
composed
of Digital
Raster
Graphics
data.

You can view the map by itself or both the map and its location data. Use one of the following methods:

✔ View the map by opening the DRG file with any current graphics program that supports large TIFF files.

✔ Use the DRG file with a mapping program that supports GeoTIFF to view the map and access its location data.

For more technical details about USGS digital map data, check out the agency's product Web site:

```
mapping.usgs.gov/products.html
```

Who is Mr. Sid?

This question is more accurately stated as *what is MrSID?* MrSID is the Multi-Resolution Seamless Image Database. It's a file format used for distributing large images over networks, originally developed by a company called LizardTech. Graphics in MrSID format are compressed with a *lossless compression algorithm* (a method of compressing data that guarantees the original data can be restored exactly) designed to produce relatively small, high-resolution images.

The file format is perfect for aerial and satellite images that have large file sizes, and the government is increasingly using it for distributing data. (The Library of Congress is even using it for electronic versions of paper documents.) A number of free viewers support MrSID; use Google to find download sites. (One of my favorites is IrfanView, which is available at www.irfanview.com.)

Digital Orthophoto Quadrangle (DOQ)

Digital Orthophoto Quadrangle (DOQ) data consists of a computer-generated image of an aerial photograph. The image is corrected so that camera tilt and terrain relief don't affect the accuracy. DOQs combine the image characteristics of a photograph with the geometric qualities of a map. Figure 2-15 shows a DOQ map of Mt. Bachelor, Oregon, from the TerraServer-USA Web site.

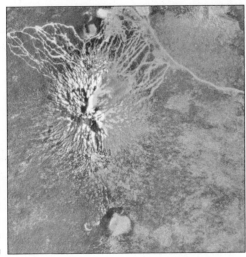

Figure 2-15:
A Digital
Orthophoto
Quadrangle
map.

The USGS has DOQs available for the entire United States. Most are grayscale, infrared photos; there are higher-resolution color photos for a few large U.S. metropolitan areas.

A booming business provides high-resolution, color aerial photographs to individuals, government agencies, corporations, and educational and non-profit organizations. Companies like AirphotoUSA (www.airphotousa.com), Keyhole (www.keyhole.com) and DeLorme's TopoBird subsidiary (www.topobird.com) provide imagery with quality and resolution that's close to what was only available to intelligence agencies. If you want aerial photographs for business or government purposes, check these commercial sources.

Satellite data

Satellites are the most exotic source of data for digital maps. Orbiting several hundred miles above the earth, satellites provide photographs and other sensor data. NASA's Landsat, the Space Shuttle, and other satellites collect raster data for most of the earth. It's available both free and commercially.

I spy

The highest resolution commercial satellite imagery available is .61 meters, from Digital-Globe's QuickBird satellite (www.digital globe.com).

By 2006, commercial satellites are expected to have resolution as high as 0.25 meters. That's pretty close to the resolution of spy satellites, which are thought to have a resolution of 0.1 meters. (The best spy satellites can reputedly discern objects about the size of a baseball. Despite what you see in the movies, license plate numbers are too small to be read by spy satellites, especially considering they don't face up toward space.)

Resolution defines the smallest object a satellite can distinguish. A satellite with one-meter resolution can distinguish objects down to a meter (a little under 40 inches) in size.

Figure 2-16 is a ten-meter resolution SPOT satellite data of Mt. Bachelor, from DeLorme's Spot 10 collection of satellite data. (SPOT, which stands for Systeme Pour l'observation de la Terre, is a French commercial satellite program that started in 1986.)

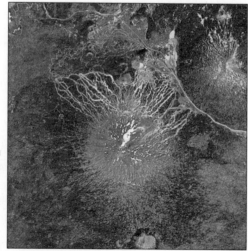

Figure 2-16:
A ten-meter resolution satellite image.

Although most free satellite imagery doesn't come close to the resolution of some commercial sources, the government is relying increasingly on private companies to acquire data. I expect that government sources eventually will release high-resolution, color imagery to the public.

Part II
All About GPS

The 5th Wave   By Rich Tennant

@RICHTENNANT

"Someone want to look at this manuscript I recieved on email called, 'The Embedded Virus That Destroyed the Publishers Servers When the Manuscript was Rejected.'?"

In this part . . .

GPS stands for Global Positioning System, which is a nifty satellite system that tells you your location anywhere on planet earth. This part is all about GPS. We'll start with a broad overview of the satellite system and work our way back down to earth and discuss handheld, consumer GPS receivers. By the end of the part you'll understand the technology behind GPS (without needing to be a rocket scientist), be able to navigate through the jungle of GPS receivers on the market, and have the skills and knowledge to practically use a GPS receiver without being intimidated or confused by it.

Chapter 3

GPS Fundamentals

You've heard about GPS and probably know that it has something to do with handheld gadgets and satellites that tell you where you're located. That's great for starters, but to understand and use GPS, you need a bit more detailed knowledge. Follow this chapter to go through some of the fundamentals of GPS so you have a better grasp of what it is and how you can use it.

What Is GPS?

GPS stands for *Global Positioning System.* A special radio receiver measures the distance from your location to satellites that orbit the earth broadcasting radio signals. GPS can pinpoint your position anywhere in the world. Pretty cool, huh? Aside from buying the receiver, the system is free for anyone.

You can purchase an inexpensive GPS receiver, pop some batteries in it, turn it on, and presto! Your location appears on the screen. No map, compass, sextant, nor sundial is required. Just like magic. It's not really magic, though, but has evolved from some great practical applications of science that have come together over the last 50 years.

Other satellite Global Positioning Systems are either in orbit or planned, but this book uses the term *GPS* for the Global Positioning System operated by the United States government.

A short history of GPS

Military, government, and civilian users all over the world rely on GPS for navigation and location positioning, but radio signals have been used for navigation purposes since the 1920s. LORAN (Long Range Aid to Navigation), a position-finding system that measured the time difference of arriving radio signals, was developed during World War II.

The first step to GPS came way back in 1957 when the Russians launched *Sputnik,* the first satellite to orbit the Earth. Sputnik used a radio transmitter to broadcast telemetry information. Scientists at the Johns Hopkins Applied Physics Lab discovered that the Doppler shift phenomenon applied to the spacecraft — and almost unwittingly struck gold.

A down-to-earth, painless example of the Doppler shift principle is when you stand on a sidewalk and a police car speeds by in hot pursuit of a stolen motorcycle. The pitch of the police siren increases as the car approaches you and then drops sharply as it moves away.

American scientists figured out that if they knew the satellite's precise orbital position, they could accurately locate their exact position on Earth by listening to the pinging sounds and measuring the satellite's radio signal Doppler shift. Satellites offered some possibilities for a navigation and positioning system, and the U.S. Department of Defense (DoD) explored the concept.

By the 1960s, several rudimentary satellite-positioning systems existed. The U.S. Army, Navy, and Air Force were all working on independent versions of radio navigation systems that could provide accurate positioning and all-weather, 24-hour coverage. In 1973, the Air Force was selected as the lead organization to consolidate all the military satellite navigation efforts into a single program. This evolved into the NAVSTAR (Navigation Satellite Timing and Ranging) Global Positioning System, which is the official name for the United States' GPS program.

The U.S. military wasn't just interested in GPS for navigation. A satellite location system can be used for weapons-system targeting. Smart weapons such as the Tomahawk cruise missile use GPS in their precision guidance systems. GPS, combined with contour-matching radar and digital image-matching optics, makes a Tomahawk an extremely accurate weapon. The possibility of an enemy using GPS against the United States is one reason why civilian GPS receivers are less accurate than their restricted-use military counterparts.

The first NAVSTAR satellite was launched in 1974 to test the concept. By the mid-1980s, more satellites were put in orbit to make the system functional. In 1994, the planned full constellation of 24 satellites was in place. Soon, the military declared the system completely operational. The program has been wildly successful and is still funded through the U.S. DoD.

How GPS Works

The intricacies of GPS are steeped in mathematics, physics, and engineering, but you don't need to be a rocket scientist to understand how GPS works. GPS is composed of three parts (as shown in Figure 3-1):

✔ Satellites

✔ Ground stations

✔ Receivers

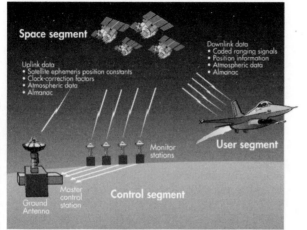

Figure 3-1:
GPS is
composed
of satellites,
ground
stations, and
receivers.

Eyeing satellites

In GPS jargon, a satellite is the space segment. A constellation of 24 GPS satellites (21 operational and 3 spares) orbits about 12,000 miles above the Earth (as shown in Figure 3-2). The satellites zoom through the heavens at around 7,000 miles per hour. It takes about 12 hours for a satellite to completely orbit the Earth, passing over the exact same spot approximately every 24 hours. The satellites are positioned where a GPS receiver can receive signals from at least six of the satellites at any time, at any location on the Earth (if nothing obstructs the signals).

A satellite has three key pieces of hardware:

✔ **Computer:** This onboard computer controls its flight and other functions.

✔ **Atomic clock:** This keeps accurate time within three *nanoseconds* (around three-billionths of a second).

✔ **Radio transmitter:** This sends signals to Earth.

Figure 3-2:
The constellation of NAVSTAR satellites and their orbits.

GPS satellites don't just help you stay found. All GPS satellites since 1980 carry NUDET sensors. No, this isn't some high-tech pornography-detection system. NUDET is an acronym for NUclear DETonation; GPS satellites have sensors to detect nuclear-weapon explosions, assess the threat of nuclear attack, and help evaluate nuclear strike damage.

The solar-powered GPS satellites have a limited life span (around 10 years). When they start to fail, spares are activated or new satellites are sent into orbit to replace the old ones. This gives the government a chance to upgrade the GPS system by putting hardware with new features into space.

GPS radio signals

GPS satellites transmit two types of radio signals: C/A-code and P-code. Briefly, here are the uses and differences of these two types of signals.

Coarse Acquisition (C/A-code)

Coarse Acquisition (C/A-code) is the type of signal that consumer GPS units receive. C/A-code is sent on the L1 band at a frequency of 1575.42 MHz.

C/A broadcasts are known as the Standard Positioning Service (SPS).

C/A-code is less accurate than P-code (see the following section) and is easier for U.S. military forces to jam and *spoof* (broadcast false signals to make a receiver think it's somewhere else when it's really not).

The advantage of C/A-code is that it's quicker to use for acquiring satellites and getting an initial position fix. Some military P-code receivers first track on the C/A-code and then switch over to P-code.

Precision (P-code)

P-code provides highly precise location information. P-code is difficult to jam and spoof. The U.S. military is the primary user of P-code transmissions, and it uses an encrypted form of the data (Y-code) so only special receivers can access the information. The P-code signal is broadcast on the L2 band at 1227.6 MHz.

P-code broadcasts are known as the Precise Positioning Service (PPS).

Covering ground stations

Ground stations are the control segment of GPS. Five unmanned ground stations around the Earth monitor the satellites. Information from the stations is sent to a master control station — the Consolidated Space Operations Center (CSOC) at Schriever Air Force Base in Colorado — where the data is processed to determine each satellite's ephemeris and timing errors.

An *ephemeris* is a list of the predicted positions of astronomical bodies such as the planets or the Moon. Ephemerides (the plural of *ephemeris*) have been around for thousands of years because of their importance in celestial navigation. Ephemerides are compiled to track the positions of the numerous satellites orbiting the earth.

The processed data is sent to the satellites once daily with ground antennas located around the world. This is kind of like syncing a personal digital assistant (PDA) with your personal computer to ensure that all the data is in sync between the two devices. Because the satellites have small built-in rockets, the CSOC can control them to ensure that they stay in a correct orbit.

GPS receivers

Anyone who has a GPS receiver can receive the satellite signals to determine where he or she is located.

Satellite data

GPS units receive two types of data from the NAVSTAR satellites.

Almanac

Almanac data contains the approximate positions of the satellites. The data is constantly being transmitted and is stored in the GPS receiver's memory.

Ephemeris

Ephemeris data has the precise positions of the satellites. To get an accurate location fix, the receiver has to know how far away a satellite is. The GPS receiver calculates the distance to the satellite by using signals from the satellite.

Using the formula *Distance = Velocity x Time*, a GPS receiver calculates the satellite's distance. A radio signal travels at the speed of light (186,000 miles per second). The GPS receiver needs to know how long the radio signal takes to travel from the satellite to the receiver in order to figure the distance. Both the satellite and the GPS receiver generate an identical pseudo-random code sequence. When the GPS receiver receives this transmitted code, it determines how much the code needs to be shifted (using the Doppler-shift principle) for the two code sequences to match. The shift is multiplied by the speed of light to determine the distance from the satellite to the receiver.

Multiple satellites

A GPS receiver needs several pieces of data to produce position information:

- **Location:** A minimum of three satellite signals is required to find your location.

- **Position:** Four satellite signals are required to determine your position in three dimensions: latitude, longitude, and elevation.

Receiver types

GPS receivers generally fall into five categories.

Consumer models

Consumers can buy practical GPS receivers in sporting goods stores. They're easy to use and are mostly targeted for recreational and other uses that don't require a high level of location precision. The Big Three manufacturers in the consumer GPS market are Garmin (www.garmin.com), Magellan (www.magellangps.com), and Lowrance (www.lowrance.com). Consumer GPS receivers are reasonably priced, from less than $100 to $400 in the U.S.

This book emphasizes the features of and how to use the consumer-oriented, handheld types.

When you buy a consumer receiver, opt for a 12-channel GPS model over an older 8-channel model:

- **12-channel parallel receivers:** These acquire satellites faster and operate better under foliage and tree-canopy cover.

- **8-channel receivers:** These are slow when acquiring satellite signals and have difficulty operating even under light tree cover.

Selective Availability (SA)

The average GPS user didn't always have 15-meter accuracy. In the 1970s, studies showed that the less-accurate C/A-code for nonmilitary use, was more accurate than the U.S. government intended. Originally thought to provide accuracy within 100 meters, experiments showed that C/A accuracy was in the range of 20–30 meters. To reduce the accuracy of C/A-code, the U.S. government developed *Selective Availability (SA)*. SA adds errors to NAVSTAR satellite data and prevents consumer GPS receivers from providing an extremely precise location fix.

Selective Availability was temporarily turned off in 1990 during the Persian Gulf War. There weren't enough U.S. and allies military P-code GPS receivers, so the Coalition troops used civilian GPS receivers. The Gulf War was the first use of GPS in large-scale combat operations.

On May 2, 2000, SA was turned off permanently. Overnight, the accuracy of civilian GPS users went from 100 meters to 15 meters. Turning off SA on a global scale was directly related to the U.S. military's ability to degrade the C/A-code on a regional basis. For example, during the invasion of Afghanistan, the American military jammed GPS signals in Afghanistan to prevent the Taliban from using consumer receivers in operations against American forces.

Don't consider purchasing an 8-channel receiver. Even if you were given one for free, it's like running the latest version of Windows on a 386 computer.

U.S. military/government models

GPS units that receive P-code and Y-code are available only to the government. These portable units are Precision Lightweight GPS Receivers (PLGRs — or, more fondly, *pluggers*). First-generation PLGRs were big and boxy and provided accuracy within four meters. The newest precise GPS receivers are DAGRs (Defense Advanced Global Positioning System Receivers) and are smaller, more accurate, and have mapping features like consumer GPS units. For the specifications of U.S. military GPS receivers, including pictures of different units, visit http://army-gps.robins.af.mil.

Mapping/resource models

These portable receivers collect location points and line and area data that can be input into a Geographic Information System (GIS). They are more precise than consumer models, can store more data, and are much more expensive.

Survey models

These are used mostly for surveying land, where you may need accuracy down to the centimeter for legal or practical purposes. These units are extremely precise and store a large amount of data. They tend to be large, complex to use, and very expensive.

Commercial transportation models

These GPS receivers, not designed to be handheld, are installed in aircraft, ships, boats, trucks, and cars. They provide navigation information appropriate to the mode of transportation. These receivers may be part of an Automated Position Reporting System (APRS) that sends the vehicle's location to a monitoring facility.

Trimble Navigation (www.trimble.com) is one of the biggest players in the nonconsumer GPS receiver market. If you're interested in discovering how commercial and higher-end GPS units work and the features they support, check out the Trimble Web site.

How accurate is a GPS receiver?

According to the government and GPS receiver manufacturers, expect your GPS unit to be accurate within 49 feet (that's 15 meters for metric-savvy folks). If your GPS reports that you're at a certain location, you can be reasonably sure that you're within 49 feet of that exact set of coordinates.

GPS receivers tell you how accurate your position is. Based on the quality of the satellite signals that the unit receives, the screen displays the estimated accuracy in feet or meters. Accuracy depends on

✔ Receiver location

✔ Obstructions that block satellite signals

Even if you're not a U.S. government or military GPS user, you can get more accuracy by using a GPS receiver that supports corrected location data. Corrected information is broadcast over radio signals that come from either

✔ Non-GPS satellites

✔ Ground-based beacons

Two common sources of more accurate location data are

✔ Differential GPS (DGPS)

✔ Wide Area Augmentation System (WAAS)

I cover both DGPS and WAAS in the following section on GPS receiver features.

Table 3-1 shows the accuracy you can expect from a GPS receiver. These numbers are guidelines; at times, you may get slightly more or less accuracy.

Table 3-1	GPS Accuracy	
GPS Mode	*Distance in Feet*	*Distance in Meters*
GPS without SA	49	15
GPS with DGPS	10–16	3–5
GPS with WAAS	10	3

GPS errors

A number of conditions can reduce the accuracy of a GPS receiver. From a *top-down* perspective (from orbit down to ground level), the possible sources of trouble look like this:

✔ **Ephemeris errors:** Ephemeris errors occur when the satellite doesn't correctly transmit its exact position in orbit.

✔ **Ionosphere conditions:** The *ionosphere* starts at about 43–50 miles above the Earth and continues for hundreds of miles. Satellite signals traveling through the ionosphere are slowed down because of *plasma* (a low density gas). Although GPS receivers attempt account for this delay, unexpected plasma activity can cause calculation errors.

✔ **Troposphere conditions:** The *troposphere* is the lowest region in the Earth's atmosphere and goes from ground level up to about 11 miles. Variations in temperature, pressure, and humidity all can cause variations in how fast radio waves travel, resulting in relatively small accuracy errors.

✔ **Timing errors:** Because placing an atomic clock in every GPS receiver is impractical, timing errors from the receiver's less-precise clock can cause slight position inaccuracies.

✔ **Multipath errors:** When a satellite signal bounces off a hard surface (such as a building or canyon wall) before it reaches the receiver, a delay in the travel time occurs, which causes an inaccurate distance calculation.

✔ **Poor satellite coverage:** When a significant part of the sky is blocked, your GPS unit has difficulty receiving satellite data. Unfortunately, you can't say that if 50 percent (or some other percentage) of the sky is blocked, you'll have poor satellite reception; this is because the GPS satellites are constantly moving in orbit. A satellite that provides a good signal one day may provide a poor signal at the exact same location on another day because its position has changed and is now being blocked by a tree. The more open sky you have, the better your chances of not having satellite signals blocked.

Building interiors, streets surrounded by tall buildings, dense tree canopies, canyons, and mountainous areas are typical problem areas.

If satellite coverage is poor, try moving to a different location to see whether you get any improvement.

Although survey-grade GPS receivers can provide accuracy of less than two centimeters, they are very specialized and expensive, require a lot of training, and aren't very portable. Their accuracy is achieved with DGPS and post-processing collected data to reduce location errors. The average GPS user doesn't need this level of precision.

Clouds, rain, snow, and weather don't reduce the strength of GPS signals enough to reduce accuracy. The only way that weather can weaken signals is when a significant amount of rain or snow accumulates on the GPS receiver antenna or on an overhead tree canopy.

Information from GPS Receivers

GPS receivers provide your location and other useful information:

- ✔ **Time:** A GPS receiver receives time information from atomic clocks, so it's much more accurate than your wristwatch.

- ✔ **Location:** GPS provides your location in three dimensions:

  - Latitude (x coordinate)

  - Longitude (y coordinate)

  - Elevation

    The vertical (elevation) accuracy of consumer GPS receivers isn't that great. It can be within 15 meters, 95 percent of time. Some GPS units incorporate more accurate barometric altimeters for better elevation information.

  Your location can be displayed in a number of coordinate systems, such as

  - Latitude/longitude

  - Universal Transverse Mercator (UTM)

  I cover coordinate systems in Chapter 2.

- ✔ **Speed:** When you're moving, a GPS receiver displays your speed.

- ✔ **Direction of travel:** A GPS receiver can display your direction of travel if you're moving.

  If you're stationary, the unit can't use satellite signals to determine which direction you're facing.

  Some GPS units have electronic compasses that show the direction the receiver is pointed whether you're moving or standing still.

- ✔ **Stored locations:** You can store locations where you've been or want to go with a GPS receiver. These location positions are *waypoints*. Waypoints are important because a GPS unit can supply you with directions and information on how to get to a waypoint. A collection of waypoints that plots a course of travel is a *route,* which can also be stored. GPS receivers also store *tracks* (which are like an electronic collection of breadcrumb trails that show where you've been).

In Chapter 4, I show how to create and use waypoints, routes, and tracks.

✔ **Cumulative data:** A GPS receiver can also keep track of information such as the total distance traveled, average speed, maximum speed, minimum speed, elapsed time, and time to arrival at a specified location.

All this information is displayed on different pages of the GPS receiver's display screen. One page shows satellite status, another page displays a map, another displays trip data, and so on. With buttons on the receiver, you can scroll to an information page to view the data that you're interested in seeing.

GPS Receiver Features

A number of GPS receivers are on the market. Usually a GPS receiver with more features costs more.

GPS manufacturers have done a pretty good job making user interfaces easy to use. After you know the basic concepts of GPS receivers and are familiar with a manufacturer's user interface, a GPS unit is usually as easy to use as a cellphone and easier to use than a personal computer.

Display and output

GPS receivers have three choices for information display or data output:

✔ **Monochrome LCD screen:** Most GPS receivers have a monochrome liquid crystal display (LCD) screen.

✔ **Color screen:** These are especially useful for displaying maps.

Color screens usually have shorter battery lives than monochrome ones.

✔ **No screen:** Some GPS receivers only transmit data through an expansion slot or a cable; a receiver with a cable is often called a *mouse* GPS receiver because it resembles a computer mouse. Such receivers are designed to interface with a laptop computer or PDA running special software. Figure 3-3 shows a DeLorme Earthmate GPS unit attached to a laptop. All GPS data is sent to the laptop and processed there with mapping software. A Magellan SporTrak GPS receiver is shown on top of the laptop for comparison.

Most GPS receivers that have screens can output data to a PC or PDA.

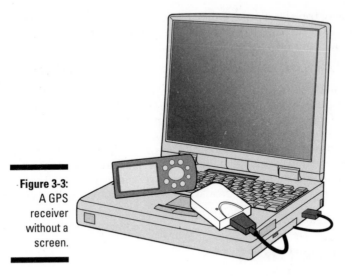

A GPS receiver's screen size depends on the receiver's size. Smaller, lighter models have small screens; larger units sport bigger screens.

Generally, a bigger screen is easier to read. Different models of GPS receiver also have different pixel resolutions; the higher the screen resolution, the more crisp the display will be. For night use, all screens can be backlit.

Alarms

A GPS receiver alarm can transmit a tone or display a message when you approach a location that you specify. This feature can be especially useful when you're trying to find a place and visibility is limited by darkness or inclement weather — or you're busy doing something else and aren't looking at the GPS receiver screen.

Built-in maps

Every GPS receiver has an information page that shows waypoints and tracks. The page is a simple map that plots travel and locations. It doesn't show roads, geographic features, or man-made structures. Figure 3-4 shows two GPS receiver screens: simple location plotting on the left, and a more sophisticated, uploaded map on the right.

Figure 3-4:
Simple and
sophisti-
cated GPS
receiver
screens.

Some GPS receivers have maps that show roads, rivers, cities, and other features on their screens. You can zoom in and out to show different levels of detail. The two types of map receivers are

- ✔ **Basemap:** These GPS units have a basemap loaded into read-only memory that contains roads, highways, water bodies, cities, airports, railroads, and interstate exits.

 Basemap GPS receivers aren't expandable, and you can't load more detailed maps to the unit to supplement the existing basemap.

- ✔ **Uploadable map:** More detailed maps can be added to this type of unit (in either internal memory or an external memory card). You can install road maps, topographic maps, and nautical charts. Many of these maps also have built-in databases, so your GPS receiver can display restaurants, gas stations, or attractions near a certain location.

 Chapter 9 covers features and how to use GPS receiver manufacturer mapping programs to upload maps to your GPS unit.

Refer to Figure 3-4 to see screens from a GPS receiver with a simple plot map and another GPS unit with an uploadable map.

GPS receivers that display maps use proprietary map data from the manufacturer. That means you can't load another manufacturer's or software company's maps into a GPS receiver. However, clever hackers reverse-engineered Garmin's map format. Programs on the Internet can create and upload your own maps to Garmin GPS receivers; GPSmapper is popular.

A handheld GPS receiver's screen is only several inches across. The limitations of such a small display certainly don't make the devices replacements for traditional paper maps.

Electronic compass

All GPS receivers can tell you which direction you're heading — that is, as long as you're moving. The minute you stop, the receiver stops acting as a compass. To address this limitation, some GPS receivers incorporate an electronic compass that doesn't rely on the GPS satellites.

Operation

Like with an old-fashioned compass, you can stand still and see which direction your GPS receiver is pointing toward. The only difference is that you see a digital display onscreen instead of a floating needle.

On some GPS receivers, you need to hold the unit flat and level for the compass to work correctly. Other models have a three-axis compass that allows the receiver to be tilted.

Paying attention to these factors can improve the performance and convenience of an electronic compass:

- ✔ **Magnetic fields:** Metal objects, cars, and other electronic devices reduce the accuracy of any electronic or magnetic compass.
- ✔ **Battery life:** Using an electronic compass can impact battery life. Some GPS receivers have settings that turn off the compass or only use it when the receiver can't determine a direction from satellite data.

Calibration

Electronic compasses need to be calibrated whenever you change batteries. If your GPS unit has an electronic compass, follow your user guide's instructions to calibrate it. Usually, this requires being outside, holding the GPS unit flat and level, and slowly turning in a circle twice.

Altimeter

The elevation or altitude calculated by a GPS receiver from satellite data isn't very accurate. Because of this, some GPS units have *altimeters,* which provide the elevation, ascent/descent rates, change in elevation over distance or time, and the change of barometric pressure over time. (The rough-and-ready rule is that if barometric pressure is falling, bad weather is on the way; if it's rising, clear weather is coming.) Calibrated and used correctly, barometric altimeters can be accurate within 10 feet of the actual elevation. Knowing your altitude is useful if you have something to reference it to, such as a topographic map. Altimeters are useful for hiking or in the mountains.

On GPS units with an electronic altimeter/barometer, calibrating the altimeter to ensure accuracy is important. To do so, visit a physical location with a known elevation and enter the elevation according to the directions in your user's guide. Airports are good places to calibrate your altimeter or get an initial base reading; their elevation is posted for pilots to calibrate their airplanes' altimeters. If you're relying on the altimeter/barometer for recreational use, I recommend calibrating it before you head out on a trip.

Increasing accuracy

Some GPS receivers have features that allow you to increase the accuracy of your location by using radio signals not associated with the GPS satellites. If you see that a GPS receiver supports WAAS or Differential GPS, it has the potential to provide you with more accurate location data.

WAAS

Wide Area Augmentation System (WAAS) combines satellites and ground stations for position accuracy of better than three meters. Vertical accuracy is also improved to three to seven meters.

WAAS is a Federal Aviation Administration (FAA) system, so GPS can be used for airplane flight approaches. The system has a series of ground-reference stations throughout the United States. These monitor GPS satellite data and then send the data to two master stations — one on the west coast and the other on the east coast. These master stations create a GPS message that corrects for position inaccuracies caused by satellite orbital drift and atmospheric conditions. The corrected messages are sent to non-NAVSTAR satellites in stationary orbit over the equator. The satellites then broadcast the data to GPS receivers that are WAAS-enabled.

GPS units that support WAAS have a built-in receiver to process the WAAS signals. You don't need more hardware. Some GPS receivers support turning WAAS on and off. If WAAS is on, battery life is shorter (although not as significantly as it is when using the backlight). In fact, on these models, you can't use WAAS if the receiver's battery-saver mode is activated. Whether you turn WAAS on or off depends on your needs. Unless you need a higher level of accuracy, you can leave WAAS turned off if your GPS receiver supports toggling it on and off. WAAS is ideally suited for aviation as well as for open land and marine use. The system may not, however, provide any benefits in areas where trees or mountains obstruct the view of the horizon.

Under certain conditions — say, when weak WAAS satellite signals are being received or the GPS receiver is a long way from a ground station — accuracy can actually worsen when WAAS is enabled.

WAAS is only available in North America. Other governments are establishing similar systems that use the same format radio signals such as

- ✔ European Euro Geostationary Navigation Overlay Service (EGNOS)
- ✔ Japanese Multi-Functional Satellite Augmentation System (MSAS)

Differential GPS

Surveying and other work that demands a high level of precision use Differential GPS (DGPS) to increase the position accuracy of a GPS receiver. A stationary receiver measures GPS timing errors and broadcasts correction information to other GPS units that are capable of receiving the DGPS signals. Consumer GPS receivers that support DGPS require a separate beacon receiver that connects to the GPS unit. Consumers can receive DGPS signals from free or commercial sources.

Unless you're doing survey or other specialized work, you really don't need DGPS capabilities. For consumer use, the increased accuracy of DGPS has mostly been replaced with WAAS.

Coast Guard DGPS

DGPS signals are freely broadcast by a series of U.S. Coast Guard stations in the United States. Whether you can receive these Coast Guard broadcasts depends on your location.

For more information on DGPS, including coverage maps, pay a visit to www.navcen.uscg.gov/dgps/coverage/default.htm.

Commercial DGPS

DGPS services are offered commercially for the surveying market. You can rent or purchase electronic and radio equipment for gathering precise location information in a relatively small area.

Antennas

Well, yes, a GPS unit has to have an antenna to receive radio signals to do you any good. Several types are available, each with its advantages.

Internal antennas

All GPS receivers have one of two kinds of built-in antennas. One antenna design isn't superior to the other; performance is related to the receiver's antenna size. (Cough . . . bigger is better.)

Patch

An internal *patch antenna* is a square conductor mounted over a *groundplane* (another square piece of metal). Patch antenna models reacquire satellites faster after losing the signal.

For best performance with an internal patch antenna, hold the receiver face up and parallel with the ground.

Quad helix

An internal *quadrifilar helix antenna* (or *quad helix)* is a circular tube wrapped with wire. Quad helix antennas are more sensitive and work better under tree cover than the other types.

For best performance with an internal quad helix antenna, hold the receiver so that the top is pointing up to the sky.

External antennas

Some GPS receivers have connectors for attaching external antennas. An external antenna is useful if the GPS receiver's view of the sky is otherwise blocked, like in a boat, a car, an airplane, or a backpack.

Reradiating antennas

If a GPS receiver doesn't have a jack for connecting an external antenna, you can improve the reception with a *reradiating antenna*. These antennas work just as well as conventional external antennas that plug into a GPS receiver.

A reradiating antenna combines two GPS antennas:

- ✔ One antenna receives the GPS signal from the satellites.
- ✔ The other antenna is connected to the first and positioned next to the GPS unit's internal antenna.

Here are a couple of sources for reradiating antennas:

- ✔ **Roll your own:** If you're handy with a soldering iron, search Google for *reradiating antenna GPS* for tips on how to make one yourself.
- ✔ **Buy one:** Purchase an assembled reradiating antenna from Pc-Mobile at www.pc-mobile.net/gpsant.htm.

Internal memory

A receiver's internal memory holds such data as waypoints, track logs, routes, and uploadable digital maps (if the model supports them). The more memory the receiver has, the more data you can store in it. All the data that's been stored in the GPS receiver is retained when the device is turned off.

GPS receivers have different amounts of memory. Unlike personal computers, you can't add memory chips to a GPS unit to expand its internal memory.

External storage

Some GPS receivers aren't limited to internal memory for storage, using support memory cards that can be plugged into the receiver to store data. External memory can be either

- **Manufacturer proprietary data cards**
- **Generic (and less expensive) storage,** such as
  - MultiMediaCard (MMC; www.mmca.org)
  - Secure Digital (SD; www.sandisk.com)

Accessory programs

Many GPS receivers have built-in accessory programs that display various handy features such as

- Calendars with the best time to hunt and fish
- Sunrise, moonrise, sunset, and moonset tables
- Tide tables
- Calculators
- Games

User interface modes

Some GPS receivers have simple and advanced user interface modes.

✔ **Simple mode:** This displays only often used commands and features.

This is an excellent option for the novice user who wants to use basic GPS receiver functions without being distracted or confused by the many other features.

✔ **Advanced mode:** This shows all commands and features.

Synthesized voice

Some models of GPS receiver, designed primarily for automotive use, have a synthesized voice that provides you with route-finding information. Although this feature has been available as an option in some luxury cars for many years (for example, in the OnStar system), portable GPS units that talk to you are available. You don't have to pay monthly subscription fees for them, and you can easily move them from car to car. (Ah, progress.)

You can find more information in Chapter 5 on how to select a portable GPS receiver to use for road navigation.

If you're using your GPS receiver primarily for navigation in your vehicle, mount it securely so that it doesn't slide around the dashboard.

✔ GPS receiver manufacturers make mounting brackets for in-vehicle use.

✔ Do-it-yourself solutions can include Velcro, Silly Putty, small beanbags, or modeling clay (the nonhardening type).

Never mount your GPS unit where an airbag deploys during a crash.

GPS monopoly

The U.S. has had a monopoly on satellite-based location systems over the years (the Russian GLONASS, Global Orbiting Navigation Satellite System, has really never been a viable player), but that may soon change.

The European Union is moving toward deploying its own positioning system called Galileo. If everything goes as planned, Galileo will be operational by 2008 with a constellation of 30 stationary satellites. Position accuracy is touted as within a meter, which is ten times more precise than what GPS currently provides to civilians.

The United States isn't happy about this; as an alternative, GPS prevents the U.S. government and military from selectively degrading signals and blocking use elsewhere in the world. China, Israel, and India have expressed interest in becoming involved with Galileo. As of early 2004, after a number of negotiation sessions, the U.S. and European Union had reached a number of compromises that met both parties' needs.

```
http://europa.eu.int/comm/dgs/
    energy_transport/galileo/
    index_en.htm
```

The Future of GPS

Modern technology rapidly evolves, and the same holds true for GPS. Since consumer GPS receivers first became available in the mid-1990s, the market has grown tremendously because of cheaper receiver prices and new ways to use GPS. A peek into a crystal ball shows what the future may hold for GPS.

✔ **More accurate:** The United States has started planning the next generation of GPS, dubbed *GPS III*. Driving factors are better accuracy and reliability, improved resistance to signal jamming, and the looming European Galileo system. Increasing the number of WAAS satellites in orbit is also planned. The first GPS III satellite is tentatively planned for launch in 2012. The U.S. government budget will have an impact on plans to improve the present GPS system; the Iraq invasion delayed the launch of several satellites.

✔ **Smaller:** GPS receivers will continue to shrink. GPS units already are integrated into wristwatches, and PC Card GPS receivers can plug into a laptop or PDA.

The three limiting factors that prevent a consumer receiver from shrinking are antenna size, screen size, and power source size

✔ **Cheaper:** Prices will continue to decline as manufacturing costs decrease and production quantities increase.

✔ **Easier to use:** Simplified and less technical user interfaces will become more of a priority as GPS receivers become more appliancelike to meet the needs of specialized markets. An example is Garmin's Forerunner product, which is targeted to runners and lacks a number of features typically found in traditional GPS receivers.

✔ **Easier to view:** Improved screen technology will make GPS receiver screens brighter and easier to read.

✔ **More integrated:** GPS receivers are being integrated into cars and trucks, cellphones, PDAs, Family Radio Service (FRS) radios, and other consumer electronic devices. Expect some new products and services that take advantage of location-aware data.

✔ **Thriftier:** User-replaceable AA and AAA batteries have long powered portable GPS receivers, but expect some changes in power sources.

• Built-in Lithium ion (Li-Ion) and nickel metal-hydride (NiMH) batteries, popular in cellphones and laptops, make sense for GPS receivers. Garmin started releasing rechargeable GPS receivers at the end of 2003.

• Further on the horizon, miniature fuel cell technology will keep GPS units going and going without frequent battery changes.

✔ **Less wired:** Most GPS receivers transfer data from personal computers through a cable. Wireless technologies such as Bluetooth (www.blue tooth.com) and wireless USB are well suited for fast and easy data transfers to GPS receivers without using cables.

Chapter 4

Grasping Important GPS Concepts

In Chapter 3, I provide you with a pretty good idea of what Global Positioning System (GPS) is and how it works. In addition to knowing about the satellites, ground stations, and receivers, however, you should have a grasp of some important concepts before you start using a GPS receiver — things like coordinate systems, datums, waypoints, routes, and tracks.

Even if you already own a GPS receiver and have used it for a while, this is still a good chapter to skim through because some of these basic concepts that I discuss end up being overlooked in user manuals or can get a bit fuzzy if you don't use your GPS receiver on a regular basis. Read on while I help clarify some important terms and concepts (like datums and waypoints and routes) so you'll be (pardon the pun) moving in the right direction.

Linking GPS, Maps, and Coordinate Systems

Some people think that after they have a GPS receiver, they really don't need a map, especially if the receiver has built-in mapping capabilities. This isn't necessarily true. GPS receivers are best used in conjunction with maps, whether those maps are paper or digital. Here are some of the reasons why:

  ✔ **Detail:** Most maps on handheld GPS receivers don't offer the detail of full-size paper or digital maps, especially topographic maps and nautical charts.

✔ **Size:** A GPS receiver's screen is pretty darn small, and it's just about impossible to get the big picture that a full-size map can give you.

✔ **Backup:** If you have a paper map with you and know how to use it, the map becomes an important backup if your GPS receiver's batteries fail or if you encounter poor satellite coverage. Gadget lovers might consider a paper map and magnetic compasses primitive, but they don't require batteries — and both are lightweight and cheap, to boot.

✔ **Complementary:** After you get back home or to the office, you might want to see where you've been on a map, based on the locations that you've stored in the GPS receiver. With a digital map, you can easily plot the exact route that you took or identify the places you visited.

All maps and GPS receivers use *coordinate systems,* which are grids on maps that enable you to find locations on a map. Because GPS receivers are designed for use with maps, they support a number of coordinate systems that correspond to those commonly found on maps. (Chapter 2 has information on using map coordinate systems.) Thus, you can take a location that you recorded on your GPS receiver and precisely locate it on a map.

By default, your GPS receiver displays positions in latitude and longitude. But you can change the settings to display locations in exotic-sounding coordinate systems such as the Finnish KKJ27 grid, the Qatar grid, or the W Malaysian R grid. You probably won't need to switch to some of these obscure coordinate systems, so you can stick with latitude and longitude or Universal Transverse Mercator (UTM), which are used pretty much everywhere. If you're fuzzy on what latitude and longitude or UTM are, check out Chapter 2, which gives an overview of the two coordinate systems.

Land navigation

Discovering how to effectively use paper maps and compasses for land navigation is both an art and a science, with complete books written on the subject. Here are two excellent, free online resources if you want to find out more.

✔ *Map and Compass for Firefighters* (NFES 2554) is a self-study course developed by the U.S. government for wildland firefighters. The course is available at `www.nwcg.gov/pms/training/map_comp.pdf`.

✔ *Map Reading and Land Navigation* (FM 3-25.26) is the U.S. Army field manual on the subject, available at `www.army.mil/usapa/doctrine/DR_pubs/dr_a/pdf/fm3_25x26.pdf`.

Another great way to become a pro land navigator is through the sport of orienteering. *Orienteering* involves using a map and compass to find control points (small flags) in the shortest amount of time as possible. Do a Web search for *orienteering* to find more about the sport and how you can participate in clubs and events in your local area.

How much latitude?

GPS units can display latitude and longitude in several different formats. Take the location at the top of Mt. Bachelor (some great skiing in Central Oregon if you're ever in the neighborhood) and see how it can be expressed.

- Degrees, minutes, decimal seconds (D° M' S"): 43° 58' 46.94" N, 121° 41' 14.73" W

- Degrees, decimal minutes (D° M.M'): 43° 58.7824' N, 121° 41.2455' W

- Decimal degrees (D.D°): 43.9797069° N, 121.6874253° W

And just for fun, here are the UTM coordinates for that same location: 10T 0605273E, 48 70240N.

Ouch! Is this confusing or what? Although it doesn't seem like it, all these coordinates refer to the exact same location. Remember, just like converting locations from one coordinate system

to another, you can also use your GPS receiver as a calculator to convert from different latitude and longitude formats. Suppose you have some coordinates in decimal degrees and need them in degrees, minutes, and seconds:

1. **Change the coordinate settings in your GPS receiver to decimal degrees.**

2. **Manually enter the coordinates as a waypoint.**

3. **Change the coordinate settings in your GPS receiver to degrees, minutes, and seconds.**

When you look at the coordinates of the waypoint that you entered, they're now displayed in degrees, minutes, and seconds. (**Note:** Because changing coordinate systems varies from model to model, check your user manual for specific instructions.)

Suppose you have your GPS receiver set to latitude and longitude, and you record some locations. When you get home, you find out that your paper map doesn't have latitude and longitude marks but uses only the UTM coordinate system. Not a problem. Look in your GPS receiver user manual for information on changing the coordinate system from latitude and longitude to UTM. Location points that you store in latitude and longitude appear as UTM coordinates. This is a quick and easy way of converting data between coordinate systems. Or you can visit the Graphical Locator Home Page at Montana State University (www.esg.montana.edu/gl/index.html) to perform online conversions of latitude and longitude and Township and Range.

Although Township and Range is a popular coordinate system used on many maps in the United States, don't expect your GPS receiver to support this system. Unlike the latitude and longitude and UTM grid systems, which were mathematically derived, grids in the Township and Range system may not always be the same size, thus making it difficult for a GPS receiver to determine coordinates in this system. Most maps that have Township and Range information also have latitude and longitude or UTM marks. If you have a location reported in Township and Range, you'll need to spend a bit of time looking at a map, manually figuring out the position that the coordinates point to, and then plot that position by using a different coordinate system.

Understanding GPS and Datums

As I discuss in Chapter 2, a *datum* is a frame of reference for mapping. Because the earth isn't flat, geographic coordinate systems use *ellipsoids* (think of a sphere that's not perfectly spherical, much like the shape of the Earth) to calculate positions on our third planet from the sun. A datum is the position of the ellipsoid relative to the center of the earth.

Unless you're a cartographer or geographer, that probably hurts just thinking about it. Sparing you a long and detailed technical description (which you can get in Chapter 2), here are the two important things that you need to know:

✔ **All maps have a datum.** Hundreds of different datums are in use. Most good maps used for navigation — and highway maps don't count — usually state which datum was used in making the map.

✔ **You can set what datum your GPS receiver uses.** An example of a GPS map datum page is shown in Figure 4-1.

Figure 4-1:
A GPS
receiver
map datum
page.

The default datum for GPS receivers is WGS 84, more formally known as the World Geodetic System 1984. WGS 84 was adopted as a world standard and is derived from a datum called the North American Datum of 1983.

Most USGS topographic maps that you use for hiking are based on an earlier datum called the North American Datum of 1927, or NAD 27. This datum is divided into different geographic areas, so if you're in the United States — at least in the lower 48 states — use a version of NAD 27 that mentions the continental U.S.

So why is all this datum stuff so important? In the United States, if a position is saved in a GPS receiver by using the WGS 84 datum and the same coordinates are plotted on a map that uses the NAD 27 datum, the location can be off as much as 200 meters. That's more than a couple of football fields off. The latitude and longitude coordinates will be identical, but the location is going to end up in two different spots.

Datum lessons learned

Here's a quick story from my Forest Service fire-fighting days that illustrates the importance of being aware of datums. A fire was reported in a mountainous area of eastern Oregon, and my partner and I helicopter-rappelled in to put out the fire. Because the fire was bigger than expected, we requested some smokejumpers to assist. They were down from Alaska, helping out during the lower 48's fire season, and they all had new handheld GPS receivers, which were pretty state of the art back then (1998). The fire continued to grow, and we called in a small air tanker to stop the fire's spread. One of the Alaska jumpers pulled out his GPS unit, and we called in an exact set of coordinates for the pilot to hit. As the tanker approached, the pilot radioed us, asking whether we were sure that was where we wanted the retardant to go. Turns out that the jumper still had his GPS unit set with an Alaska map datum (that didn't match the local datum on the pilot's GPS receiver), and the coordinates that the Bureau of Land Management (BLM) jumper gave were on the other side of the ridge, nowhere near the fire. Fortunately, the pilot used his own initiative and dumped his load right where it needed to go.

The moral of the story is to make sure that the datums on your GPS receiver and maps are the same. Or, if you're with a group of people using GPS receivers, make sure that all your datums match.

Not having the map datum match the GPS receiver datum is one of the biggest errors that new users of GPS receivers make. I can't emphasize this point strongly enough: Make sure that the two match!

Setting Waypoints

A *waypoint* is GPS lingo for a location or point that you store in your GPS receiver. Some manufacturers also call them *marks or landmarks.* A waypoint consists of the following information:

- ✔ **Location:** The location of the waypoint in whichever coordinate system the GPS receiver is currently using. Some receivers also store the elevation of the location.

- ✔ **Name:** The name of the waypoint. You get to choose your own name; the length varies between GPS receiver models from six characters on up.

- ✔ **Date and time:** The date and time the waypoint was created.

- ✔ **Optional icon or symbol:** An optional icon or symbol associated with the waypoint that appears on the GPS receiver's map page when the area around the waypoint is displayed. This could be a tent for a campground, a boat for a boat launch, or a fish for a favorite fishing spot.

All GPS receivers can store waypoints, but the maximum number that you can save varies from model to model. As a general rule, as the price of a GPS receiver goes up, so does the number of waypoints that can be stored. Lower-end consumer GPS receivers store 100–250 waypoints, and top-of-the-line models can store 1,000 or more.

Saving waypoints

The two types of waypoints you can enter and save to your GPS receiver are

- **Current location:** GPS receivers have a button on the case or an onscreen command for marking the current location as a waypoint. (Check your user manual for details.) After the waypoint is marked, the GPS receiver screen displays a waypoint information page where you can name the waypoint and associate an icon with it.

- **Known location:** If you know the coordinates of a location that you want to save as a waypoint, you can manually enter it in the GPS receiver. Most GPS receivers also allow you to mark wherever the cursor is on the map page as a waypoint. A known location could be a good fishing spot that a friend saved to his GPS receiver or perhaps a lake you want to visit that you got the coordinates from a digital map. Again, check your user manual for directions on how to manually enter a waypoint. In Figure 4-2, you can see a Lowrance iFINDER waypoint page that's displayed when you press its ENT button.

Always use meaningful names when you save a waypoint. GPS receivers typically assign a sequential number as the default waypoint name. Although numbers and cryptic codes might make sense when you enter them, I guarantee you that you probably won't remember what they mean a couple of weeks down the road.

Some GPS units have a MOB function, which has nothing whatever to do with tommy guns or cement shoes. MOB stands for *Man Overboard* and was designed for boaters to use in case someone fell into the water. (Go figure.) After seeing or hearing the splash, the captain can press a button (that creates a waypoint appropriately named MOB) and then turn around and head back to the exact location of the unlucky sailor.

Although a GPS receiver is good for letting you know where you are, waypoints are important for helping you get somewhere you'd like to go. GPS receivers have a number of features that can help you navigate to a waypoint that you've entered.

Maybe you decide to go for a hike. Before you leave the trailhead, you save the location of the parking lot as a waypoint, naming it PRKLOT. ***Note:*** Some GPS receivers support waypoint names only in uppercase characters; others allow you to use both uppercase and lowercase characters.

Figure 4-2:
A waypoint
page.

As you hike down the trail, you hear the call of a rare ivory-billed wood-pecker and head off into the brush, intent on getting a sighting of the very elusive bird. After an hour of tromping around in the dense woods, you dis-cover two things. First, the bird was just a robin; second, you're totally turned around and are somewhat lost. But fortunately, because you have a GPS receiver with you (and have read this book), you know that you'll be able to easily find your way back to the car and be home in time for dinner. The following sections show you how.

Using the waypoint list

GPS receivers have an information page that lists all the waypoints that you've created and stored. (Again, check your user manual for information on how to access and use this list.) The waypoints can be listed by name or those closest to your current location. By selecting a waypoint, no matter where you are, you can find your way to it.

✔ **The distance to the waypoint,** such as a parking lot or trailhead.

✔ **The compass direction in degrees** that you'll need to head to get to the waypoint.

In Figure 4-3, see a GPS receiver screen providing information on how to get to a selected waypoint.

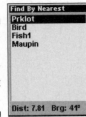

Figure 4-3:
A GPS
receiver
waypoint list
screen.

Any of the waypoints in the list can be deleted or edited. See your user manual for specific instructions.

If you roam around the Internet searching for information about GPS, you'll come across handy collections of waypoints that you can enter into your GPS receiver. There are all manner of waypoint lists, from fishing spots to pubs in England. If you're planning a vacation, consider doing a Web search ahead of time to see whether there are any waypoints associated with your destination. Then bring your GPS receiver along with you as a personal tour guide.

GPS receivers designed for outdoor use always assume a straight line as the route between two points. That might be convenient for airplanes and boats, but it doesn't take into account cliffs, rivers, streams, fences, and other obstacles on land. GPS receivers designed for automobile navigation are a bit smarter, having built-in databases of road information that's used in suggesting and measuring appropriate routes from Point A to Point B.

Depending on the GPS receiver model, other waypoint-related information that you may be able to display includes

- ✔ **Travel time:** The amount of time it will take you to reach the waypoint based on your current speed.

- ✔ **Compass:** A picture of a compass that displays the waypoint direction heading.

- ✔ **Directional arrow:** An arrow that points in the correct direction that you should be heading.

- ✔ **Navigational hints:** A picture of a road that moves as you travel. If the road is centered onscreen, your destination is straight ahead. If the road veers to the right or the left, you need to correct your course so that the road is centered. A symbol associated with the waypoint will grow larger as you get closer to it.

Some GPS receivers come with databases of cities, highways, airports, landmarks, and other geographic features. These are just waypoints stored in memory that you can't edit or delete to free up memory for new waypoints.

Most GPS receivers support mapping. At the very least, a GPS receiver has a simple plot display, a map page that shows waypoints, tracks (see the upcoming section, "Making Tracks"), and your current position. More advanced (and expensive) GPS receivers support more sophisticated maps; your waypoints and tracks appear along with roads, rivers, bodies of water, and whatever built-in features the map has. When the map page is displayed, you can zoom in, zoom out, and move around the map with an onscreen cursor that you control with buttons on the GPS receiver.

A map page can be orientated two ways: so either the top of the screen always faces north or the top of the screen faces the direction you're traveling. Orientating the screen to the north is probably the easiest if you're used to working with maps, which usually are orientated with their tops to the north.

Following Routes

A *route* is a course that you're currently traveling or plan to take. In GPS terms, a route is the course between one or more waypoints (see Figure 4-4). If multiple waypoints are in a route, the course between two waypoints is a *leg*. A single route can be made up of a number of legs.

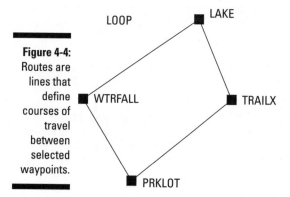

Figure 4-4: Routes are lines that define courses of travel between selected waypoints.

Suppose it was a beautiful day, and you went hiking, deciding to make a loop: hike from a parking lot trailhead to a scenic waterfall, go over to a lake for some lunch on a sandy beach, and finally head cross-country until you reach a trail intersection that would take you back to your starting point at the parking lot. You've hiked in the area before; in fact, you've visited each of your planned destinations and marked them as waypoints in your GPS receiver. However, you've never hiked this particular loop before, so you decide to make a route called LOOP with the following legs that you've already previously entered as waypoints:

> PRKLOT to WTRFALL
>
> WTRFALL to LAKE
>
> LAKE to TRAILX
>
> TRAILX to PRKLOT

After you create your route, the GPS receiver tells you how long each leg will be and also the total distance of the route. When you *activate* the route (tell the GPS receiver you're ready to use it), this information is displayed:

✔ **Direction:** The direction you need to travel in order to reach the next waypoint in the route

✔ **Distance:** How far away the next waypoint is

✔ **Duration:** How much time it's going to take to get there

After you reach a waypoint in the route, the GPS receiver automatically starts calculating the information for the next leg. This continues until you reach your final destination.

To route or not to route

A fair number of GPS receiver owners don't use routes and find them to be an overrated feature. After all, after you reach your first destination, you can easily select the next location from the waypoint list and be on your way. In addition, if you want to record where you've been, just using tracks is much easier. I discuss this in the section, "Making Tracks." However, here are a couple of situations when you should consider using routes:

✔ If you're traveling to the same location on a regular basis (such as a guide leading clients on established trips).

✔ If you're planning on sharing a route with other GPS receiver owners. Think of this as being a virtual tour guide. Routes can be downloaded and then uploaded to other GPS receivers.

✔ If you have a mapping program, you can plan a trip ahead of time and create routes on your computer by simply clicking your mouse where you want to go. When you're finished, you can upload the route to your GPS receiver.

Using routes is a personal preference. Try creating and using routes to see whether they meet your needs. If they don't, you can get by with waypoints and tracks.

Don't confuse a route with an *autoroute,* which applies to GPS receivers that can provide you with turn-by-turn street directions to a destination you're driving to. AutoRoute is also the name of a Microsoft European street mapping program.

Routes can be created ahead of time or entered while you're traveling. Like with waypoints, after you create a route, you can delete or edit it, including removing or adding waypoints within legs.

Whenever you're using a route or navigating to a waypoint, you don't need to leave your GPS receiver on all the time. You can shut it off every now and then to conserve batteries. When you turn the GPS receiver back on, just select the waypoint or route that you were using, and the GPS receiver recalculates your present position and gives you updated information about how to reach your destination.

The number of routes and the number of waypoints that a route can consist of vary from one GPS receiver to another. Some inexpensive GPS receivers don't support routes, but a high-end consumer GPS unit might have up to 50 routes with up to 125 waypoints in each route.

Making Tracks

Remember the story of Hansel and Gretel, the kids who dropped breadcrumbs in the forest to try to find their way back home? Their story would've had a different ending if they had a GPS receiver because all newer GPS receivers leave electronic breadcrumbs (called *tracks* or *trails* depending on the manufacturer) while you travel. Every so often, the GPS receiver saves the coordinates of the current position to memory. This series of tracks is a *track log* or *track history.* (Because various GPS models handle tracks differently, check your user manual for specific details.)

Note these differences between tracks and waypoints:

- ✔ **Names and symbols:** Although tracks and waypoints are both location data points, tracks don't have names or symbols associated with them and can't be edited in the GPS receiver.

- ✔ **Autocreation:** Unlike waypoints — that you need to manually enter — tracks are automatically created whenever a GPS receiver is turned on (that is, if you have the track feature enabled).

If track logging is enabled, tracks are shown on the GPS receiver's map page while you move, like a trail of breadcrumbs. The GPS receiver constantly collects tracks while it's powered on, so you need to clear the current track log before you start a new trip. If you want, you can save a current track log.

If you turn your GPS receiver off or if you lose satellite reception, the GPS receiver stops recording tracks. When it's turned back on again or good satellite coverage resumes, the GPS receiver continues recording tracks, but it will assume that you traveled in a straight line between the last track location saved, before satellite reception was lost, and your current position.

Some GPS receivers allow you to set how often tracks are saved, either by time or distance intervals. For example, you could specify that a track be saved every minute or each time that you travel a tenth of a mile. Leaving the default, automatic setting for track collection should work for most occasions. However, if you're using your GPS receiver for specialized purposes (such as mapping a trail), you may want to experiment with different intervals to give you the level of detail that you need.

When you reach your final destination, your GPS receiver can optionally use the track log to help you navigate back to your starting point by using the track data to guide you retracing your steps. Check your user manual for model specific instructions on how to do this.

Tracks are probably one of the most useful GPS receiver features if you're working with digital maps. From a number of free and commercial mapping programs, you can overlay your tracks on top of a map to see exactly where you've been. Figure 4-5 shows an example of track data collected during a trail run and then uploaded to a mapping program.

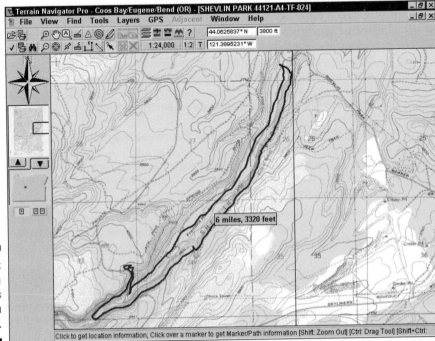

Figure 4-5:
Track data
shows
where you
traveled.

GPSBabel

You won't find any standards when it comes to GPS receiver waypoint, route, and track formats. Each GPS receiver manufacturer seems to have its own data format. To further complicate things, software companies that make mapping programs also use their own data formats. This can make exchanging GPS data between different receivers and software a very big challenge.

In order to help address this, the folks at topoGraphix (www.topographix.com), a GPS and map software company, developed GPX. GPX stands for *GPS Exchange,* which is a lightweight, XML (eXtensible Markup Language) data format for exchanging waypoints, routes, and tracks between applications and Web services on the Internet. GPX is slowly building up

momentum and is being adopted by both software vendors and Web service providers.

However, until a standard is widely adopted (and I'm personally not holding my breath), your best bet to exchange GPS data is the free GPSBabel utility. This versatile program converts information created by one type of GPS receiver or software program into formats that can be read by others. GPSBabel is available for a number of different operating systems as a command line utility, and you can find easy-to-use Windows front-ends if you prefer a mouse and menus.

To get more information about GPSBabel and download the utility, visit http://gpsbabel.sourceforge.net.

Depending on the model, GPS receivers can store between 1,000 and 10,000 tracks and up to 10 track logs. If you exceed the maximum number of tracks, the GPS receiver will either stop collecting tracks or begin overwriting the oldest tracks that were collected first with the most current ones. (Some GPS receivers let you define what action to take.) The number of tracks collected over time depends completely on your activity, speed, GPS coverage, and the GPS receiver's track setting. Just to give you a ballpark idea, when I go trail running with a Garmin Geko 201, the receiver typically collects around 250 tracks an hour on its default track setting.

Some GPS receivers reduce the number of tracks in saved track logs. For example, if you have 5,100 track points in the active track log, the number might be reduced to 750 track points when you save the log. This is done to save memory. You'll still have a general sense of where you've been, but you lose detail. If you need a high level of detail — such as if you were mapping a trail — always download the active track log to a computer first before saving the track log to your GPS receiver.

You can download waypoints, routes, and tracks to your personal computer. The data can then be stored on your hard drive, used with digital mapping programs, or loaded into other GPS receivers. You can also upload waypoints, routes, and tracks that you create on your computer to your GPS receiver. See Chapter 9 for tips on how to interface your GPS receiver to a computer.

Chapter 5

Selecting and Getting Started with a GPS Receiver

- -

- -

*T*his chapter is about selecting a GPS receiver and getting started using it. Choosing a GPS receiver can be quite an overwhelming experience. If you look at handheld, portable GPS receivers that the Big Three (Garmin, Magellan, and Lowrance) currently offer, you'll have around 50–60 GPS receivers to choose from. That's a lot of choices. And that's only the beginning. After you purchase one, you still need to find out how to use it.

This chapter should take some of the confusion out of buying a GPS receiver and help you come up to speed using it. (*GPS For Dummies* isn't meant to replace your user manual, though, which you should refer to while you're reading the "Becoming Familiar with Your New GPS Receiver" section of this chapter.)

When it comes to selecting a GPS receiver, I won't recommend that you buy a particular brand or model or tell you which is best for hiking, *geocaching* (the best Easter egg hunt in the world; see Chapter 9), or other activities. Rather, I follow more of a Socratic method, in which I ask you a number of questions that should help you make a pretty good and informed purchasing decision.

Selecting a GPS Receiver

Before you purchase a GPS receiver, you should spend some time kicking the proverbial tires. Don't rush out and buy a receiver based on one or two good Internet reviews without having a chance to hold that very GPS receiver in your hands to see how it works. Spend some time comparing different brands and models to determine which one works best for you. Because GPS units are sold in most sporting goods stores and many large retail chains, you shouldn't have to buy a receiver sight unseen.

The three largest manufacturers of consumer GPS receivers in the United States are Garmin, Magellan (a part of Thales Navigation), and Lowrance. All these manufacturers have extensive Web sites that provide detailed information about their products. If you're in the market for a GPS receiver, definitely spend some time browsing through product literature. The Web site addresses for these manufacturers are

- ✔ **Garmin:** www.garmin.com
- ✔ **Magellan:** www.magellangps.com
- ✔ **Lowrance:** www.lowrance.com

And don't just look at the marketing literature. Download the user manuals for the models you're interested in to better understand their features.

All GPS receiver manufacturers offer free Adobe Acrobat PDF versions of their product user manuals on their respective Web sites. If you're in the market for a GPS receiver, these are excellent resources for comparing features and seeing what the user interface is like because the manuals have instructions as well as screenshots.

Friends with GPS receivers are also a good source of information; ask to take their different brands and models out for a test drive.

Here are the two big questions that you should ask yourself before you begin your GPS receiver search:

- ✔ **What am I going to use it for?** Think about what activities you'll be doing with your GPS receiver: hiking, biking, fishing, sales trips on the road, and so on. What will you expect your GPS receiver to do? Navigate streets or the wilderness, store favorite fishing spots, or find *geocaches* (hidden goodies from the popular electronic treasure hunting sport of geocaching)? When you get specific with your answers, you start to identify features that your GPS receiver should have to meet your needs.

✔ **How much do I want to spend?** How much money you've got in your wallet or purse is obviously going to influence which models you end up considering. The more features a GPS receiver has, the more it's going to cost. So if you can figure out exactly what you're going to use the receiver for (see the preceding bullet) as well as which features you really need (versus those that are nice to have), you'll end up saving some money. Generally, figure on spending anywhere from a little under $100 to $500 for a handheld GPS receiver, although note that a few specialized automotive and aviation models can cost up to $1,000.

For the most part, the cost of a GPS receiver really has nothing to do with accuracy. An expensive GPS receiver isn't more accurate than a cheaper model. The only exceptions to this rule are GPS receivers that support Wide Area Augmentation System (WAAS), which can be more accurate than GPS receivers that don't have these enhanced location features.

Figuring out how much you want to spend and what you want your GPS receiver to do narrows your options considerably, but you're likely still going to be faced with a number of choices. The next step is to narrow down the list of candidates with some more questions and things to consider, including

✔ **Map display:** *Do you want to view maps on your GPS receiver?* If so, you definitely need a *mapping model* — a GPS receiver that displays maps. See the later section, "To map or not to map."

✔ **Function:** *Will you use your GSP receiver primarily for road navigation or outdoor recreation?* Models are better suited for one or the other. See the upcoming section, "Road warriors."

✔ **Accessories:** *Does your budget include accessories such as cases, cables, vehicle mounting brackets, a case, and uploadable maps?*

✔ **Battery needs:** Consider the following questions:

- *How many hours does the GPS receiver run on a set of batteries?* Remember two things: Different models (and their features) have different battery diets, and different battery types have varying life spans. (See the upcoming section, "Battery basics," for the skinny on the different types of batteries and their life expectancy.)

- *Will you need to carry spare batteries (always a good idea), and if so, how many?* I recommend always carrying at least one fresh set of spare batteries.

- *Will you be using a cigarette lighter power adapter as an alternative to using batteries?*

✔ **Memory:** *How much memory does the GPS receiver have and is it expandable?* This is a critical question if you're interested in a GPS receiver that supports uploadable maps. Visit the GPS receiver manufacturer Web site to get an idea of how much memory maps can take up. Or better yet, check some of the Internet GPS information sources listed in Chapter 21, where users talk about how much memory they need for loading different types of maps.

✔ **Display screen:** Find out the following:

• *How big is the screen and how well can you read it?* Make sure to consider visibility at night, in bright sunlight, and in poor weather conditions. The size of the screen is directly related to the overall size of the GPS receiver, so if you want a larger, more readable screen, expect a larger GPS receiver to go with it.

• *Do you really need a color screen?* A color screen makes reading maps easier because different colors are associated with map features. ***Note:*** Color is more of a preference than a requirement.

✔ **User interface:** *Does operating the GPS receiver make sense to you?* Sure, some learning is required to come up to speed, but using a GPS receiver should mostly be intuitive. Be sure to compare different brands and models because user interfaces are far from standardized.

✔ **External controls:** Look at different designs:

• *Are the buttons and controls on the GPS receiver easy to use?* Naturally, this is also related to the user interface.

• *Are the controls hard to operate while wearing gloves or mittens?*

✔ **Weight and size:** *Do you want absolutely the smallest package you can get?* Note that there's only about a 7-ounce weight difference between the lightest and heaviest handheld GPS receivers.

✔ **Computer interface:** *Do you plan to connect your GPS receiver to a computer to download and upload data?* If so, make sure that the receiver can interface with a computer to exchange data; I think this feature is a must so you can upgrade the GPS receiver's firmware. See Chapter 9 for more details on connecting GPS receivers to computers.

To map or not to map

In terms of features, probably the biggest decision you'll need to make is whether to get a GPS receiver that displays maps. If you plan to use your GPS receiver for on-the-road navigation, you need a mapping model. If you're primarily using your GPS receiver for outdoor activities, you need to decide whether to spend the extra money and get a model that displays maps. Quite honestly, no matter what a salesperson might tell you, a GPS receiver with built-in maps isn't required for activities such as hiking, geocaching, fishing, bird watching, kayaking, or other outdoor pursuits. Using waypoints (see

Chapter 4) and tracks are all you need to navigate and successfully stay found. (Of course, you have a paper map and compass with you, and know how to use them, right?) Even though your GPS receiver doesn't display maps, if it can interface with a PC, you can still download information on where you've been and have it show up in a digital mapping program.

That said, mapping GPS receivers are pretty handy because they give you a quick, big-picture view of where you're located in relation to other features. And just the sight of a map, even though it's tiny and lacks a lot of detail, can be pretty reassuring at times; even for a seasoned outdoors-person.

Although I'm a firm believer that a mapping GPS receiver should never take the place of a paper map and compass, if your budget allows a mapping GPS receiver along with the digital maps to load with it, I'd say buy it. I personally use a mapping model for outdoor navigation and treat the map feature as just another tool in my bag of navigation tricks. In Chapter 10, find out more about the type of maps that you can use with GPS receivers.

Road warriors

If you'll use your GPS receiver primarily in a car or truck for road navigation, your feature criteria is a bit different than a GPS receiver designed primarily for outdoor recreational use. Although any GPS receiver with a base map or uploadable street maps can help you stay found on the road, some models are more suited to automobile navigation. And although some GPS receivers are designed primarily for automotive use, I prefer handheld GPS receivers that offer versatility because they can be used in a car or for outdoor recreation.

Some important features to look for in a GPS receiver that you're going to use for road navigation include

- ✔ **Automatic route selection:** A GPS receiver designed for street navigation allows you to find addresses, street intersections, and highway exits. Just enter where you want to go, and the receiver calculates the shortest or fastest way to get there. Pretty slick, isn't it? The selected route is highlighted on the map screen, and your progress is displayed as you travel. If you encounter a traffic jam or other road problem, you can instruct the receiver to recalculate a new route from your present position and avoid the problem.

- ✔ *Turn here* **directions:** The GPS receiver lists all the streets and roads in your route at which you'll need to make turns, including the street name, an arrow that points to the correct turning direction, how far ahead the turn is, and how long it's going to take to arrive at the turn. The GPS receiver gives an audible or visual signal prior to when you need to turn.

- ✔ **Points of interest:** Maps that are used with road navigation GPS receivers have databases of information about gas stations, restaurants, freeway exits, hotels, attractions, entertainment, shopping, and emergency services along your route. These are dubbed *Points of Interest* (POIs); the GPS receiver can display information about specific POIs.

✔ **External antenna support:** Because the metal body of a car or truck might interfere with satellite signals, an external antenna might be required to connect to the GPS receiver. An external antenna also provides you with more mounting location options because only the antenna (and not the GPS receiver) needs to be mounted someplace with a clear view of the sky. *Note:* Some heated windshields can block satellite signals. In cases like that, you'll probably need to use an external antenna with a magnetic roof mount.

If you're a GPS road warrior, you'll definitely want a 12-volt cigarette lighter adapter so you don't go through a lot of batteries during a trip.

And finally, if you're more of an urbanite (versus an outdoors) adventurer, another option is to use a PDA, such as a Pocket PC or Palm with GPS hardware and street navigation software. Chapter 6 discusses the ins and outs of using PDAs with GPS.

Matching GPS receiver features to your activities

Aside from a few portable, specialized, single-purpose automotive and aviation GPS receivers, most GPS receivers are pretty versatile and can be used for a wide range of activities. However, some features make some GPS receivers more suited to certain activities than others.

Table 5-1 contains a list of activities in which people typically use GPS receivers as well as a list of features that could be useful for each activity. Just remember that these features aren't necessarily required and that a bare-bones GPS receiver will serve you equally well for basic navigation needs.

Table 5-1	Recommended GPS Receiver Features by Activity
Activity	*Useful Features*
Hiking, mountain biking, cross-country skiing	Altimeter/barometer Electronic compass Sunrise/sunset table Uploadable topographic maps
Geocaching	Electronic compass Uploadable topographic maps

Activity	Useful Features
Hunting	Hunting and fishing calendar Sunrise/sunset table Uploadable topographic maps
Fishing	Fishing calendar Floats (it's buoyant) Saltwater tide table Sunrise/sunset table Waterproof
Boating (inland and offshore)	External power supply Floats NMEA* output (for autopilots) Saltwater tide table Sunrise/sunset table Uploadable nautical charts Waterproof
Canoeing, kayaking (inland and coastal)	Floats Saltwater tide table Sunrise/sunset table Uploadable nautical and topographic maps Waterproof
4 x 4-ing, motorcycling, ATV-ing	Electronic compass External power supply Uploadable topographic maps
Flying	External power supply Jeppesen database** WAAS
Mapping, data collection	Area calculation Differential GPS External antenna Helix versus patch antenna*** Large number of waypoints and tracks WAAS
Caving, scuba diving, visiting art museums	Sorry, you're out of luck! You need a clear view of the sky for a GPS receiver to work.

*National Marine Electronics Association.
**Jeppesen (www.jeppesen.com) is the leading U.S. supplier of pilot information. Its databases include information about airports, radio frequencies, and other flight-planning data.
***If there's tree cover, most users prefer the increased sensitivity of a helix antenna. See Chapter 3 for more information about the differences between helix and patch antennas.

GPS receivers that are advertised as waterproof typically comply with the IEC (European Community Specification) Standard 529 IPX7. This standard states a device can be immersed in up to one meter (a little over three feet) of water for up to 30 minutes before failing. You can count on all handheld GPS receivers to be weatherproof (moisture-resistant), but if I'm doing an activity where my waterproof IPX7 GPS receiver might end up taking a dunking, I carry it in water-proof bag that floats just for added security.

If you're a pilot, you've probably figured out I don't include much information about GPS and flying in this book. If you want the lowdown on selecting and using GPS receivers for aviation, check out www.cockpitgps.com. John Bell, a commercial pilot, has written an excellent book — *Cockpit GPS* — that he makes available as a shareware PDF file. Highly recommended.

After you narrow down your choices to a couple of different GPS receivers, check out what people have to say about the models you're considering. Both www.amazon.com and http://reviews.cnet.com have lots of com-ments from consumers who have purchased popular GPS receivers. Perform a search for the manufacturer and model and read online feedback.

Becoming Familiar with Your New GPS Receiver

After considering all the options, making your list, checking it twice, and find-ing out which GPS receivers are naughty and nice, you've finally come to that blessed event where you're the proud owner of a GPS receiver. But before you step out the door for a 100-mile wilderness trek or cross-country road trip, intent on relying on your new electronic gadget as a guide, be sure spend some time getting to know your GPS receiver.

A good place to start your GPS familiarization process is with the user manual. Many GPS receivers have a quick-start guide that gets you up and running in a matter of minutes. These guides are perfect for those impatient, got-to-have-it-now people; however, I suggest that you also take the time to read the full user manual. Otherwise, you could miss out on some important information contained in the full user manual.

In addition to the user manual, this section will also help you become familiar with your GPS receiver so you can get the most out of it. Obviously, because so many GPS receiver models are on the market, don't expect to find detailed operating procedures for your specific model here: You need your user manual for that. What you can expect is basic information that applies to most GPS receivers, including some things most user manuals don't mention.

Based on a number of years of search and rescue experience, I can list numerous occasions when hunters and hikers thought that their GPS receiver was some kind of magic talisman that would prevent them from getting lost. And quite often when the search teams finally found them, they had no clue whatsoever how to properly use their GPS receiver. If you're going to rely on a GPS receiver for navigating outside of urban areas, take the time to find out how to use it so the friendly, local search-and-rescue people don't have to come looking for you. I'll step off my soapbox now, thank you.

Powering Your GPS Receiver

Before you can start using your GPS receiver, you obviously need to give it some power. For portable GPS receivers, that usually means AA or AAA batteries. Manufacturers all give estimated battery lifetimes for their GPS receivers, but the actual number of hours a GPS receiver will run depends on how it's being used. For example, with the backlight on, battery life goes down because more power is consumed. In addition, what type of batteries you're using can also make a difference.

Battery Tech 101

You can really get geeky with batteries and powering your GPS unit. If you get a charge out of electricity, here are some links to nitty-gritty information sources that cover voltage, milliamperes, and GPS drainage rates:

✔ **Battery drain for selected GPS receivers:** www.gpsinformation.net/main/ bat-5.txt. This site offers the lowdown on just how much juice different GPS receiver models consume.

✔ **The Great Battery Shootout!:** www. imaging-resource.com/ACCS/BATTS/ BATTS.HTM. This site is more orientated to digital cameras (not GPS receiver-specific),

but you'll find some good data on how different types of batteries perform.

✔ **Newsgroups:** sci.geo.satellite-nav. Do a Google Groups search in this USENET newsgroup for batteries and be prepared to spend a couple of hours reading through educational (and sometimes controversial) posts.

When you check these sources, you'll run into *mAh,* which means *milliampere-hours.* Most rechargeable batteries like NiMH have the mAh rating printed on their label. This rating is the battery capacity. Typically, the higher the mAh number, the longer the battery will last.

Battery basics

Although batteries may have the same size and shape, they definitely don't perform the same. In Table 5-2 are the pluses and minuses of some of the different types of batteries that you can use with your GPS receiver.

Table 5-2		Battery Comparison	
Type	*Rechargeable?*	*Plus*	*Minus*
Alkaline	No	You can get these popular batteries just about anywhere. They're cheap (especially in quantity) and have a relatively long life	Can't be reused.
Lithium	No	These batteries are lighter and work better under extreme cold conditions. They have the longest life and can be stored for up to ten years. These are different than the rechargeable lithium ion (Li-Ion) batteries found in laptops and cellphones. GPS receivers are starting to appear on the market with nonreplaceable Li-Ion batteries, though.	Can be up to ten times more expensive than alkaline batteries; can't be recharged.
Nickel cadmium (NiCad)	Yes	NiCads were the first generation recharge batteries, and they can be charged about 500 times.	Only have about one-third to one-quarter the life of an alkaline battery. Can develop a *memory* (can't be fully recharged). Have to buy a charger. Probably going the way of the dinosaur, replaced by NiMH batteries.

Type	Rechargeable?	Plus	Minus
Nickel metal-hydride (NiMH)	Yes	NiMH batteries are much better than Ni-Cads because they have a longer life (although not as long as alkalines), don't suffer from memory problems, can be recharged up to around 1,000 times, and are reusable.	Depending on the milliampere capacity (usually the higher the better), can cost a bit more than lithium batteries. Have to buy a charger.
Rechargeable alkaline	Yes	Usually last about one-Have to buy a charger. half to two-thirds as long as regular alkaline batteries and are rechargeable up to 100 times.	Cost roughly the same as NiMHs but aren't as popular.

Expect to pay about $4 for a four-pack of alkalines (the more you buy in a single pack, the cheaper they are) and about $15 for NiMH. Chargers can run you anywhere from $20–$50. (Some chargers come bundled with a set or two of batteries.) When it comes to batteries and chargers, online prices are almost always cheaper than full retail, so be sure to shop around.

Battery saver mode

Some GPS receivers have a battery saver mode that can greatly extend the life of your batteries. (Check your user manual to see whether your model has this feature and how to turn it on.) Normally, a GPS receiver processes satellite data every second and determines your speed and location. Based on this information, the GPS receiver predicts where you should be the next time it gets satellite data. If the prediction is close to your actual position and battery saver mode is turned on, the GPS receiver will start receiving satellite signals every five seconds or so instead of every second. In addition, some of the internal electronics are turned off during this wait period. Because a reduced amount of power is needed, the battery life is extended.

The GPS receiver continues to access satellite data every five seconds until the predicted location isn't accurate anymore, at which time it switches back to receiving data every second, starting the process over again. (Some GPS receivers provide you with a number of choices of how often satellite data is received. The more seconds, the more battery efficient the receiver is.)

If you're environmentally conscious or want to save some money over the long term, use NiMH rechargeable batteries in your GPS receiver. Although a charger and pack of batteries obviously cost more than disposable alkalines, rechargeable batteries are a wise investment because they can be recharged hundreds of times before they end up in a landfill.

Power to the people

After you select the type of batteries you're going to use, you should be aware of some other issues when it comes to powering GPS receivers:

- **Battery life gauges:** In the GPS receiver's setup information page, you can specify what type of battery you're using, such as alkaline or NiMH. The battery type setting helps the GPS receiver make an accurate guess how long the battery will last. Remember that different battery types have different discharge rates. All GPS receivers also have an onscreen battery gauge that shows you how fully charged the batteries are. If you set the wrong type, the worst that will happen is that the gauge won't be accurate. See how to extend battery life with some GPS receiver models in the sidebar, "Battery saver mode."

Always check the battery level of your GPS receiver before you head out on a trip and also remember to carry spare batteries. One way to tell which batteries are new or charged is to put a rubber band around the good ones. By feeling around in your pack or pocket, you can instantly tell which ones are fresh. *Note:* Rechargeable batteries discharge faster than alkaline batteries when they're not in use, so if you haven't used your GPS unit in a couple of months, don't be surprised if those rechargeable batteries are dead or don't have much life left in them.

- **Cigarette lighter adapters:** If you're primarily using your GPS receiver in a car or truck, you can save on battery costs by powering the GPS receiver with a cigarette lighter adapter. These handy devices run a GPS receiver from your car's electrical system. You can buy a generic version or one made for your model (sold by that GPS receiver manufacturer). Depending on the model, adapters cost between $20–$40, with the generic versions a bit cheaper than the manufacturer models.

Cigarette lighter power adapters have straight or coiled cables. Although coiled cables are tidier, if your cigarette lighter isn't close to the dashboard, a coiled cable can pull your GPS receiver off the dashboard if it's not securely mounted. Adapters with straight cables don't have this problem; you can tidy up any slack in the cable with a plastic zip tie.

Initializing Your GPS Receiver

Your GPS now has power, so it's ready to go, right? Well, almost. After you put batteries in your GPS receiver and turn it on for the first time, don't expect it to instantly display your location. A GPS receiver first needs to go through an initialization process before it can tell you where you are. The type of initialization and the amount of time it takes depends on what information the GPS receiver has previously received from the satellites and when.

The process is mostly all automatic, and you don't need to do much as your GPS receiver starts up and begins to acquire satellites. Your GPS user manual may contain model-specific initialization information.

To initialize a new GPS receiver, take it outside to someplace that has an unobstructed view of the sky (such as a large field or a park) and turn on the power. (You did install the batteries first, right?). After the start-up screen displays, the receiver will begin trying to acquire satellites.

It can take anywhere from 5–30 minutes for the GPS receiver to gather enough satellite data to get a position fix for the first time (usually more toward the 5 minutes end of the scale). Don't worry; your GPS receiver isn't going to be this slow all the time. After the GPS receiver is first initialized, it usually only takes 15–45 seconds to lock on to the satellites when you turn it on in the future.

GPS receiver initialization nitty-gritty

You really don't need to know this technical information to operate your GPS receiver, but to start acquiring satellites to get an accurate location fix, a GPS receiver needs the following satellite data:

- A current almanac (rough positions of all the satellites in orbit)

- The GPS receiver's current location

- The current date and time

- *Ephemeris* data (precise position of individual satellites)

If some or all the data is missing or out-of-date, the GPS receiver needs to get updated information from the satellites before it can accurately fix a current position. The types of data that are out-of-date or missing determine how long the GPS receiver takes to initialize. If the GPS receiver is brand new, out of the box, several hundred miles away from where it was last used, or has been stored for a prolonged period of time, initialization will take longer.

In order to speed up the location fix for the first time or when the GPS receiver has been moved hundreds of miles since it was last turned on, many GPS receivers have an option where you move a cursor on an onscreen map of the United States or world to show your general location. Providing a general location helps the GPS receiver narrow its search for satellites that are visible from your present location, speeding up the initialization process.

Manufacturers often use the terms *cold start* and *warm start* to describe different GPS receiver start-up states and times. Unfortunately, their definitions of these terms can be different, which makes comparative information about start times not very useful. Just remember that under the same conditions, with a similar view of the sky and with their antennas optimally orientated, most modern GPS receivers generally take the same amount of time to acquire satellites and fix a location.

Most GPS receivers have a satellite status page that's displayed while the receiver is acquiring satellites; see an example status page in Figure 5-1. This page typically consists of two circles that represent a dome of sky above your head. The outer circle is the horizon, the inner circle is 45 degrees above the horizon, and the center of the inner circle is directly overhead. The N on the page represents north.

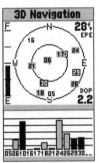

Figure 5-1: A GPS receiver satellite status page.

Based on the almanac information, the GPS receiver shows the position of satellites within the circles, representing them with numbers. As a signal from a satellite is acquired, the number is highlighted or bolded.

Underneath the circles are a series of bar graphs with numbers underneath them that represent signal strength. The numbers correspond to the satellites that the GPS receiver has located. The more a bar is filled in, the better the GPS receiver is receiving signals from that particular satellite.

Trimble planning software

During certain times of the day, you might have better satellite coverage than at other times because of the number of satellites that are in view and the position of a single satellite relative to the GPS receiver and other satellites in the constellation.

Trimble Navigation (www.trimble.com), one of the largest manufacturers of commercial and professional GPS receivers, has a free Windows program called Planning, shown in the figure here. Planning is designed for surveyors who need to know when the best time is to use GPS surveying instruments. Just enter the latitude and longitude coordinates of a location and the date, and Planning gives you information on

✔ **DOP:** Dilution of Precision describes how accurate a reported GPS position is. The smaller the DOP number, the higher the accuracy.

✔ **Satellites:** You can see how many satellites are in view if the sky is unobstructed, the optimum times of satellite visibility, and the satellite orbit paths.

You don't need to be a surveyor to use this information. Knowing optimal GPS times is useful for all sorts of outdoor activities. For example, if you're serious about geocaching, you can select the best time of day to look for caches when your GPS receiver gives you the most accuracy.

Planning is easy to use and works for any location in the world with all the GPS satellite information presented in graphs or lists.

To download Planning, go to www.trimble.com/planningsoftware_ts.asp?Nav=Collection-8425.

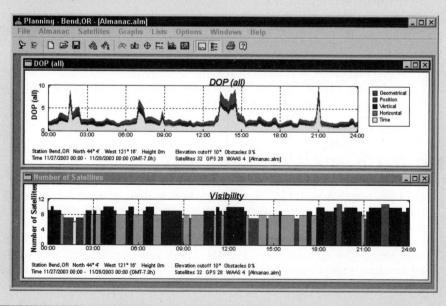

Try moving your GPS receiver to watch the satellite signal strength change. If signals are weak or you get a message about poor satellite coverage, move to another location and change the position of the receiver to better align it with the satellites that are shown onscreen. If you're successful, you'll see new satellites acquired, the signal strength increase, or both. The more satellites you acquire and the stronger the signals, the more accurate your receiver is.

Holding the GPS receiver properly will optimize signal reception. If your GPS receiver has a patch antenna, hold it face up, parallel to the ground. If your GPS receiver has a quad helix antenna, hold it straight up so that the top of the receiver is pointing toward the sky. Chapter 3 covers the differences between patch and quad helix antennas.

After the GPS receiver gets enough information from the satellites to fix your location, the screen typically displays an Estimated Position Error (EPE) number. Based on the satellite data received, this is the estimated error for the current position. The smaller the number displayed, which will be in feet or meters, the more accurate your position.

Estimated Position Error (EPE) is a bit confusing. If you see an EPE of 20 feet, it doesn't mean that you're within 20 feet of the actual coordinates. You're actually within up to two times the distance of the EPE (or even more) from the actual location. For example, if you have an EPE of 50, your location could be 1–100 feet of the actual coordinates. EPE is not a maximum distance away from the actual location; it's only a measurement estimate based on available satellite data. To complicate things even further, different GPS receiver manufacturers use different formulas for determining EPE, so if you set three different GPS receiver brands next to each other, they all display different EPE numbers. Some manufacturers are conservative with their numbers, and others are optimistic. Don't get too caught up with EPE numbers; just treat them as ballpark estimates — and remember, the smaller the number, the better.

Changing Receiver Settings

After you initialize your GPS receiver for the first time, you need to change a few of the receiver's default system settings. You only need to do this once, and a few GPS receivers will prompt you to make some of these changes as part of the initialization process. These changes are mostly to customize settings based on your location and needs. Check your user manual for specific information on how to change the system settings described below. An example of a GPS receiver system settings page is shown in Figure 5-2.

Figure 5-2:
A GPS
receiver
system set-
tings page
showing
time options.

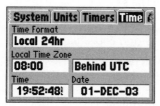

System	Units	Timers	Time

Time Format
Local 24hr

Local Time Zone
08:00 | **Behind UTC**

Time | Date
19:52:48 | **01-DEC-03**

Although GPS receivers have a number of system settings that you can change, here are some of the important settings you'll want to initially adjust:

- **Time:** Your GPS receiver gets very precise time data from atomic clocks aboard the satellites, but it's up to you how the time will be displayed. You need to specify

  - Whether to use 24-hour (military time) or 12-hour (AM and PM) time

  - Whether Daylight Savings Time is automatically turned on and off

  - What your time zone is (or your offset from UTC)

  Your GPS receiver gets time data from the satellites in the UTC format. UTC stands for Coordinated Universal Time (no, the acronym doesn't match the meaning), an international time standard. UTC is a time scale kept by laboratories around the world, using highly precise atomic clocks. The International Bureau of Weights and Measures uses time data collected from the labs to establish UTC, which is accurate to approximately one *nanosecond* (about a billionth of a second) per day. In 1986, UTC replaced Greenwich Mean Time (GMT) as the world time standard. The Greenwich meridian (prime meridian, or zero degrees longitude) is the starting point of every time zone in the world. GMT is the mean time that the earth takes to rotate from noon to the following noon. These observations have been kept since 1884 at the Royal Observatory in Greenwich, England. In hours, minutes, and seconds, UTC and GMT always have the same values.

- **Units of measure:** Your GPS receiver can display distance information in statute (such as feet and miles), nautical (knots), or metric (meters and kilometers) formats. The default setting for GPS units sold in the United States is statute, so unless you're boating or want to use the more logical metric system, leave the setting as-is.

- **Coordinate system:** By default, your GPS receiver displays positions in latitude and longitude. If you want to use location coordinates in a different format, now's the time to change the setting.

✔ **Datum:** The default datum for all GPS receivers is WGS 84. Unless you're planning on using your receiver with maps that have a different datum, leave the default setting. (See Chapter 4 for more information on types of datums and their impact GPS position coordinates.)

✔ **Battery type:** The default battery setting on most GPS receivers is alkaline. If you're using another type of battery, select the correct type. The battery type setting doesn't affect the GPS receiver's operation; it only ensures that the battery life is correctly displayed on the screen because different types of batteries have different power characteristics.

✔ **Language:** Most GPS receivers are multilingual, so if you'd rather view the user interface in a language other than English, it's as simple as selecting a different language from a menu.

Using Your GPS Receiver

Finally! After you initialize your GPS receiver and change some of the system settings, it's time to use it. Start with

✔ Going through the GPS receiver's different onscreen pages and see what information is displayed.

✔ Walking around and watching what happens to the numbers and your position on the GPS receiver's mapping and trip pages. (Do this outside, of course.)

✔ Pressing buttons and seeing what happens. You may want to have your user manual nearby in case you get lost between information screens.

GPS receivers are pretty robust, and you're not going to hurt your new purchase by being curious.

GPS receiver screens can be scratched relatively easily. Investing in a carrying case will keep the screen scratch-free; many cases have a clear plastic face that allows you to use and view the GPS without taking it out of the case. Another way to keep the screen from being scratched is to buy thin, clear plastic sheets used to protect PDA screens, cut them to shape, and place the sheet on top of the GPS receiver screen.

The following are some simple exercises you can try that will help you become familiar with your GPS receiver. When you first start using your GPS receiver, take the user manual with you. If you forget how to do something or have a question, the manual will be right there for reference.

Coming home

Everyone has opinions and like to know where people stand on different things, so here's an exercise to let you know exactly where you stand — when you're outside your backdoor.

1. **Take your GPS receiver outside where you live and create a waypoint for the spot where you're standing.**

   See Chapter 4 for the skinny on creating waypoints.

2. **Name the waypoint HOME.**

3. **Turn the GPS receiver off and go for a walk.**

   How far is up to you, but at least travel far enough that you can see your starting point.

4. **When you're ready to head back home, turn the GPS receiver back on and use it to navigate back to the HOME waypoint.**

    Be sure to move through the different onscreen pages to watch the direction and distance change as you head back home.

After you enter the HOME waypoint, no matter where you are, if you have your GPS receiver with you, you can always tell exactly how far away home is. Remember, this is in a straight line as the crow flies unless you've got a GPS receiver that supports autorouting.

How far, how fast?

Your GPS receiver also contains a very accurate trip computer that displays information about distance, speed, and time. After you read your user manual on how to reset and start the trip computer, here are some ideas for getting familiar with how it works:

- ✔ **When exercising:** When you run, jog, bike, or whatever, take your GPS receiver with you on your favorite course to see just how far you go. At the end, check your average and maximum speed. (Chapter 23 is filled with tips on using GPS if you're an athlete.)

- ✔ **When on walks:** If you have children and they walk to school, go with them on their route to see exactly how far it is. (And then tell them you used to have to walk at least ten times that distance . . . in the snow . . . uphill both ways . . . when you were young.)

- ✔ **When doing lawn work:** The next time you cut the grass, take your GPS receiver with you and see just how far you push your lawn mower.

Finding your ancestors

A lot of people are into genealogy these days, and your GPS receiver can be a helpful tool in tracking your ancestors. When you visit a cemetery looking for long-lost kin, bring your GPS receiver with you to record the exact locations of tombstones and grave plots. You can pass the latitude and longitude on to other relatives doing their own genealogical research. The coordinates can be extremely useful for someone locating a small out-of-the-way cemetery in the countryside, or a relative buried in a cemetery with thousands of plots.

Simulating navigation

Some GPS receivers have a simulator or demonstration mode. This is probably one of the most overlooked (but coolest) features on a GPS receiver. The simulator mode acts as if the receiver is actually acquiring GPS satellite information. You select a speed and a direction, and the GPS receiver pretends you're moving. Because the receiver isn't relying on acquiring satellite data, you can comfortably sit inside the house in your favorite chair, getting familiar with your new purchase.

Depending on where you live or work, how many windows you have, and your view of the sky, your GPS receiver might (might) work indoors (or at least close to windows). Although you're limited to what you can do with a GPS receiver indoors, it's fun to see just how much GPS coverage you can get walking around inside a building.

There are lots more things you can do with a GPS receiver besides using it for basic navigation. Think outside the box. Some examples include

- ✔ Take digital pictures of cool places and record their coordinates with your GPS receiver. You can post them on a Web site or e-mail them to friends.

- ✔ If you have a small GPS receiver (like a Garmin Geko), securely attach it to your dog's collar and track where Fido goes for the day. (You can also find commercial GPS pet locator products on the market.)

- ✔ Use your track log to create art. Some GPS users express themselves as artists by using their GPS receiver to record their movements as they walk around trying to create shapes or pictures. (Don't believe me? Check out www.gpsdrawing.com.)

Your goal should be to become confident using your GPS receiver and to have fun in the process.

Virtual GPS

Lowrance (www.lowrance.com) has a unique series of simulators for its sonar and GPS products that run on your computer. Just download and run a program from the Internet, and a life-like replica of the product appears onscreen. The GPS receiver simulators don't actually track satellites, but other than that, work just like the real thing. Use your mouse to click buttons, and the keyboard arrow and Enter keys to select menu items and change settings.

Although Lowrance designed the simulators as a way for potential customers to become familiar with their products (and for owners to practice with them), GPS receiver simulators are an excellent way to find out about concepts and functions that are common to all GPS receivers, no matter

what the brand or model. The user interface and features vary between brands and models, but key GPS receiver concepts such as datums, coordinate systems, waypoints, routes, and tracks remain the same. The Lowrance simulator, shown in the figure here, lets you come up to speed on basic GPS receiver operations without even owning a receiver; plus it's fun to play with. (If you download a simulator, get a copy of the real product's user manual so you can understand and try all the features. These can be downloaded from the Lowrance site as well.)

To download Lowrance simulators, go to www.lowrance.com/software/pcsoftware/demos.asp.

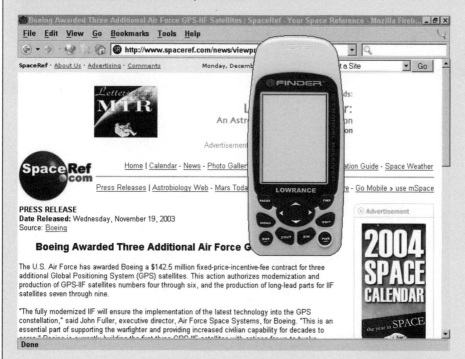

Chapter 6

Using GPS with a PDA

*P*ersonal digital assistants (PDAs), such as a Pocket PC or Palm, are a popular way of accessing GPS information. The PDA processes satellite data from a GPS receiver and then displays your current location in a mapping program.

You can use many different types of GPS receivers with PDAs, including handheld, mouse, wireless, and card. This chapter helps you navigate through the PDA/GPS maze by reviewing the different hardware and software options and comparing common, handheld GPS receivers (such as those discussed in Chapter 5) with PDAs that use GPS. I start things off by discussing some of the advantages and disadvantages of PDA-based navigation systems.

Choosing between a GPS Receiver and a PDA

You might wonder why anyone would you want to use a PDA instead of a handheld, consumer GPS receiver. That's a very good question; you gadget junkies out there who have your hands raised and are answering, "Because it's cool," please put your hands down and continue reading.

You'll find compelling advantages and disadvantages to using a PDA with GPS that are based on your intended use and needs. To see whether you should even be considering a PDA navigation system, review some of the pros and cons right from the start.

PDA advantages

Aside from being cool, a PDA might make sense for you as part of a personal navigation system for a number of reasons. Some of the advantages include

- ✔ **Larger screens:** PDAs have larger, higher-resolution, color screens compared with handheld GPS receivers. This is a big plus if your eyesight isn't as good as it used to be — and it's really important if you're using the PDA while driving. You want to be able to quickly glance at a map on the screen, determine your location, and then get your eyes back on the road.

- ✔ **More maps:** Most of the maps that you can upload to GPS receivers don't have a lot of detail; especially the topographic maps. These maps tend to be vector line maps and don't have the resolution or detail found on paper maps that you'd use for hiking. Several mapping programs are available for PDAs that support all types of maps, and you can even create your own custom maps. With a PDA, you can use more detailed maps, like scanned, color 1:24,000 topographic maps. ***Bonus:*** You're not locked in to using only a GPS receiver manufacturer's proprietary software and maps.

- ✔ **Expandable memory:** Unlike many GPS receivers, which have fixed amounts of memory, most PDAs support expandable memory with plug-in memory cards. The only limitation to the number of the maps and amount of data that you can store is the size of the memory card.

- ✔ **Usability:** Although handheld GPS receivers are fairly easy to use, the user interfaces found on PDAs are even simpler. Using a touch screen and stylus to enter data and commands is a lot faster and easier than using the buttons on a handheld GPS receiver.

- ✔ **Custom programs:** Developers can easily write custom programs for PDAs that access the data output from a GPS receiver. If you're collecting information that's based on location data, this can make your job much easier than pressing buttons on a GPS receiver and then handwriting remarks in a field notebook.

- ✔ **PDA features:** PDAs have all sorts of useful programs such as address books, contact lists, and databases designed for readily storing data. A fair amount of this information tends to be location based (like addresses), and having a single information/navigation device is the definition of practical.

PDA disadvantages

After reading through advantages of using a PDA as your navigation system of choice, you're probably sold on a using a PDA. However, they definitely aren't for everyone. Some of downsides include

✔ **Ruggedness:** Handheld GPS receivers are designed to take more abuse than PDAs, which often fail when they're dropped or knocked around. Although you can buy *ruggedized* (with special enclosures that make them waterproof, drop-proof, bear-proof, and kid-proof) PDAs, they're considerably more expensive than off-the-shelf models; expect to spend at least several hundred dollars more.

✔ **Weather/water resistance:** Unlike GPS receivers, PDAs aren't designed to be waterproof or even weatherproof. This can be a major issue if you plan on using your PDA navigation system outdoors in damp, rainy, or snowy weather, you're around water, or you have a leaky water bottle in your backpack.

✔ **Power considerations:** Most PDAs use internal batteries that are recharged through a docking cradle. If you're away from a power source, this can be a serious issue because you can't swap out dead or dying batteries for a convenient set of spare AA or AAA batteries like you can with a handheld GPS receiver.

When it comes to weighing the pros and cons of PDA navigation systems, you really have to examine your needs and planned use. If you plan on using a GPS receiver exclusively for road navigation, you should definitely consider a PDA. However if you're going to be using GPS primarily in an outdoor setting, you're probably better off with a handheld GPS receiver.

TIP

OtterBoxes

Although PDAs are relatively fragile and don't get along well with water, you can find products on the market to protect them when exposed to harsh environments. Among my favorites are OtterBox cases. For a well-spent $20–25 for the lower-end models, these plastic containers defend a PDA or other electronic devices from Mother Nature as well as not-too-careful owners.

OtterBox has two products that let you operate a PDA (including using its stylus) while encased in a waterproof and crushproof housing. One model, the Armor 3600 shown in the figure here, has a waterproof portal that allows you to connect the PDA to an external GPS receiver with a serial cable. There are also accessories that accommodate the oversize external antennas of GPS receiver cards and sleeves. Tests performed by the U.S. Forest Service indicated no satellite signal degradation when GPS receivers were used in the Armor cases.

The Armor series of cases do add bulk to the size of your PDA. However, considering the protection that they offer, the rugged cases are well suited for anyone who wants to venture out into the wilds and use a PDA without worrying about it breaking. A 3600 Armor model will set you back about $100; OtterBox also has other Armor cases from $20–50.

I like to think of the OtterBox Armor products as accessories that turn your meek and mild PDA into a tough and rugged Humvee. To find out more about the products, check out www.otter box.com.

If you're leaning toward a PDA navigation system (or already have one) and want to operate it out in the elements, at least buy an OtterBox or some type of protective bag. See the sidebar, "OtterBoxes." (I also like the Voyageur waterproof and padded bags, see `http://voyageur-gear.com` for product details.) I guarantee that your repair and replacement bills will be considerably less compared with stowing your PDA in a jacket pocket.

Interfacing Your PDA to a GPS Receiver

If you've decided that a PDA navigation system meets your needs (or maybe you just love cool high-tech toys), the first step is to decide how you're going to use to get GPS data into your PDA. Options for doing so include

- ✔ Handheld GPS receivers connected to the PDA with a serial (or USB) cable.
- ✔ *Mouse* GPS receivers (a GPS receiver with no display screen and a serial or USB cable).
- ✔ GPS receivers built into PC or memory cards.
- ✔ GPS receiver *sleeves* (expansion devices that slide on the back of certain models of PDAs).
- ✔ Wireless GPS receivers that transmit data with Bluetooth radio signals. Read more about these in the upcoming section, "Bluetooth GPS receivers."
- ✔ Integrated GPS receivers built directly into a PDA.

I'm assuming you already have a PDA or are currently shopping for one and have a pretty good idea what you're going to buy. It's outside the scope of this book to make suggestions on which PDA you should use. (Plus I'm not going to pick sides in the Palm versus Pocket PC brand-loyalty wars.) Just keep in mind that most PDAs can be interfaced with a GPS receiver one way or another.

Look at the types of GPS receivers you can use with a PDA. Most of the GPS receivers designed for use with PDAs cost as much as low-end to mid-range handheld GPS receivers. Some also work with laptop computers, which provide the ultimate big-screen GPS display.

Handheld GPS receivers

If your PDA has a serial port, you can easily interface the PDA to a general purpose, handheld GPS receiver. Most of the information on connecting a personal computer to a GPS receiver that I discuss in Chapter 9 also applies to PDAs.

GPS and cellphones

You can't talk about PDAs and GPS without mentioning cellular phones, especially as features and functionality of the two electronic devices start to converge.

GPS will play a large role in the future of cellphones. The U.S. government has mandated that calls placed by cellphones to 911 emergency operators must reveal where the call was made, just like landline telephones. This new program works by either triangulating a mobile phone's position via cellular phone network antenna towers or with a GPS receiver built into the cellphone that transmits its location.

In 2003, the first GPS-enabled cellular phones started to appear on the U.S. market. Phones like the Motorola i730, i88, and i58sr cell phones all have GPS receivers built inside them and are capable of broadcasting their location. Internet sites and tracking software are available that can provide you with the location of a GPS-enabled phone that's subscribed to a location reporting service.

As GPS-enabled phones start to become more common, it's only a matter of time before navigation and map programs start to appear on the phones, which will bring a whole new meaning to using your phone to get directions.

Because you're using the handheld GPS receiver exclusively as a data input source — and really don't care about what's appearing on its screen — just about any GPS receiver that can communicate with a computer via a serial port will fit the bill. You don't need a lot of features and whistles and bells on the GPS receiver if you're primarily using it this way. This option makes a lot of sense because the GPS receiver can be used independently of the PDA, especially outdoors during bad weather.

The primary disadvantage is that you have to contend with two electronic devices and the cable that connects them together. This can sometimes get a bit messy in a car, with hardware and power and interface cables scattered all over your dashboard. Also, this type of PDA navigation setup is a bit cumbersome to deal with if you're walking around.

One of the best sources of GPS receiver interface cables for a wide variety of PDAs is Pc-Mobile. Check out its extensive product Web site at http://pc-mobile.net.

Mouse GPS receivers

GPS receivers that don't have a display screen but connect to a computer with a serial or USB cable are often called *mouse* receivers because of their resemblance to a computer mouse. A mouse GPS receiver acts as an input device for a PDA or laptop and only sends satellite data that it's currently receiving.

Mouse GPS receivers are about half the size of the smallest handheld GPS receivers (Figure 6-1 shows the size differences between several GPS receivers), but even so still have good satellite reception with open skies. Another advantage to a mouse GPS receiver is you can place it in an optimal spot on your car's dashboard for satellite reception and then mount the PDA in the most visible place for driving. Depending on the model and type, a mouse GPS receiver can be powered by a cigarette lighter adapter, rechargeable batteries, or the device it's plugged in to.

Although mouse GPS receivers are smaller than handheld GPS receivers, you still face the cable clutter issue, plus you can't use the mouse receiver to get satellite data unless it's connected to a PDA or laptop.

Some of the vendors of mouse GPS receivers (and their Web sites where you can get product information) include

✔ **DeLorme:** www.delorme.com

✔ **Haicom:** www.haicom.com.tw

✔ **Holux:** www.holux.com

✔ **Mapopolis:** www.mapopolis.com

GPS receiver cards

Some GPS receivers take the form of a card that you can plug into a PDA expansion slot. The two types of GPS receiver cards are

✔ **Memory cards:** Most PDAs have a memory card slot that supports a Compact Flash (CF) or Secure Digital (SD) type of memory card. Both of these card formats also support hardware devices that can be embedded into the card: in this case, a GPS receiver. (PDAs without internal memory card slots might have optional *expansion packs* that plug into the PDA and provide a memory card slot.)

✔ **PC Cards:** A PC Card (also called a PCMCIA card) is a hardware expansion card designed for laptops. PC Card devices include hard drives, modems, and GPS receivers. These receiver cards are mostly used with laptops, but some PDAs support expansion packs for using PC Card devices.

Using a GPS receiver card with your PDA means that you don't need to worry about an external GPS receiver or cables. You just plug the card into a slot, and the GPS receiver starts accessing satellite data. However, note these drawbacks:

✔ **Slot competition:** CF and SD memory cards that function as GPS receivers take up the expansion slot that's used for additional PDA memory.

✔ **Battery hogs:** GPS receiver cards quickly run down your PDA's battery if you're not connected to an external power source.

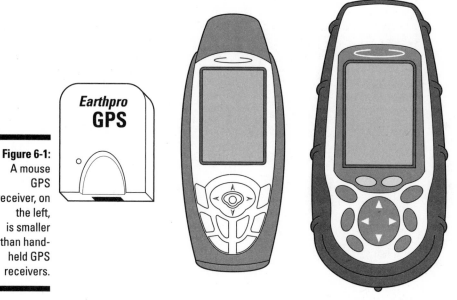

Figure 6-1:
A mouse
GPS
receiver, on
the left,
is smaller
than hand-
held GPS
receivers.

Some of the main GPS receiver card manufacturers (and their Web sites) are

- **Deluo:** www.deluo.com
- **Fortuna:** www.fortuna.com.tw
- **Haicom:** www.haicom.com.tw
- **Holux:** www.holux.com
- **Pharos:** www.pharos.com

GPS receiver sleeves

Certain models of iPAQ Pocket PCs and Palm OS PDAs have a proprietary expansion slot into which you can plug hardware devices. These add-on pieces of hardware are often called *sleeves* because they fit around the PDA. See a GPS receiver sleeve in Figure 6-2.

The same advantages and disadvantages found with GPS receiver cards (they're convenient but can run down the PDA's battery quickly) also apply to GPS sleeves. Additionally, a sleeve adds a lot of bulk to the size of a normally slim PDA.

The main producer of Pocket PC and Palm sleeves is Navman. Expect to spend around $200–$250 for a GPS sleeve. Find more about these products at www.navman.com.

Figure 6-2:
A Navman
GPS
receiver
sleeve that
slides on to
the back of
a PDA.

Bluetooth GPS receivers

If your PDA supports *Bluetooth* (a wireless communication standard; www.
bluetooth.com), you have yet another GPS receiver option. Bluetooth GPS
receivers are pretty slick because they don't

✔ **Rely on the PDA's batteries for power**

   They have their own power source and will run from 6–10 hours when
   fully charged, depending on the model.

✔ **Use up one of the PDA's expansion slots**

✔ **Need cables that can get all tangled up**

   Bluetooth devices have about a 30-foot range, and the GPS receiver can
   be placed in an optimal position on the dashboard to receive satellite
   signals.

Just place your Bluetooth GPS receiver (about the size of a mouse GPS
receiver) anywhere with an open view of the sky, and it will broadcast GPS
data to your Bluetooth-enabled PDA. (If you have an older PDA that doesn't
support Bluetooth, there are Bluetooth receivers that plug into your PDA's
memory card slot.)

Many of the companies that manufacture GPS receiver cards, listed previously, also make Bluetooth GPS receivers. Some other companies that offer
Bluetooth receivers include

   ✔ **ALK Technologies:** www.alk.com

   ✔ **DeLorme:** www.delorme.com

   ✔ **EMTAC:** www.emtac.com

For outdoor use, you can easily mount your Bluetooth GPS receiver on a high spot, such as on top of a pack (or some other location that's in an optimal position to receive satellite signals) and wirelessly record GPS data with your PDA. OtterBox also makes waterproof cases for Bluetooth GPS receivers that don't degrade the transmitted radio signals so you can create a rugged wireless PDA navigation system for use in harsh conditions. (See the sidebar, "OtterBoxes.")

For an extensive list of the GPS receiver devices available for Pocket PC PDAs, including reviews and detailed specifications, check out www.gpspassion.com/en/hardware/gpslist.htm.

GPS-integrated PDAs

The most expensive option when creating a PDA navigation system is to purchase a PDA that comes with a built-in GPS receiver. In 2003, Garmin introduced the *iQue 3600,* a PDA that runs the Palm OS and features an integrated GPS receiver.

The iQue 3600 looks like a normal PDA but has a flip-up, adjustable antenna that pops out of the top. It has extensive mapping capabilities, including turn-by-turn voice directions and integration with the calendar and address book programs in which you can click an address and get instant directions. For more information about the iQue 3600, visit www.garmin.com.

If the iQue becomes popular, look for other integrated GPS PDAs to be released by Garmin and other manufacturers in the future; especially as GPS receiver components become smaller and cheaper. As this book went to press, Taiwanese manufacturer MiTAC announced the *Mio 168,* an integrated GPS/Pocket PC.

Reviewing PDA Mapping Software

If you buy a GPS receiver specifically designed for PDA use, it will probably come bundled with mapping software that includes map data and a program that displays the maps and interfaces with the GPS receiver.

In addition to the program that runs on your PDA is a program that runs on your PC; this program installs the maps on your PDA and can be used for route planning. You select the maps that you want to install on your PC and then upload the selected map data to your PDA. Because the maps are typically stored in the PDA's memory card, the more memory you have, the more maps you'll be able to use.

Most PDA navigation software is designed for street navigation (see Figure 6-3 for screenshot of a typical PDA street map program), and has features for getting around on roads and highways, including

- **Autorouting:** By inputting starting- and ending-point addresses, the map program creates a route for you to follow to reach your destination. (You usually can choose between fastest or shortest routes.) The route is outlined on the map, and the program also provides turn-by-turn directions to get to your destination.

- **POI data:** In addition to maps, most programs have extensive databases of POIs (Points of Interest) information, including gas stations, restaurants, shopping locations, and other useful travel data. POIs appear as icons on the map that you can click to get more information. You can also search for specific POIs by geographic location.

- **Real-time tracking:** When your PDA is connected to a GPS receiver, an arrow moves on the screen, giving you real-time information about your current position as well as displaying where you've been.

- **Voice prompts:** In addition to displaying turn-by-turn directions on the screen, many programs provide voice prompts that tell you when to make turns to reach your final destination. This is a nice safety feature because you can pay more attention to the road and less attention to the PDA screen.

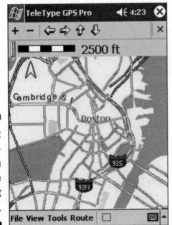

Figure 6-3:
Map display from TeleType GPS Pocket PC software.

A number of PDA mapping programs are on the market, and I could easily devote an entire book to discussing them all. Because this chapter provides only a general review of using PDAs with GPS, Table 6-1 lists of some of the more popular PDA mapping programs; including which types of PDAs they work with and a Web site address to get more product information. Most of these programs are sold individually or might come bundled with a GPS receiver. Expect to pay anywhere between $40–$150 for a software package.

Table 6-1	Popular PDA Mapping Programs		
Program	*Pocket PC*	*Palm*	*Web Site*
DeLorme Street Atlas USA Handheld	X	X	www.delorme.com
Destinator	X		www.destinator1.com
Intellinav	X		www.intellinav.com
Mapopolis Navigator	X	X	www.mapopolis.com
Microsoft Pocket Streets	X		www.microsoft.com
Quo Vadis		X	www.marcosoft.com
TeleType	X		www.teletype.com
TomTom Navigator	X		www.tomtom.com

One of the challenges in using a PDA in a car is dealing with the stylus. It can be quite a coordination test holding the stylus in your hand, tapping commands on the PDA with it, and driving at the same time. One slick solution is the Stinger Stylus, which is a cross between a plastic ring and an artificial finger-nail. Just slip the Stinger over your finger, and your fingertip takes the place of a stylus. For more information on the Stinger, go to www.stingerstylus.com.

Most of the software and maps that come bundled with the PDA GPS receivers are designed for road navigation. But what if you want to display topographic or nautical charts on your PDA or use real-time GPS tracking off the road?

You're in luck because several PDA programs fill this need. Topographic map display is one area that PDA mapping software far exceeds handheld mapping GPS receivers. Your PDA can display full-color, detailed 1:24,000 scale maps that look exactly like the USGS paper versions. Compared with the 1:100,000 scale vector maps typically used on mapping GPS receivers, there's no comparison when it comes to the amount of map detail that a PDA can display.

If your journeys take you off the beaten path, here are four products you should be aware of:

- **FUGAWI:** FUGAWI was one of the first Windows desktop mapping programs and now works with Pocket PCs and Palms. The product comes bundled with U.S. street maps and nautical charts, or you can import maps of your own, such as USGS Digital Raster Graphics topographic maps. For additional product details, go to `www.fugawi.com`.

- **Maptech Outdoor Navigator:** The Maptech Outdoor Navigator is unique. Instead of being bundled with map data or requiring you to create your own maps, (with purchase) you receive a year-long subscription to download all the USGS topographic maps and NOAA nautical charts that you want from Maptech's Internet servers. Nice. Versions of Outdoor Navigator are available for Pocket PCs and Palms. You can find more about the product at `www.maptech.com`.

- **SkyEye:** This is a slick shareware Pocket PC program that displays aerial photographs and topographic maps that you can download from the Internet or create on your own. The program also interfaces with Garmin GPS receivers to provide real-time mapping capabilities. For more about SkyEye's features, visit `www.etree.com/tech/notsofreestuff/skyeye/index.html`.

- **TeleType GPS:** Although originally designed for street navigation, TeleType's PDA mapping program supports importing aerial photographs and digital maps from the TerraServer-USA Web site. For more information on the software, visit `www.teletype.com`.

- **OziExplorerCE:** OziExplorerCE is a Pocket PC version of the popular OziExplorer mapping program. The CE version allows you to import maps that you've created with OziExplorer on your PC to your PDA. See a review of the PC version OziExplorer in Chapter 15. For more information on the CE edition, go to `www.oziexplorer.com`.

Here are several excellent Internet resources that can provide you with more information:

- **Dale DePriest's Navigation and GPS Articles:** Dale DePriest is a longtime contributor to the `sci.geo.satellite-nav` USENET newsgroup and the comprehensive `gpsinformation.net` Web site. He has a considerable amount of practical information on using Palms, Pocket PCs, and GPS at `www.gpsinformation.org/dale`.

- **Pocket GPS World:** Check out this European Web site for news, information, and forums devoted to mobile GPS products. The site has an extensive review section of PDA GPS receivers and is located at `www.pocketgpsworld.com`.

- **GpsPasSion:** This European site is devoted to Pocket PCs and GPS with forums, links, news, and more. To visit the site, go to `www.gpspassion.com`.

Chapter 7

Geocaching

*P*robably the fastest way for you to get real-world experience with your GPS unit is by going geocaching. This new, high-tech sport gets you out of the house and into the fresh air as you use both the computer in your GPS unit and also the one in your head to find hidden treasure. Geocaching is a fun and challenging activity that combines modern technologies like GPS and the Internet, with primitive outdoor navigation and search skills that people have been using for thousands of years. The sport also gives you a good reason to visit places you've never been.

Geocaching is pronounced *GEE*-oh-*cash*-ing. Don't pronounce cache as ca-*shay*, even if you're French. Unless you want funny looks, stick with *cash*.

Geocaching: The High-Tech Scavenger Hunt

When the U.S. government turned off GPS Selective Availability (SA) in May 2000, it was like magic. Suddenly civilian GPS receivers that were formerly accurate to about 300 feet were accurate to 30 feet. This level of accuracy offered some creative possibilities. Three days after SA was turned off, the following message appeared in the sci.geo.satellite-nav USENET newsgroup:

```
From: Dave (news2yousNOneSPAM@hotmail.com.invalid)
        Subject: GPS Stash Hunt... Stash #1 is there!
        Newsgroups: sci.geo.satellite-nav
        Date: 2000/05/03

Well, I did it, created the first stash hunt stash and here
        are the coordinates:

N 45 17-460
W122 24.800

Lots of goodies for the finders. Look for a black plastic
        bucket buried most of the way in the ground. Take
        some stuff, leave some stuff! Record it all in the
        log book. Have Fun!

Stash contains: DeLorme Topo USA software, videos, books,
        food, money, and a slingshot!
```

Earlier that day, in the same newsgroup, Dave Ulmer had proposed a world-wide *stash hunt,* where people would post GPS waypoints on the Internet to lead searchers to hidden goodies. While Ulmer envisioned thousands of stashes tucked in places all over the world, he had no idea how popular his idea would become.

Starting with a humble little bucket full of goodies in Oregon, Ulmer's idea took off like wildfire. Within weeks, caches were hidden in Washington, Kansas, California, New Zealand, Australia, and Chile. A newsgroup and Web site that hosted the coordinates of the stashes soon popped up as the word started to get around.

The original caches: letterboxes

The whole geocaching concept isn't that new. Over 100 years ago, something similar developed in England: *letterboxing.* Letterboxing comprises placing a blank logbook and a custom-made rubber stamp in a waterproof container and then hiding it. Clues are distributed with the container's location, and searchers armed with inkpads and notebooks try to find the hidden box. If they are successful, they stamp the logbook in the box with their own personal rubber stamp and also stamp their logbook with the box's stamp. This low-tech version of geocaching is still very popular. Depending on whom you talk to, 10,000–40,000 letterboxes are hidden in England, and around 5,000 are lurking in the United States. Read more about letterboxing at www.letterboxing.org.

By the end of May, in a Yahoo! Group devoted to the new sport, member Matt Stum suggested that the sport be called *geocaching* in order to avoid some of the negative connotations associated with drugs and word *stash*. (A *cache* is a hidden place where goods or valuables are concealed.) Geocaching had a nice ring to it, and it didn't sound like a bad Cheech and Chong movie.

Today, geocaching has grown popular, and the rules are still pretty much the same: Take some stuff, leave some stuff, record it in the logbook, and have fun! Relatively cheap and accurate GPS receivers and widespread Internet access have helped the sport flourish. As of November 2003, the www.geocaching. com site (currently the largest geocaching site on the Net) had over 72,500 active caches in 188 countries listed in its database. That's a lot of caches out there to find! (Figure 7-1 shows a typical cache.)

OFFICIAL GEOCACHE

PLEASE DO NOT DISTURB!

Cache Name: _____

Figure 7-1:
Geocaches
hold a
logbook and
goodies.

Getting Started Geocaching

Just about anyone can participate in geocaching; gender, age, and economic status don't much matter. The main requirements are a spirit of adventure, a love of puzzles and mysteries, and a sense of fun. This section discusses what you need to geocache, how to select caches to look for, and how to find them.

What you need to geocache

Geocaching sounds pretty intriguing, doesn't it? But before you can try it out, you need a few things. You probably already have many pieces of the required gear, and your biggest investment will be a GPS receiver if you don't already have one. (Read Chapter 5 for the lowdown on selecting a receiver.) With that in mind, here's a list of basic things you need.

I start off with the technology-related items:

- **Cache location:** Obviously, you need to know where to look for a cache: a set of latitude and longitude or UTM (Universal Transverse Mercator) coordinates. You'll find tens of thousands of caches freely listed on the Internet. For information on locating a geocache, see the appropriately named section, "Selecting a cache to look for," later in this chapter.

- **Geocaching alias:** Most people who geocache use a registered *handle* (alias) instead of their real name when they sign cache logs or make Internet posts. The aliases are cool-sounding names like Navdog, Wiley Cacher, or Moun10Bike. Be imaginative and come up with an alias that fits your personality. The aliases are all unique: If you try to register an alias on one of the popular geocaching Web sites and someone else already has registered the alias, you need to select another name.

- **GPS receiver:** You can certainly find caches by using only a map and compass (my adventure racing team does this to practice our navigation skills), but it's sure a lot easier when using a GPS receiver. You don't need an expensive GPS unit with lots of whistles and bells to geocache; a basic model around or under $100 will work just fine; receivers that support WAAS (Wide Area Augmentation Service, as described in Chapter 3) usually are more accurate than those that don't.

  Don't forget to bring the GPS receiver user manual, especially if you just purchased your receiver and are still trying to figure out how to use it.

A few other things can make your outing a little more enjoyable:

- **Map and compass:** A fair number of geocachers use only their GPS receiver to get them to a cache, but a good local map of the area can be very helpful. Although a receiver can lead you directly in a straight line to cache, it's probably not going to tell you about the river, deep canyon, or cliffs between you and the cache. Even GPS receivers that display topographic maps often won't show enough detail that can help or hinder you on your way to a cache. Additionally, a map and compass serve as a backup just in case something goes wrong with your GPS. (Just make sure you know how to use them.)

- **Pen or pencil and paper:** Carry a small pad of paper and a pen or pencil for taking notes about your route or things that you see on the way. Some geocachers keep an ongoing journal of their adventures, and you never know — you might turn into a geocaching Hemingway.

- **Something to leave in the cache:** When you locate a cache, you'll find all sorts of *swags,* which are treasures other people have left. Don't expect diamonds, gold bullion, or Super Bowl tickets, though. (You're far more likely to find baseball cards, costume jewelry, or corporate marketing giveaways.) Just remember that one man's trash is another man's treasure. The best things to leave in a cache are unique, out-of-the-ordinary items (such as foreign coins, fossils, exotic matchbooks, or anything that has a high cool factor). And, please, avoid leaving *McToys,* geocaching lingo for junk that you reasonably expect to find with fast-food kid's meals. For more of the lingo, check out the section, "GeoJargon: Speaking the lingo," later in this chapter.

✔ **Appropriate clothes and footwear:** There are no geocaching fashion police, so wear clothes that are comfortable, weather appropriate, and suitable for getting dirty. Even if it's the middle of summer, it's not a bad idea to bring along a jacket in case of an unexpected rain shower or drop in the temperature. Also, make sure you're wearing sturdy and comfortable footwear if the cache is outside an urban area. High heels and wingtip loafers generally aren't recommended.

✔ **Food and water:** Some caches take all day to find, so be prepared with enough food and water to get you through your search; you can even plan a picnic lunch or dinner around your outing.

✔ **Walking stick/trekking poles:** If the terrain is really rough, a good walking stick or set of trekking poles can make life much easier when going downhill and negotiating uneven surfaces. A stick or a pole is also useful for poking around in rock cracks looking for a cache, just in case there's a creepy-crawly inside.

✔ **Digital camera:** Although definitely not a required piece of geocaching gear, a number of cachers tote along a digital camera to record their adventures or to post pictures on the Web.

✔ **Small pack:** It's much easier to put all your geocaching gear in a small daypack rather than stuffing your pockets full of stuff.

Don't forget a few safety-related items. As the Boy Scouts say, be prepared:

✔ **Flashlight:** This is a must-have for looking in cracks and crevices where a cache might be hidden — and also in case you run out of daylight. If you're smart, your flashlight uses the same type of batteries as your GPS receiver, giving you even more spare batteries.

✔ **Cellphone:** You probably have a cellphone, so bring it along (preferably with the battery fully charged). Just a note of advice, from my search and rescue experiences: I've found at times that people think of their cellphones as an absolute insurance policy against trouble. They can fail, cellphone batteries go dead, and you might have really bad cell coverage out in the middle of nowhere. So although a cellphone is great to have along, be prepared to take care of yourself!

✔ **Spare batteries:** I always bring along spare batteries for anything that uses them. (In this case, that means your GPS receiver and flashlight — and if you're really safety conscious, your cellphone, too.)

That's the basic gear you need for geocaching. The whole key with gear lists is to find out what works best for you. You'll probably end up carrying too much stuff in your pack at first. After you've geocached for a while, check your pack and see what you're not using so you can lighten your load.

Most geocaches are located in pretty tame, civilized areas (usually 100 feet or so off a main trail or road), but I advise letting someone know where you're going, when you'll be back, and what to do if you're late. Twisted ankles and broken-down cars seem to happen a lot in areas without cellphone service. If you haven't spent much time in the great outdoors, check out a list of The Ten Essentials (which has been expanded to 14 over the years) at www.back packing.net/ten-essl.html.

Selecting a cache to look for

After you get all your gear together, ready to venture out into the wilds, comes this one small detail: How do you know where to look for a geocache?

Like most other modern-day searches for information, start with the Internet. Many Web sites have listings of geocaching caches. I list some of the best Internet resources in the upcoming section, "Internet Geocaching Resources."

Geocaching.com (www.geocaching.com) is currently the most widely used site and has the largest database of geocaches all over the world; most of the information in this chapter is orientated toward that site. However, if you use another geocaching Web site, you'll find most of the same general techniques described here for selecting a cache also apply to other sites.

You can set up a free user account on Geocaching.com to log caches that you find, as well as to be informed of new caches that are placed in your area. Anyone with Internet access can freely view the cache locations without an account. Site owner Jeremy Irish also has Premium Member subscription services ($30 per year) and sells products to help keep the site running.

To start, go to www.geocaching.com. Finding caches is as simple as entering the ZIP code for where you're interested in geocaching. You can also search for caches by state, city, country, latitude, longitude, or by street address (only in the United States). The basic search screen is shown in Figure 7-2.

After you enter where you'd like to search for caches, a list of geocaches in that area is displayed (see Figure 7-3). The list is sorted by how far away the cache is from the search criteria you entered; the closest geocaches are displayed first. The name and type of the cache is shown, when it was first placed, when it was found last, and how difficult the cache is to get to and find. You can scroll through the list of geocaches until you find one that looks interesting. Cache names that are lined out are no longer active.

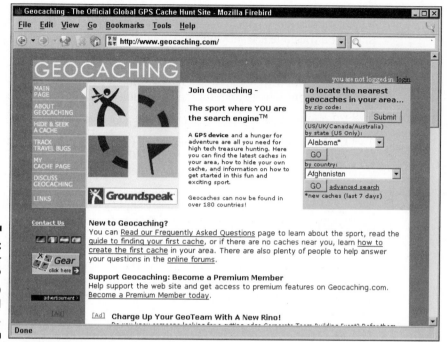

Figure 7-2:
Just enter
your ZIP
code to
get started
geocaching.

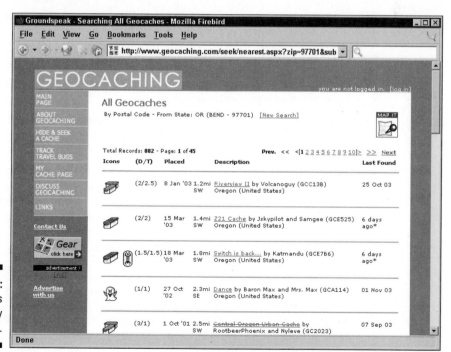

Figure 7-3:
Geocaches
are listed by
closest first.

Just click the name of a cache displayed in the list about which you want more information to see a page with the following information. (Cache details displayed on the page are shown in the upcoming Figures 7-4 and 7-5.)

✔ **Cache name:** The name of the cache (usually the cache name has something to do with the area where it's hidden, who hid it, or a play on words). *Bonus:* If you hide a cache, you get to name it.

✔ **Who placed the cache:** This is usually a cacher's alias.

✔ **Cache type:** Caches can be *traditional* (a single container), *multicaches* (where clues in a single cache point to one or more other caches), or *virtual* caches (a cool location that doesn't have a container).

✔ **Cache coordinates:** These record where the cache is located in latitude and longitude and UTM coordinates; these coordinates use the WGS 84 datum, so be sure your GPS receiver is set to this datum.

✔ **When the cache was hidden:** The date the cache was originally placed.

✔ **Cache waypoint name:** All caches in the Geocaching.com database have a unique name: for example, *GC* followed by the numeric order the cache was added to the database. You can use this to name a GPS waypoint for the cache location.

✔ **Difficulty:** The difficulty rating is how hard the cache placer thinks the cache will be to find; 1 is easiest, and 5 is the most difficult. Whoever places the cache decides the difficulty level, based on some general criteria, such as how steep or rocky the terrain is or if you have to go through very much underbrush to reach the cache.

✔ **Terrain:** The terrain rating is how difficult the terrain is. 1 is flat, easy, and level; 5 could be very steep and rocky with lots of underbrush and generally miserable travel conditions. Like with the difficulty rating, it's up to the cache placer to rate the terrain.

✔ **General description of the cache:** Cache descriptions range from a couple of sentences to stories and history lessons about the location. Clues often appear in the description, so check it closely.

✔ **Map location of the cache:** At the top of the page is a small state map from which you can take a general idea of where the cache is. A larger map with more detail appears at the bottom of the page. You can click the larger map and go to the MapQuest Web site, where you can zoom in on the cache site.

✔ **Hints:** The cache placer can optionally add hints to help a geocacher narrow his search. The hints are in code; I discuss these in the following "Finding the cache" section.

✔ **Logged visits:** This is a list of all the comments about the cache from people who have visited it and then logged Web site comments.

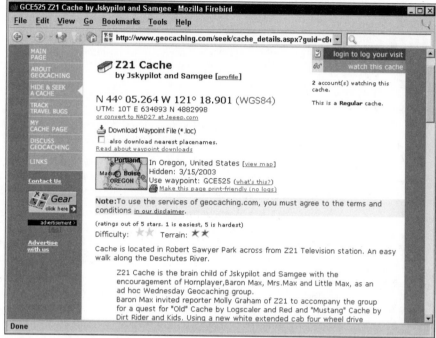

Figure 7-4:
Information
about a
cache
includes its
name, its
location,
and a
description.

Some of these logged visit comments may contain *spoilers,* which are hints that may make it easier to find the cache. Although most cachers try not to spoil the fun for others, sometimes a clue accidentally appears.

Before heading out to search for a cache, check the last time someone found it. Although Geocaching.com tries to keep track of inactive caches, sometimes caches that have been stolen or kidnapped by space aliens slip through the cracks. If you're just getting started geocaching, go after caches that have had some recent activity. This increases the odds that they'll still be hiding where they're supposed to be when you go looking for them.

Finding the cache

After you select a cache you want to search for, the next step is finding it. This might be a little bit more challenging than you think. Remember that your GPS receiver will only get you within 10–30 feet of the cache location — perhaps even farther away if you have poor satellite coverage or the cache hider's coordinates are a little off. After your GPS unit gets you to the general vicinity of the cache, start using your eyes and your brain, which at times might be more reliable than your GPS receiver.

Sometimes a series of caches are located close together, usually separated by at least a tenth of a mile. Because you're already in the neighborhood, consider trying to find several instead of going for just a single cache. Check out the link on the cache description page that displays all the nearby caches and how far away they are from each other.

Finding a cache boils down to following these general steps:

1. **Enter the cache coordinates in your GPS receiver as a waypoint and then add a name for the waypoint on your GPS receiver.**

   The methodology for entering waypoints differs from model to model. Check your user manual for specific instructions about how to enter and name a waypoint on your GPS model. Read more about this in Chapter 4.

   You can use the six-character waypoint name on the cache description Web page for the name of the waypoint. Double-check that you've entered the correct coordinates. Many caches haven't been found on the first try because of an typo in the coordinates in a GPS unit.

   If you have an account on Geocaching.com, you can download the cache waypoint to your computer from a link on the cache description page and then upload the waypoint directly to your GPS receiver. Doing so helps to eliminate errors caused by typos in GPS coordinates.

2. **Print a copy of the cache description Web page so you can bring all the information you need to find the cache with you.**

   If your printer is out of ink or you're being frugal, scribble down the coordinates and any other information that you think might be useful in locating the cache.

3. **Gather your equipment, including your GPS receiver, map, compass, food, water, and other essential items mentioned in this chapter.**

4. **Head out to the cache's starting point.**

   Drive or bike as close to the cache as you can get. Sometimes the cache descriptions give you exact instructions, like at which parking lot or trailhead to start from. The more challenging caches give you only the coordinates, and it's up to you to decide where you'll start from and how you'll get there. One of the pleasures of geocaching is it's usually not a timed event (although a few timed competitions are starting to crop up), and you can take as long as you want to reach the cache site, stopping to smell the roses and enjoy interesting sights.

5. **Turn on your GPS receiver and get a satellite lock.**

   Hopefully! If not, you brought that map and compass, right?

6. **Save a waypoint for your starting point.**

   Getting back to your car can sometimes be a challenge after finding a cache, and saving a waypoint with your car's location can make life much easier (and get you home in time for dinner). Your GPS manual contains details for setting a waypoint for your particular model.

7. **Double-check to make sure that you have the coordinates, cache description, hints, and the rest of your geocaching equipment in your possession. (Keeping it all together in a backpack is convenient.)**

   From personal experience, I can tell you it's never any fun arriving at the cache and remembering that I left vital clues in the cache description that's now a couple of miles away in the car.

8. **Activate the cache's waypoint.**

   Activating a waypoint tells the receiver to calculate the distance and direction from your current spot to the waypoint's location. Your GPS unit will let you know how far away the cache is and what direction you need to head to get there. (This often is as simple as pressing a button on the GPS receiver and selecting the waypoint you want to go to.)

9. **Follow the direction arrow, road map display, or compass ring on your GPS receiver toward the cache.**

   A local map can come in handy as you move toward the cache because you can use it to figure out what the terrain is like and whether any rivers, cliffs, or mountains lie between you and the cache. You can use some of the online digital maps discussed in Chapter 19 for preplanning or print them out to use in the field.

   Don't feel compelled to always head in the direction your GPS unit tells you to go. It might make more sense to walk around a pile of rocks or downed trees than to go over the top of them. After you get around an obstacle, you can check your receiver again to get on the right course.

   Watch your step! As you head toward the cache, don't get so caught up in staring at your GPS receiver that you fall off a cliff or trip over a tree root. And watch the scenery, too. Sometimes the journey is the reward.

10. **When your receiver says you're within 30 feet or so of the cache, move around and find the place that reports the closest distance to the cache.**

    Begin your search at that spot. This is where the real fun starts. You now shift from relying on technology to using your powers of observation and common sense. A cache could be inside a cave, tucked in a tree hollow, hiding behind a rock outcropping, or concealed under a pile of brush. Some caches are easy to find, and others are devilishly difficult.

Geocaching stats

Just like any sport, geocaching has statistics (stats). In this case, *stats* refer to the number of caches that you've found and hidden. When you sign up for a free or premium account at Geocaching.com, you can log the caches you've found as well as add caches that you've hidden to the site's extensive database. The Web site tracks the finds and hides for you and displays them on a user profile page. Other members can check out your stats, and the number of caches that you've found appears next to your alias when you log your comments about a cache you've visited. Some geocachers are competitive and are in to racking up as many cache finds as possible. Others are more blasé about the whole numbers thing and could care less. Like so many other aspects of geocaching, it's up to you how you want to play the game.

As you start looking around, you can do a few things to help improve your odds of finding the cache:

- ✔ **Find out the maximum distance to the cache.** Check the Estimated Position Error (EPE) to see how accurate your GPS receiver currently is, based on the satellite coverage. *Remember:* The bigger the number, the less accuracy. This helps you roughly determine how large your search area is. For example, if the EPE is 20 feet, your search area is a circle with a 40-foot diameter, with the center at the closest location that you can get to the cache waypoint.

- ✔ **Follow a magnetic compass.** When you're within 30 feet of the waypoint and your GPS receiver is showing a consistent bearing to the cache (tree cover and poor satellite coverage can cause the distance and direction numbers to jump around), use a magnetic compass to guide yourself to the cache. As you slow down, unless your receiver has an electronic compass, the direction that your receiver shows to the waypoint becomes less precise, and you can easily veer off-course. Handheld magnetic compasses or electronic compasses built into the GPS unit don't rely on satellite signals, and won't have this problem.

- ✔ **Think about the container.** Knowing what kind of container the cache is stored in can be a big help in identifying and eliminating possible hiding spots. Sometimes the cache description lists the container type (ammo can, plastic ware, bucket, or whatever), which can narrow your search based on the container size and shape. For example, you shouldn't be looking for an ammo can in a three-inch-wide crack in a rock.

- ✔ **Think about the terrain.** Look at the surrounding environment to get a general idea of where a cache might be hidden. What natural (or man-made) features make a good hiding place? Remember, unlike pirate booty hiding, geocaching has a rule against burying cache containers, so you shouldn't be burrowing holes like a gopher.

✔ **Split up the work.** If you're geocaching with other folks, assign areas for people to check. Although you don't need to precisely measure and grid-off squares, divvying up an area to search is faster and more efficient than randomly wandering around.

✔ **Think like a cache hider.** If you were going to hide a cache, where would you hide it? Sometimes trusting your intuition can be more effective than trying to apply logic. After you check the ordinary places, start looking in the unordinary spots.

There's an old safety saying in wildland firefighting that goes, "Look up, look down, look all around." The same advice applies to geocaching, which is an excellent way to improve your overall awareness and observation skills.

Going in circles

This will happen: You find the general cache location, but after a couple of hours of wandering around in circles, you still can't find the cache container. You've double-checked the coordinates, the satellite coverage is good, and you're starting to get a bit frustrated. Take a deep breath. Here's what to do.

You can always resort to using a hint. Most cache description pages have a short hint, but you have to work for it because it's encoded. The reason for the spy stuff is so the hint doesn't spoil the fun for another cacher who doesn't want to use the hint as part of his search. Fortunately, the hint is encoded with a simple substitution code (for example, A = M, B = N, C = O, and so on), so you don't need to work for the NSA to be able to break it. The decoding key is on the right side of the page, and it's pretty easy to figure it out by hand. See Figure 7-5 for what a coded hint and decoding key look like.

One of the more challenging types of caches to find is a *microcache*. Instead of using large containers, smaller ones — like small pill bottles, 35mm film canisters, or magnetic hide-a-keys — are used that only hold a piece of paper that serves as the log. These caches are typically in urban areas and can be cleverly hidden to avoid detection by nongeocachers passing by.

In addition to the hint, you can also look through the logged visit comments that other people have posted who have already found the cache. Although most geocachers try to avoid including *spoilers* (way-too-obvious hints or commentary) into their comments, sometimes enough information leaks through that can help you narrow your search.

How you go about finding the cache is up to you. Some purists will use only the coordinates and basic description of the cache, never using the hints or the comments. Other cachers decrypt the hint and read all the comments before they head out the door on a search. It's up to you.

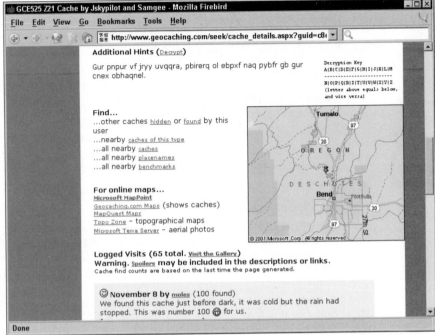

GCE525 Z21 Cache by Jskypilot and Samgee - Mozilla Firebird

File Edit View Go Bookmarks Tools Help

http://www.geocaching.com/seek/cache_details.aspx?guid=c8...

Additional Hints (Decrypt)

Gur pnpur vf jryy uvqqra, pbirerq ol ebpxf naq pybfr gb gur cnrx obhaqnel.

Decryption Key

A|B|C|D|E|F|G|H|I|J|K|L|M

N|O|P|Q|R|S|T|U|V|W|X|Y|Z
(letter above equals below,
and vice versa)

Find...
...other caches hidden or found by this user
...nearby caches of this type
...all nearby caches
...all nearby placenames
...all nearby benchmarks

For online maps...
Microsoft MapPoint
Geocaching.com Maps (shows caches)
MapQuest Maps
Topo Zone - topographical maps
Microsoft Terra Server - aerial photos

©2001 Microsoft Corp. All rights reserved

Logged Visits (65 total. Visit the Gallery)
Warning. Spoilers **may be included in the descriptions or links.**
Cache find counts are based on the last time the page generated.

☺ **November 8 by** moles **(100 found)**
We found this cache just before dark, it was cold but the rain had stopped. This was number 100 ⊕ for us.

Done

Figure 7-5:
If you're stumped (ha!), go for a hint.

There's no shame in a DNF (Did Not Find); it happens to everyone. Go back to the cache location another day and try again. Geocaching is supposed to be fun, so don't take it too hard if you can't locate a cache. Consider bringing someone else with you next time: Two heads are better than one, and a different set of eyes might find something you overlooked. Don't be shy about logging a DNF for the cache at the Geocaching.com site. If a cache owner hasn't visited the site in a while, a number of logged DNFs could mean that the cache has been moved or stolen by someone. Unfortunately, cache vandalism and thievery happen: For example, the cache you were looking for might have been stolen, and the database hasn't been updated yet.

Lost but now found

In more cases than not, after looking around for a while, behold! You find an old, olive-drab ammo can tucked behind some rocks. Congratulations, you found your first geocache! Now what?

✔ **Savor the moment.** There's definitely a sense of accomplishment when you find a cache and a little bit of childlike wonder as you open up the container to see what types of treasures are inside.

✔ **Sign the logbook.** Write down the date, a few sentences about your experiences finding the cache, what you took and/or added, and your geocaching alias. Some people who are really into geocaching have custom business cards or stickers made up for placing in the cache log.

✔ **Read the logbook.** It's fun to read about other cachers' adventures and when they discovered the cache.

✔ **Exchange treasures.** If you take something from the cache, leave something. If you forgot your goodies, just sign the logbook. Quite a few geocachers are more into the hunt for the cache than for the loot inside.

Trading up means leaving something in the cache that's better than what you take. There's always been a considerable amount of discussion in the geocaching community about how caches start out with cool stuff but soon end up filled with junk (broken toys, beat-up golf balls, cheap party favors, and so on). Some geocachers even take it upon themselves to remove anything from a cache that doesn't meet their personal quality bar. If you can, trade up to make the finds more interesting for everyone.

✔ **Cover your tracks.** Seal the cache container up and put it back where you found it, making sure that it's hidden just as well as it was before you found it.

✔ **Go home.** Use the track-back feature of your GPS receiver to follow your exact path back to your car. Better yet, activate the waypoint that you set for your car (but see some different sights by taking a new route back to where you started).

✔ **Share your experiences.** When you get back to your computer (if you're a member of Geocaching.com), log your find on the Web site so the whole world knows you found the cache. Go to the cache description page and click the Log Your Visit link at the top of the page. (This is completely optional. Some geocachers prefer operating under a low profile, keeping their discoveries and adventures to themselves.)

✔ **Do it again (and again, and . . .).** After you have your first cache find under your belt, you're ready to venture out into the brave new world of geocaching and find even more caches. As your experience with a GPS receiver grows and your skills in navigation and cache finding improve, you'll likely want to start challenging yourself more by going after caches that are more difficult to find and reach.

The force is strong with this one

A *Star Wars* Darth Vader action figure, Travel Bug, started his travels in an Arkansas geocache in February, 2002. By the time he was returned to his owner nine months later, he had journeyed 17,534.64 miles, including tagging along on aerial missions in Afghanistan, pub-hopping in England, and working on his tan in Florida. At last report, Darth was getting some R&R in Texas.

GeoJargon: Speaking the lingo

Like any sport or pastime, geocaching has its own language. Because the sport is so new, the jargon is still evolving, but here are some terms to be familiar with so when you talk to other people about geocaching, you sound like a pro.

- **Archived:** Caches that no longer exist but still appear in a Web site database for historical purposes. A cache can be archived because it has been stolen, is no longer maintained, or does not abide by the guidelines for where caches should be placed.

- **Cache machine:** A preplanned event in a local area, where geocachers look for caches. The event can last hours or days. This is a marathon-endurance session of geocaching, where you try to find as many caches as you can in a set amount of time. The event is named after a dedicated geocacher. BruceS, a true cache machine, found 28 caches in 24 hours, totaling 86 finds in 5 days.

- **DNF:** Did Not Find (as in, *did not find the cache*). It happens to everyone. If you didn't find the cache, try again on another day.

- **FTF:** First To Find. This means bragging rights that you were the first person to find a newly placed cache.

- **GPSR/GPSr:** GPS receiver. Many people drop the R and just call a GPS receiver a *GPS*.

- **Hitchhiker:** An object that moves from cache to cache. A hitchhiker is marked with some instructions, telling the finding geocacher to take it and place it in another cache.

- **McToys:** Cheap trinkets left in a cache, like the toys that appear in fast-food kids' meals. There are better things to leave in caches.

- **Muggles:** People you encounter on the trail who aren't geocachers; from the Harry Potter stories.

- **Neocacher:** An inexperienced or newbie geocacher.

- **Signature item:** Something unique that a particular geocacher always places in a cache that he or she finds.

- **Spoiler:** Information that might give away the location of a cache.

- **Swag:** Goodies that you find in a cache; from the marketing term *swag* (or schwag) used to describe the promotional trash and trinkets (tchotchkes) handed out at trade shows.

- **TNLN:** Took Nothing, Left Nothing. Just what it sounds like. Also, *TNLNSL*, which means that the geocacher signed the cache log.

✔ **Travel Bug (TB):** A type of hitchhiker that you mark with a special dog tag purchased from Geocaching.com. When TBs are found, their journey is tracked on the Geocaching.com Web site. Travel Bugs can have specific goals (as in, getting from Point A to Point B) or are just released into the world to see how far they can travel.

Hiding a Cache

After a while, you might get the urge to set up a cache of your own. This section discusses how to create and hide your own cache. It's not that difficult, and most cache hiders spend $10 or less to set up their cache, which is some pretty cheap entertainment these days. It's also a way to give something back to the sport.

Don't rush out and hide a cache before spending some time finding caches. Searching for other caches will give you some good ideas and set expectations for creating your own. Check out Geocaching.com for the FAQs there as well as a complete set of guidelines for hiding and placing caches.

Selecting a container

First things first. You need something to house your cache in. The only real requirement for the container is that it needs to be waterproof, although sometimes cachers use plastic bags inside a nonwaterproof container. The size of the container determines where you'll be able to hide the cache and how full you'll be able to fill it with trading trinkets. Any container that you can think of has probably been used for geocaching, including plastic buckets with lids, breath mint tins, margarine tubs, 35mm film canisters, pill bottles, plastic Army decontamination kit boxes, and PVC piping. You've probably got a suitable geocaching container lying around the house or garage. Just for the record, the two most popular types of cache containers are

✔ **Ammo cans:** Made of military surplus steel, ammunition (ammo) cans work great because they're sturdy and waterproof. They typically come in two sizes, based on the machine gun ammunition they once held:

- *50 caliber:* 11 inches long, 5.5 inches wide, and 7–5 inches deep.

- *30 caliber:* 10 inches long, 3.5 inches wide, and 6.75 inches deep. (The narrow cans tend to fill up with trinkets quicker.)

Depending on the terrain and vegetation, the olive-drab color makes ammo cans difficult to spot. You can typically get ammo cans for around five dollars or less from local or online Army surplus stores.

✔ **Tupperware:** Rectangular Tupperware or other plastic storage containers are also a popular choice but aren't quite as rugged as an ammo can.
Sometimes a geocacher won't reseal the lid very well. Plastic containers
are cheaper and more available than ammo cans, and you can easily
match a size to go with any cache. Some cache hiders spray paint the
containers to make them blend better with the surroundings.

Location is everything

Just like in real estate or retail sales, location is everything when it comes to
placing a cache. After you select a container, figure out where to put it. The
location of your cache usually defines its success and popularity.

I recommend doing some initial research to locate a general area to hide your
cache. For many geocachers, visiting a new place with some unique feature,
incredible scenery, or just gorgeous view is every bit as important as finding
a cache. Keep this in mind as you use maps, travel guides, or memories from
your own explorations to help you select a good cache location.

An important part of your homework is discovering where caches are and are
not permitted. The geocaching community tends to be very aware that the
continued growth and success of the sport depends on good relationships
with landowners.

If you want to place a cache on private property, always first ask the owner's
permission. Because geocaching is so new, many people don't know what it
is, so take the time to explain how the sport works.

Always check with a governmental agency before placing caches on its land.
You can contact the agency directly, try a Google search to see whether its
geocaching policies are published on the Web, or talk with other geocachers
in your area to get their experiences in dealing with different agencies. For
example, the U.S. Bureau of Land Management recognizes geocaching as a
recreational activity and tends to be friendly toward cache hiders who want
to locate a cache in places other than wilderness or wilderness study areas.
The U.S. National Park Service, on the other hand, prohibits placing geocaches
on the land that it manages; if you're caught hiding a cache on such land, it's
a federal offense. Yipes.

After you figure out the land ownership issues, the next step is to ensure that
your cache appears in the Geocaching.com database. The site has a series of
common-sense criteria that a cache must meet to be added to its database.
Generally a cache can't be

- ✔ **Buried:** Covering it with braches or leaves is okay, but no digging, please.

- ✔ **Placed in environmentally sensitive areas:** This includes archaeological and historic sites.

- ✔ **Placed in national parks or designated wilderness areas:** This is a no-no. Sorry; them's the rules.

- ✔ **Placed within 150 feet of railroad tracks:** Umm, this is for safety reasons.

- ✔ **Placed anywhere that might cause concerns about possible terrorist activities:** Use your post-9/11 brain. This includes areas near airports, tunnels, military facilities, municipal water supplies, and government buildings or bridges.

- ✔ **Placed within one-tenth of a mile of another cache:** This is a rule for adding a cache to the Geocaching.com database as well as simple geo-caching etiquette.

- ✔ **Of a commercial, political, or religious nature:** Keep it neutral; don't cache something promoting some business or cause.

The geocaching community polices itself fairly well. If you put a cache where it shouldn't be, a cacher will probably let the Geocaching.com administrators know about it, and the cache will be removed from the database.

After you select a good general location to put the cache, visit the area to figure out exactly where you're going to hide the cache. Use your creativity to find a challenging hiding place: in a tree hollow, underneath bushes, wedged in rocks, and so on. The more experience you have finding caches, the more ideas you'll have for good hiding places.

After you find your secret hiding spot, you need to determine the cache's coordinates as precisely as possible. (Use the WGS 84 datum; see Chapter 4 for more on this.) This can be challenging because of less-than-perfect satellite coverage. You might find the location's coordinates changing on your GPS receiver every few seconds. Many GPS units have an averaging feature that compares coordinates at a single spot over a period of time and then averages the result. If your receiver does do averaging, get it as close to the cache as possible, let it sit for five or ten minutes, and then copy down the cache coordinates and enter them as a waypoint.

A manual approach to averaging is to set a waypoint for the cache location, walk away, and then come back and set another waypoint. Repeat this until you have 6–12 dozen waypoints; then examine the list of waypoints, and pick the one that looks the most accurate (generally the value in the middle of the list).

Taking geocaching to the extreme

Although geocaching usually doesn't require a high degree of fitness or special skills, a few caches out there might be labeled *extreme geocaching*. A cache might be perched midway down a cliff face, requiring climbing equipment to rappel down to reach it. And a handful of caches are underwater and can only be reached by scuba diving. (GPS doesn't work underwater, so this would be the spot for a boat to anchor.) Obviously, these types of caches limit the number of finders but can be quite unique if you're into challenging and technical outdoor sport.

Stocking the cache

Here are the basics of what to cache in your cache.

   ✔ **Logbook and writing utensil**

   At the very minimum, your cache should contain a logbook and a pen or pencil so other cachers can write about their discovery. (Pencils work better in cold climates because the ink in most pens will freeze); mechanical pencils are the best because they don't need sharpening. The logbook is usually a spiral notebook with the name of the cache written on the cover. Some cache hiders paste their personal logo or some other graphic to the notebook cover. As the cache founder, you should write some profound thoughts about the cache on the first page.

   ✔ **Identifying information**

   The cache should have some information that identifies it as a geocache, describes what geocaching is, and provides instructions to the finder. (Non-geocachers often stumble upon a cache.) The Geocaching.com site has an information sheet in a number of different languages that you can print out and place in your cache; laminating this sheet is a good idea. Be sure to mention the cache's name and its coordinates.

   ✔ **Treasures**

   Add some treasures to your cache. These should be unique and interesting items. Because geocaching is a family sport, initially put a mix of things in it that appeal to both adults and children. You don't need to fill the container up like a stocking at Christmas. Many caches start out with 6–12 small items. If you want, you can add a hitchhiker or a Travel Bug. (Read more about both of these critters in the earlier section, "GeoJargon: Speaking the lingo.")

Even though your storage container may be waterproof, always put your logbook and cache goodies into resealable plastic storage bags. This prevents your cache from turning into a soggy mush when someone inevitably forgets to seal the container's lid.

Submitting the cache

Time for a little advertising. It doesn't do much good if people don't know about your cache after you place it. The Geocaching.com Web site currently has the largest database of caches and is where most people go to find information about caches. You need to have a free or premium account at the site to be able to post your cache, so if you don't have an account yet, go to the site and sign up. (I promise that it's quick and painless.)

After you log on to the site, submitting a cache is just a matter of filling out an online form about your new pride and joy. You enter things like the cache's name (think of something creative), its coordinates, the date it was placed, and other information similar to what you find when you're looking at a cache description Web page.

 If you're having trouble trying to determine the terrain and difficulty ratings, head over to geocacher ClayJar's online terrain and difficulty calculator, at `www.clayjar.com/gcrs`.

After you enter all the cache information, submit the form. Volunteers will check things like whether all the information needed is present, the coordinates are generally correct, and the cache meets the general submission guidelines. Keep in mind that volunteers don't physically visit the cache because that would require thousands of people all over the world with a considerable amount of free time on their hands. The approval process can take up to a couple of days but is usually shorter. If you're approved, your cache is added to the database. If you're not approved, you'll be informed why, and you can either address the problem and resubmit or discuss the issue with the staff.

 If you're handy with HTML and your Internet provider supports Web hosting, you can associate a Web site with your cache. The Web site might have digital photos, detailed maps, or anything else that supplements or complements the standard information found in a cache database entry.

Cache hiders checklist

When you hide caches, you bring along most of the same things you have when you search for caches. Here are a few other things not to forget:

✔ Waterproof cache container

✔ Cache log (spiral notebook)

✔ Pencils and/or pens to leave in the cache

✔ Resealable plastic bags

✔ Trinkets to stock the cache

✔ Notebook to record information about the cache to submit to the Geocaching.com database

The Oregon Hell Hole

It all started in June when Croaker posted a message in a Geocaching.com Web forum, asking about something called *The Oregon Hell Hole.* He remembered seeing a public television show about it several years back. The Hell Hole was considered such a dangerous place that the U.S. Forest Service didn't want anyone to know where it was located.

A geocacher named Moun10Bike mentioned that he had an old newspaper article that described a 200-foot-deep rift in the forest floor somewhere in the Willamette National Forest, above the North Fork of the Middle Fork of the Willamette River. The location had been deliberately kept out of tourist books and omitted from government maps since the 1930s,and there were ominous quotes from a Forest Service geologist about how easy it would be for someone to get killed because of the crumbling rock around the deep hole.

Geocachers are by nature very curious people, and the thought of a spectacular geologic formation that was being covered up by the government got the forum all riled up. Soon there were posts from people examining aerial photographs (some conspiracy theorists offered that likely even aerial photos had been doctored), visiting university libraries in search of old maps, asking relatives employed by the Forest Service for information, and trying to find a copy of the TV show to see whether it might offer any clues to the location of the secretive Hell Hole. Thirteen days after Croaker's original post, Navdog solved the mystery when he located a videotape of the TV show at the library.

By pausing the video at a key point where a map and aerial photograph were shown, like Sherlock Holmes, Navdog put these and other clues together and posted a series of maps where he believed the Hell Hole was located. A few hours later, Uplink confirmed Navdog's hypothesis, posting a scanned map from 1937 that had the words *Hell Hole* printed exactly where Navdog thought the rift was.

There was much discussion about getting a group of geocachers together to visit the place — not to descend into the Hell Hole but just to see what it was like. Almost everyone agreed that placing a cache there wouldn't be a good idea. (Most geocachers are sensitive to their sport being potentially overly regulated by federal land managers, and if the Forest Service had been trying to keep the Hell Hole secret for all these years, it would be like thumbing your nose at them by advertising a cache there.)

After several failed attempts by others, Grin'n' Bearit and Lef-t made it to the Hell Hole on July 19. After about five hours of searching and bushwhacking, the geocachers found the Hell Hole and left a cache there.

The cache's listing in the database generated a storm of controversy in the forum, with fears about safety and getting the Forest Service angry about their once secret place now revealed to the world. There was a heated debate, as each side weighed in with their opinions.

In the end, Grin'n'Bearit returned to the Hell Hole. Instead of the tangle of underbrush he initially encountered, he found a new path from a different road. It was a three-minute walk from where he parked to the edge of the Hell Hole. He reported well-used trails, all leading to the hole. He moved the cache to a safer spot and changed the description in the database.

The story of the Oregon Hell Hole is a testament to the ingenuity, creativity, and community spirit of geocachers as well as the struggles involved in trying to do the right thing for their sport. Although perhaps not as dramatic, lesser versions of this story happen every day.

Maintaining the cache

After you hide your cache and it appears in the database, your work isn't over yet. You now have the responsibility of maintaining the cache. This means visiting the cache every now and then to verify that it's there and in a good state of repair. You may even need to restock it with some trinkets if the supply is running low. During your visits, check that the area around the cache isn't being extremely impacted by people searching for the cache. If the site is being disturbed, consider either moving the cache to a new location or pulling the cache entirely. (If you decide to temporarily or permanently remove a cache, be sure to post a log entry to let other geocachers know when they look up information about the cache. Also, let the Geocaching.com administrators know so they can update their database.)

In addition to physically checking the cache, you should also check your cache online and read the comments posted from people who have visited the cache. These comments can alert you when it's time to make a maintenance call to the cache. Patience, Grasshopper! Sometimes it can take a while for someone to first find your cache and post about it.

Geocaching Etiquette

For the most part, there aren't a whole lot of rules when it comes to geocaching. It mostly boils down to respecting other cachers and the land that you play on. Consider these etiquette points when you're out geocaching:

- **Always respect private property.** Need I say more?

- **Don't leave food in a cache.** Food can attract animals as well as get smelly and messy, and plastic cache containers have been chewed through to get at a tasty snack.

- **Never put anything illegal, dangerous, or possibly offensive in a cache.** Geocaching is a family sport, so be responsible.

- **Always trade up or replace an item in the cache with something of equal value.** Don't be a Scrooge; what's the fun in that?

- **Be environmentally conscious when searching for and hiding caches.** Tread lightly on the land. Check out the Leave No Trace site at www.lnt.org for more information.

- **Geocaching is a pretty dog-friendly sport.** Keep it that way by having Fido tethered in leash-only areas. And no matter how good your dog is, have a leash ready in case other people or animals are around.

✔ **Cache In, Trash Out (CITO).** If you see any litter on your way to or from a cache, get some additional exercise with a deep-knee bend, pick it up, and pack it out.

✔ **Say thank you.** After you visit a cache, send a quick e-mail, thank-you message to the geocacher that placed the cache or acknowledge him or her in your cache comments.

Internet Geocaching Resources

Because geocaching is very much a sport of the Internet community, the Internet contains some terrific sites about the sport. Here's a sample:

✔ **Geocaching.com** (www.geocaching.com): This is the primary geocaching site on the 'Net. In addition to an extensive database of caches and FAQs about the sport, the site also has a large number of forums dedicated to different geocaching topics.

✔ **Navicache.com** (www.navicache.com): This is the second-largest Web site dedicated to geocaching, but it's still currently quite a bit smaller than Geocaching.com in terms of caches listed. The site has many of the same features as Geocaching.com and is often viewed as an alternative to the more mainstream, larger site. There's not much duplication in the cache listings between the two big sites, so be sure to check both their listings when searching for caches.

✔ **Buxley's Geocaching Waypoint** (http://brillig.com/geocaching): This site has a comprehensive set of maps that provides a bird's-eye view of caches in your area. Just click a dot on the map for cache information.

If you want to socialize with other geocachers in your area, local and regional clubs and Web sites have sprung up. Many of these sites have their own lists of caches and practical information for the novice or experienced cacher. Do a Google search for *geocaching* and your city or state to search for Web sites with more information. You can also find out more about geocaching in your area by checking out the regional discussion forums at Geocaching.com.

The geocaching community is not immune to politics. Skirmishes and large-scale battles can break out between individuals and rival Web sites. It's best to duck your head, check your GPS receiver, and head to the cache waypoint.

Other caching pursuits

In addition to geocaching, a number of other GPS-related activities have sprung up on the Internet. A few that you might be interested in include

- **Geodashing:** This is a contest in which random points are selected and players need to get within 100 meters of the location. There are no caches, hints, or terrain difficulty ratings, and the points can be anywhere on Earth. In fact, some locations can be impossible to reach. A new contest takes place roughly every month. The goal of the game is for teams to collect all the points first or to get as many as they can before the contest ends. For more details, check out www.geodashing.org.

- **The Degree Confluence Project:** This is an interesting project in which people use their GPS receivers to visit places where latitude and longitude lines converge. They take a digital picture, which is then published on a Web site. The goal is to map all the major latitude/longitude intersections for the entire Earth. For more information, go to www.confluence.org.

- **Benchmark hunting:** *Benchmarks* are permanent markers installed by the government for survey purposes. Over one-half million benchmarks have been installed in the United States. The most familiar type is a small, brass disk embedded into rock or concrete. The National Geodetic Survey (www.ngs.noaa.gov) maintains a list of the benchmarks and their locations. The Geocaching.com site also provides benchmark locations and lets you log a benchmark when you find one.

- **GPS Drawing:** This is an interesting form of art based on using your GPS receiver to record where you've been. For some amazing examples, check out the gallery at www.gpsdrawing.com.

Part III
Digital Mapping on Your Computer

The 5th Wave   By Rich Tennant

"Hey you bunch of loser jocks! This happens to be a GPS receiver I got with my laptop which you wouldn't know what to do with if your life depended on it!"

In this part . . .

You get practical. This part is all about digital maps on your PC — desktop mapping so to speak. You'll find out about hardware (both basic requirements for desktop mapping and connecting a GPS receiver to a PC) and review a number of different software packages you can use to access aerial photos and topographic and street maps.

Chapter 8

Digital Mapping Hardware Considerations

• •

In This Chapter

▶ Determining hardware requirements for different mapping activities

▶ Weighing hardware and peripheral digital mapping considerations

• •

*I*f you're planning on using digital mapping software on your PC, you might wonder about computer hardware and peripheral requirements (like a printer). What kinds of computer and add-ons work best for creating and using digital maps?

Your answer depends on what type of mapping you'll be doing and what kind of software you plan to use to access and create maps. In this chapter, I lead you through your choices to give you a pretty good idea whether your current computer can meet your mapping needs or whether you need to think about investing in a new machine. I also cover how much storage you might need as well as what makes a good printer for mapmaking.

An Internet connection is a must for anyone interested in digital mapping.

Digital Mapping Software Choices

Understandably, your hardware needs are driven by your software needs. Here are the three main types of mapping programs you're most likely to use:

✓ **Commercial mapping programs:** Commercial mapping programs come bundled with maps and offer a number of powerful features but are relatively easy to use. Most commercial map programs don't have extensive hardware requirements. In fact, many of the programs on the market work fine with older computers. (I discuss GPS receiver manufacturer software in Chapter 10 and street and topographic map software in Chapters 12 and 13.)

✔ **Web-hosted map services:** Web-hosted map services are accessed with your Web browser. These map Web sites are easy to use but don't offer as many features as commercial or standalone mapping programs. Viewing Web site maps isn't a very resource-intensive activity. The speed of your Internet connection is a bigger issue than the speed of your computer's processor. (For more on using Web-hosted map services of various types, see Chapters 17, 18, and 19.)

✔ **Standalone mapping programs:** Standalone map programs are similar to commercial map software but don't come bundled with maps; you need to provide the map data yourself. If you're using a standalone program to make maps from data that you download from the Internet — especially if you'll be creating 3-D images — you want as much processor speed, memory, and storage as your budget allows. It also doesn't hurt to have a high-speed Internet connection to speed up downloads. (I talk about some standalone map programs in Chapters 15 and 16.)

Additionally, you need to factor in your processing power as well as what types of storage devices, display devices, printers, and communications equipment you'll need and use.

In most cases, if you've purchased a computer in the past couple of years that runs Windows, it's probably going to be more than adequate for computer mapping. (Always check a mapping software vendor's Web site first, though, to ensure that your computer is compatible with the program you plan to use.)

Processing Power

When it comes to software, whether it's an operating system or program, the processor and amount of memory your PC has can make a difference in performance. Some people think that just like money, you can never have enough processor speed or memory; when it comes to mapping software, though, that's not entirely true.

You don't absolutely need to have the latest cutting edge and fastest technology for computer mapping. You can easily get by using older computers and peripherals. I have an old 500 MHz Pentium with 256K of RAM running Windows 2000 that works fine for mapping. Granted, it's a bit slower performing some tasks than faster, newer computers, but it still gets the job done. With this in mind, take a look at practical processing and memory requirements for mapping software.

Processors

Most commercial mapping programs have pretty humble processor require-ments. To use these programs, your computer should have a modern Pentium or similar chip with a minimum speed of 300 MHz. That's a pretty meager amount of computing power considering that current computers offer at least six times greater processor speed, if not more. If you're using commercial mapping software, just about any contemporary computer is going to fit the bill when it comes to processor requirements.

You'll want a faster processor and more computing horsepower if you're doing a lot of 3-D mapping or processing large amounts of map data — particularly creating maps from data that you download from the Internet. This can be a processor-intensive task: The faster the chip, the quicker the map or terrain image will be rendered and displayed. (Any Pentium III or above PC with a processor speed of over 1.2 GHz should suffice for the average map user.)

Memory

If you look at the system requirements of commercial mapping software, you'll see some ridiculously low memory requirements considering what's standard in today's computers. (When was the last time you saw a computer advertised with 16, 32, or 64K of RAM? That's actually some of the stated min-imum memory requirements for a number of popular mapping programs.) Every contemporary computer should have enough memory to work with most mapping programs.

However, memory is one of those things that you can't have enough of. Although a computer with 128K of RAM is probably going to meet most of your mapping needs, more memory will improve performance. If you're run-ning Microsoft Windows XP, you should consider running at least 256K of RAM.

 Don't fret over the different types of memory. Double Data Rate (DDR) memory chips are indeed faster than conventional, synchronous dynamic RAM (SDRAM) memory. But if you're the average computer user doing typical mapping projects, you're probably not going to notice the difference.

Storage Capacity

Another important hardware consideration is storage capacity. Map data files don't tend to be small like word processing or spreadsheet documents, so you need to plan accordingly. This section gives you some advice on ensuring that your storage space is adequate for your maps.

Sweet emulation

Some mapping programs allow you to copy map data from a CD to your hard drive. This is useful because then you don't need to find misplaced data CDs or swap between CDs to view different maps. Unfortunately, many commercial mapping programs don't give you this option.

Skirt this problem with a special type of software: a *CD emulator*. This program allows you to copy the contents of a CD onto your hard drive to create a virtual CD. This tricks a mapping (or other) program into thinking that you inserted its CD when the data actually already resides on your hard drive. Sweet. Do a Google search for *CD emulator* to find information about various products. They tend to be reasonably priced — under $40.

Hard drives

In these days of cheap, large hard drives, it's easy to get a little blasé about storage space. Digital mapping can take up quite a lot of hard drive space, though, and you should be aware how much space your map software and its data can consume.

Software storage needs

A mapping program can easily install between 300–500MB on your hard drive, and that doesn't count all the map data that's contained on a CD. Depending on program options and the types of maps to be used, you can easily have up to 1GB of space taken up by a single mapping program. Always check the software hardware requirements to ensure you'll have enough storage space to install the program.

If you're running low on hard drive space, some mapping programs have a minimal install option that leaves some program data on the CD instead of writing it to the hard drive by default.

Data storage needs

Most commercial mapping programs come with map data on CDs, so you shouldn't need to worry about storage space unless you plan on copying the map data on the CDs to your hard drive.

However, if you're downloading lots of raw data from the Internet to create your own maps, you definitely need to think about your storage space needs. Map data is not small. For example, a single map data file can easily take up 5–10MB of space.

If you plan to collect lots of map data, you'll definitely need a high-capacity hard drive for storage. At 10MB per data file, 100 files quickly can consume a gigabyte of disk space. Although you can get by using smaller hard drives, I'd opt for at least an 80GB drive.

If you decide to get serious about computer mapping, I recommend that you purchase a second internal or external hard drive to exclusively store your data. A second drive provides more performance and is easier to maintain and manage files. And because a second drive currently can be had for a little more than a dollar per GB, the bigger the better.

CD and DVD drives

Just about every commercial software manufacturer uses CDs to distribute their products. Digital map manufacturers are no different; they extensively use CDs for map data. For example, the National Geographic Back Roads Explorer (a whopping 16-CD set) provides topographic maps for the entire United States. You can run these CDs on any CD drive; the higher the read speed, the faster the map data will load and display.

Having a CD drive that can write *(burn)* CD-ROMs is way useful if you plan to download large amounts of map data from the Internet. Because data files can be very large, archive the data on CDs instead of cluttering your hard drive with infrequently used files. If you're not going to be archiving map data, consider using CD-RWs (rewriteables) because you can delete files from them, using them again and again.

Computers are now commonly equipped with a DVD drive, which can read both CDs and DVDs. DVDs rock because they can store a whole lot more data than a CD; compare 4.7GB on a DVD versus a relatively paltry 700MB on a CD. As DVD drives become more commonplace on computers, expect map software companies to start offering their products on DVD media. This will make life easier for vendors who currently distribute map data on multiple CDs.

DVD soup

As this book goes to press, DVD standards have yet to be agreed on (by the manufacturers as well as the ever-important consumers). Check out this alphabet soup: There are DVD-ROM, DVD-R, DVD-RW, DVD+R, DVD+RW, and DVD-RAM formats. Some manufacturers are hedging their bets on the standards race by offering multiformat DVD drives. If you're in the market for a DVD drive, I'd certainly look for a multiformat drive until a single DVD standard emerges.

Display Equipment

Obviously you're going to want to see your maps, so you'll need a few pieces of display equipment, such as a graphics card and monitor. Again, these don't have to be anything fancy. (Are you noticing a theme here when it comes to mapping software hardware requirements?) Here are a few considerations for display hardware.

Graphics cards

Unlike computer video games, graphics card requirements for mapping programs are pretty minimal. All you need is a Super Video Graphics Array (SVGA) card, which has come standard on computers for years. If your mapping software supports 3-D terrain display, a card that has a graphics accelerator will draw map images faster. An accelerator isn't an absolute requirement because most commercial programs that support 3-D rendering take advantage of a graphics accelerator only if it is present. Check the specs of your current PC (or one you're considering purchasing) to see whether an accelerator is present.

Monitors

Just like the broad, general hardware requirements theme for mapping, bigger (that is, a bigger monitor) is better. Although most programs work fine on a 15-inch monitor, the larger the monitor, the more map area can appear onscreen. 17-inch monitors, which come standard with most computers these days, are more than adequate for digital mapping. However, if you're spending a lot of time using maps in front of a computer screen, consider a larger (19-inch or 21-inch) monitor, which is both easier on the eyes and can display much more data.

In Windows, change the display size of a monitor via the Display Properties dialog box. To access this, right-click the desktop and select Properties from the contextual menu that appears. On the Settings tab, you can change the display area to different sizes such as 800 x 600, 1024 x 768, or 1280 x 1024 pixels. Try some of these different settings to see which works best for your mapping program as well as your eyes.

Printers

At some point, you're probably going to want to print a digital map. (See Chapter 22 for some great tips on printing maps.) Expensive plotters and large format printers are important for a professional mapmaker, but any printer that can output the map in a readable fashion is fine for the average computer user. However, some printers are more suited for digital mapping than others.

✔ **Color printers:** Black-and-white printers are perfectly suitable for printing maps, but color output is usually easier to read and understand, especially when using topographic maps. A colored map produced on a cheap inkjet printer might be more useful than a crisp black-and-white map that came from an expensive laser printer. When cartographers make maps, they design them to be either black and white or color. Important information can be lost when a map program translates a color map into the inherent shades of gray in black and white.

✔ **Resolution:** The higher the print resolution in dots per inch (dpi), the better the map will appear; especially for maps that show a lot of detail. Printers designed for printing digital photos work quite well in representing topographic and other detailed maps.

✔ **Print speed:** Some printers are faster than others, and a faster printer means you get to see and use your printed map quicker. Printers are rated in *pages per minute* (ppm), which is the number of pages that can be printed in a minute. When you're comparing page per minute ratings, be sure you look at the numbers for printing graphics instead of at text.

✔ **Cost per page:** If you're frequently printing maps, it makes good economic sense to use a printer with a reasonable cost-per-page rating (the estimated cost to print a single page, considering paper and ink). Cost-per-page rates vary considerably between printers and are usually mentioned in magazine and online reviews.

Communication Capabilities

If you want your GPS receiver to be able to talk to your map software or if you plan on accessing the Internet to use Web map sites or to download map data, your PC needs to have some basic communication capabilities. Take a quick look here at communications ports and Internet connectivity.

Communication ports

You can connect most GPS receivers to your computer through the computer's serial port. (I discuss ports and connectivity thoroughly in Chapter 9.) If you want to download data from a GPS receiver to use with a digital map or upload maps and data to a GPS receiver, your computer needs a serial port and a special cable to connect the two devices. (*Note:* Some GPS receivers use a faster USB connector to interface with a computer.)

If your computer doesn't have a serial port, as is the case with a number of laptop computers, you need a USB adapter and serial cable to connect your GPS receiver to a computer. Read more about this in Chapter 9, also.

If your GPS receiver supports both a serial connection and a Secure Digital (SD) or MultiMediaCard (MMC) memory card for storing data, use the memory card when you're exchanging data. It's both faster and easier to use than a serial cable when interfacing the GPS receiver to your computer. You will need a card reader connected to your computer to transfer data to and from the memory card. See Chapter 9 for more on these memory cards and readers.

Internet connection

You need a modem and an Internet account if you want to

✔ Download mapping software updates

✔ Use Web-hosted mapping services

✔ Download data for creating maps

An Internet connection is a must for anyone interested in digital mapping.

If you plan to download digital maps and aerial photographs, you really should have a broadband Internet account (DSL or cable modem). Even when compressed, these files can be very large, and it can be painfully slow waiting for the data to arrive on a slower, dialup connection.

Chapter 9

Interfacing a GPS Receiver to a Computer

. . . .

In This Chapter

▶ Transferring data between GPS receivers and computers

▶ Dealing with cables

▶ Understanding communications settings and protocols

▶ Using GPS receiver utility programs

▶ Upgrading GPS receiver firmware

. . . .

Admittedly, your GPS receiver is pretty darned useful even if you can't connect it to your computer. With your receiver, you can find your way around as well as your way back, even if you don't know what a computer is. The ability to connect your GPS receiver to your computer, however, can make your GPS receiver even more useful . . . heck, a *lot* more useful. Essentially, a connection between your GPS receiver and your computer allows them to talk and share information, such as uploaded maps and waypoints to your receiver as well as downloaded receiver information that you store while on your adventures.

In this chapter, I show you why this interconnectivity is a fantastic addition to your receiver. You'll discover the ins and outs of the physical connections, how to get your computer and receiver to speak the same language, the lowdown on great receiver utility programs, and how to upgrade your receiver firmware.

About (Inter)Face: Connectivity Rules

If you choose to use a *mapping* GPS receiver (one that you can upload maps to from a PC), you're in the right chapter. And kudos to you to getting a model that really lets you maximize using your GPS receiver. You'll be outdoor navigating and geocaching (check out Chapter 7) in no time. Here are the very cool things you can do with a PC-compatible receiver:

✔ Back up and store GPS receiver waypoints, routes, and tracks on your computer. (Get the skinny on all these important critters in Chapter 4.)

✔ Download waypoints, routes, and tracks from your GPS receiver to your computer to use with computer mapping programs.

✔ Upload waypoints, routes, and tracks to your GPS receiver from other sources such as Internet sites, other GPS users, or mapping programs.

✔ Upload maps from your computer to your GPS receiver (if your receiver supports mapping). For more on selecting a GPS with mapping capabilities, see Chapter 5.

✔ Provide GPS data to a moving map program on a laptop for real-time travel tracking such as the ones that I describe in Chapters 12 and 13.

✔ Update your GPS receiver's firmware.

Anatomy of a Link: Understanding the Interface Process

Before I talk about how to interface a GPS receiver to a PC, you need to understand the types of data that can be passed between the two devices:

✔ **GPS receiver to PC:** Saved waypoints, routes, tracks, and current location coordinates

✔ **PC to GPS receiver:** Maps (if the GPS receiver supports them), waypoints, routes, and tracks

You can interface a GPS receiver to a computer and transfer data in two ways:

✔ **Cable:** Most GPS receivers use a special cable, with one end that plugs into the receiver and the other that plugs into the serial or Universal Serial Bus (USB) port of your computer. (See the upcoming section, "Untangling Cables.")

✔ **Memory card:** Some GPS receiver models use Secure Digital (SD) or MultiMediaCard (MMC) memory cards to store data. You transfer data between the GPS receiver and your computer with a card reader connected to the computer. (See the later section, "Managing Memory.")

If you use a Bluetooth wireless GPS receiver, you don't need a cable or memory card reader to transfer data. These are designed to be used exclusively with laptops and PDAs; I discuss these in Chapter 6.

Avoid GPS receivers that can't interface with a personal computer. The benefits of connecting to a computer far exceed the few dollars you'll save.

Untangling Cables

If your GPS receiver uses a cable to connect to a computer and you want to interface the two, you need the right type of cable. Some GPS receivers come bundled with this cable; others don't.

If you don't have a cable for your GPS receiver, get one. Cables tend to vary in design between manufacturers and models, so be sure to get the right one for your GPS receiver. (See Figure 9-1 for examples of different types of cables.) You can purchase a cable directly from the manufacturer at its Web site or through a retailer. Expect cable prices to range from $20–$45.

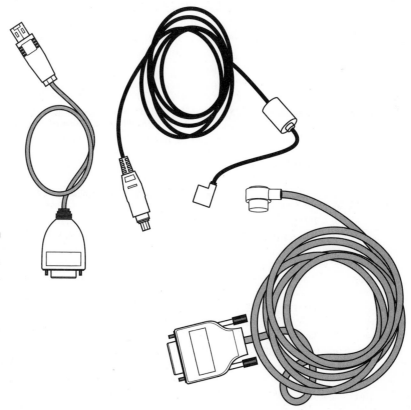

Figure 9-1:
GPS receiver cables for different models, including a USB adapter on the left.

For this connectivity, you need a *PC interface cable*. It has a connector that attaches to the GPS receiver on one end and an RS-232, 9-pin serial connector on the other end to connect to your computer.

Newer GPS receiver models support USB. If your GPS receiver supports both serial and USB interfaces, use a USB cable for much faster communications.

If you bought a GPS receiver that didn't come with a cable and you can't find a cable to buy, you're not necessarily completely out of luck. If you're handy with a soldering iron, most GPS receiver manufacturer Web sites describe the pin-out configurations of their cables so you can make your own. The tricky part can sometimes be finding the right connector for the GPS receiver because most connectors vary between manufacturers and models. A number of how-to sites on the Internet show you how to build your own cables and where to get the connectors. Do a Web search for *gps cable connector* and the brand of your GPS receiver to find different options.

Some cables are designed to both power a GPS receiver from a cigarette lighter and to connect to a computer to send and receive data. These cables are especially useful if you're using your GPS receiver with a moving map program and a laptop. Just remember that you'll also need to buy a dual, car cigarette-lighter adapter so you can plug in both your GPS receiver and laptop into a single cigarette lighter.

If you have a Garmin receiver, check out the Pfranc company for its quality Garmin-compatible cables. Larry Berg started out making shareware Garmin cable plugs, and his business grew. He now stocks a line of reasonably priced cables for all Garmin models. Check out his Web site at `www.pfranc.com`.

Understanding Ports and Protocols

Argg. You track down the right cable you need. You plug one end into your GPS receiver and the other into your computer. And nothing happens. Exactly. Nothing should happen because you need to be running some type of software on your computer that enables the two devices to talk to each other.

Before I discuss interface software, however, I have to lay some groundwork. The programs designed to communicate with GPS receivers have one thing in common: You need to specify certain communication parameters in both the program and the GPS receiver for the devices to successfully exchange data. If the settings aren't correct, you may as well try to communicate with someone a thousand miles away by sending smoke signals through a telephone line. Although setting the right communications parameters isn't that difficult, it can be a bit confusing. This section guides you through the process and also gives you some tips on smoothing out some common problems that you may encounter, beginning with ports and their settings.

Setting up communications between a GPS receiver and a PC is a one-time process. After you get everything working, no worries about the next time.

COM ports

A *COM port* is a computer serial port that's used to connect a mouse, modem, or other device, like a GPS receiver. (*COM* stands for communication, and the ports are called *serial* ports because they receive data *serially,* one character at a time.) COM ports typically have a small oval, D-shaped connector (with nine pins) and are located on the back of your computer. (If you have other devices plugged into your serial ports, you'll need to unplug them so your GPS receiver cable has a port to plug in to. You can plug the other devices back in when you're through transferring data with your GPS receiver.)

Your PC might have one or two physical serial ports that you can plug devices into, but Windows allows you to assign a COM port number to each device. These numbers usually range from 1 to 4 but might go as high as 256 if a USB adapter is used, (which I talk about in the upcoming section, "USB ports"). In most cases, you won't need to use Windows to reassign any of the port numbers. Just know that you have numbered COM ports and that you need to assign one to your GPS receiver, which I talk about next.

To get more detailed information about COM ports and Windows, including how to change settings with Windows Device Manager, head to the Microsoft support Web site at `http://support.microsoft.com` and search the Knowledge Base for *com port.* Or pick up a copy of *PCs For Dummies,* 9th Edition (Wiley) by Dan Gookin, which has an excellent chapter that clearly explains everything you need to know about the subject.

The program you're using to interface with the GPS receiver is where you need to specify which COM port number the receiver is connected to. Programs typically use a drop-down list box that shows all the COM ports; just select one from there. (Some programs have an autoselect feature that tries to establish communications on all available COM ports until the port with the GPS receiver is found.)

COM ports have properties that establish how the communication between the two devices will occur. Generally, both of the devices need to have the same settings. The COM port properties include

- **Baud rate:** *Baud* is the speed at which the port communicates with other devices. This number is in bits per second (bps): the bigger the number, the faster the speed.

- **Data bits:** This is the number of data bits that are transferred for each character, typically 7 or 8.

✔ **Parity:** This is a form of error checking that ensures the integrity of transferred data.

✔ **Stop bits:** This is how many bits follow a character and mark the end of a data transmission.

✔ **Flow control:** Sometimes called *handshaking,* this is a way for one device to stop another device from sending data until it's ready to receive the data.

Although you can set COM properties in Device Manager, I recommend making changes in the program that you're using to interface with the GPS receiver. You'll usually see an Options or Configuration menu in the program that displays a dialog box where you can set these values. (See Figure 9-2 for an example of a communications setting dialog box in a mapping program.)

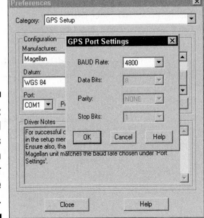

Figure 9-2: Set COM properties to match your interface program.

Unless the program specifies otherwise, here are the typical COM port settings to use when interfacing with a GPS receiver:

✔ **Baud rate:** 4,800 and 9,600 baud are almost certainly guaranteed to work with all GPS receivers. You can increase the speed to a higher rate on some types of GPS receivers. The higher the speed, the faster the data transfer. I recommend experimenting until you find the fastest, most-reliable baud rate, and then using that setting.

✔ **Data bits:** 8.

✔ **Parity:** None.

✔ **Stop bits:** 1.

✔ **Flow control:** None.

Some GPS receivers allow you to set the baud rate in the system setup page of the receiver, but other models don't give you any control of the speed. Check your GPS receiver user guide for more information about your model.

USB ports

Consumer GPS receivers first started appearing in the mid-1990s. At that time, personal computers exclusively used serial ports to interface with other devices, making it easy for hardware manufacturers to design their products to communicate through a serial port. GPS was initially popular with sailors because they could connect a GPS receiver to an autopilot or chart plotter and navigate a vessel based on GPS data. With the right cable, you can also connect your GPS receiver to a computer and download and upload data.

Serial ports are now going the way of the dinosaur, replaced by easier-to-use and faster USB ports. In fact, some laptops no longer have serial ports. However, GPS manufacturers have been slow to jump on the USB bandwagon and until recently have relied on serial port connections for getting GPS receivers and computers to talk to each other.

At some point, GPS receivers with USB connectivity will eventually become widely available in the marketplace. But until that time comes (and considering the millions of GPS receivers already manufactured that can connect only through a serial port), what do you do if your computer doesn't have a serial port?

The solution is to use a USB serial port adapter. The adapter plugs into your computer's USB port and has a standard 9-pin connector that you can connect your serial port devices to. After you install a driver for the adapter (which comes with the product on a disk or CD), Windows recognizes the adapter as a serial port. Just connect a PC interface cable to your GPS receiver and the adapter, and you're all set to send and receive data between the two devices. (See a USB adapter in Figure 9-1.)

Note this one little "gotcha" to mention regarding USB adapters: Windows might squawk that you need a driver when you plug in the adaptor, but you know you've already installed one. The fix: In the dialog box that's prompting you for the driver location, tell Windows to look in the `C:\Windows\Drivers` directory. (This path is for Windows XP; the location varies in older versions of Windows: for example, `C:\WINNT\system32\drivers` in Windows 2000.) Depending on what USB devices are running at the time, Windows XP might assign the adapter to a different COM port from the last time it was used and incorrectly assume it's a new device that needs a new driver. This above-mentioned directory is where previously installed drivers are stored, saving you from having to find the original driver distribution disk.

All GPS receiver manufacturers sell their own branded serial-to-USB adapters, albeit at a premium price. If you're on a tight budget, most any third-party adapter that you buy from a computer retailer will work. These adapters tend to be cheaper than the GPS manufacturer brand-name models.

Protocols

A *protocol* is a way for two devices to successfully talk with each other. Think of a protocol as a language with a strict set of rules. When one device sends a message to another device, it expects a certain type of response back. This structured, back-and-forth conversation takes place until one device sends a message that says the conversation is over.

Likewise, when you connect a GPS receiver to a computer, a certain protocol is used to transfer data back and forth between the two devices. You need to ensure that the same protocol has been selected for both devices. If two different protocols are used, it's like the GPS receiver speaking Russian to a computer that understands only Chinese.

The protocols typically used with GPS receivers are

- ✔ **NMEA:** The National Marine Electronics Association came up with the *NMEA 0183* standard, which is a protocol for transferring data between marine-related electronics such as GPS receivers, autopilots, and chart plotters. Virtually all GPS receivers support the NMEA 0183 standard, which uses widely documented text messages. Typical NMEA data includes latitude, longitude, time, and satellite status.

  NMEA comes in several different versions, including 1.5, 2.1, and 2.3. Make sure that this version number matches both the GPS receiver and the computer program that you're using.

- ✔ **Proprietary:** Some GPS manufacturers have their own proprietary protocols for communicating with a GPS receiver. These protocols send additional data that isn't included in the NMEA standard: for example, altitude, speed, and position error.

NMEA is the de facto standard for getting a GPS receiver to talk to a computer. However, some programs support GPS manufacturer proprietary protocols. If you have a choice between NMEA and a proprietary protocol (for example, the Garmin protocol used with Garmin GPS receivers), select the proprietary protocol because it can supply richer data to a program.

Managing Memory

If you own a GPS receiver that uses a memory card, congratulations! I personally like the versatility these receivers offer (such as stuffing a bunch of maps onto a single, large-capacity memory card). This section talks about how to get the most out of your memory card GPS receiver. If your GPS receiver uses only a cable to connect to a computer, you can skip this section. Better yet, read along to see how memory cards work for transferring data. (Figure 9-3 shows a GPS receiver with a memory card.)

If your GPS receiver supports using a memory card, you have some significant advantages when exchanging data with a computer, including

- ✔ **Upload speed:** Uploading maps from your computer to a GPS receiver is considerably faster with a memory card than via a serial port cable. Because GPS receivers communicate at a fairly low baud rate, transferring 10–20MB of map data can take a long time (up to hours depending on how the serial port is configured).

- ✔ **Affordable and practical:** Memory cards have gotten inexpensive over the years. You can load frequently used maps on several cards and not bother with repeatedly uploading data from map program CDs. You can easily pick up a 128MB memory card, which I'd recommend as a minimum size, for under $40. I like to use Froogle (http://froogle.google.com) to find the best prices online.

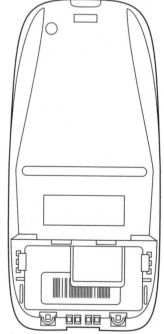

Figure 9-3:
A Lowrance
iFINDER and
an MMC
memory
card.

✔ **More storage:** Memory cards give you considerably more storage than GPS receivers with fixed amounts of internal memory. You can currently purchase memory cards that provide between 8–512MB of data storage. Handheld GPS receivers that don't support memory cards might have only 1–115MB of internal storage.

✔ **Versatility:** You can use the memory card in your PDA, digital camera, and cellphone (if all the devices support the same type of card).

✔ **Minimal settings:** When using a memory card, you don't need to worry about COM ports, baud rates, and protocols when transferring data. (However, if you're using your GPS receiver with a laptop and cable connected to a moving map program, you still have to contend with getting all the settings just right.)

Here are a few drawbacks to GPS receivers that support memory cards:

✔ **Added cost:** They add a bit more cost to the receiver price because of the built-in card reader and associated technology.

✔ **Reader:** You need a memory card reader connected to your computer to transfer data back and forth between the GPS receiver. However, some computers (notably laptops) have built-in card readers.

If your GPS receiver didn't come with a card reader, any third-party reader will work. These devices are inexpensive and easy to use. Just plug the reader into a USB port, and Windows treats the memory card like a hard drive or floppy disk. You can then copy data back and forth between your hard drive and the memory card. Card readers are inexpensive, and you can purchase a basic model for under $20.

✔ **Removal:** Memory cards can be a little tedious to swap because you need to remove the GPS receiver batteries to access the card slot.

Just like digitals cameras, GPS receivers that support memory cards usually come with a card that has a relatively small amount of storage space (8–16MB). In fact, if they both use the same type of memory card, you can swap a card between your digital camera and GPS receiver. You'll probably want to upgrade to a larger capacity card. Blank memory cards with the GPS receiver manufacturer's brand name tend to be more expensive than standard MMC and SD cards. I don't find any difference between the two, and you can save money with third-party memory cards in your GPS receiver.

Transferring GPS Data

After you have a cable and then get the ports, baud rates, and protocols all figured out (or have a memory card and card reader), the next step is getting the data transferred between the GPS receiver and your computer. This is where software comes in, and you generally have three options:

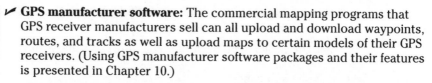

✔ **GPS manufacturer software:** The commercial mapping programs that GPS receiver manufacturers sell can all upload and download waypoints, routes, and tracks as well as upload maps to certain models of their GPS receivers. (Using GPS manufacturer software packages and their features is presented in Chapter 10.)

GPS receivers that display maps work only with proprietary maps provided by the manufacturer. You can't upload maps from third-party mapping programs into your receiver. Sometimes GPS novices believe that they can load maps from DeLorme, Maptech, National Geographic, or other mapping companies directly into their GPS receiver. You can't.

✔ **Third-party mapping software:** Most third-party, commercial map programs can also upload and download waypoints, routes, and tracks — they just can't upload a digital map that appears on your PC. This is an essential feature so you can overlay GPS data on a digital map to see where you've been or plan a trip with the mapping software and then upload waypoints and routes from your computer to a GPS receiver.

✔ **GPS utilities:** Software programs used to interface GPS receivers to computers are utility programs designed specifically to download and upload waypoints, routes, tracks, and other information. These programs are usually freeware or shareware and have a number of useful features.

GPS receiver interface programs tend to work the same way, although they have different menus, dialog boxes, commands, and appearances.

When you transfer data between your GPS receiver and PC, you'll either be

✔ Capturing current location coordinates to use with a real-time mapping program you have running on your laptop (or PDA). As you move, your location appears on the map.

✔ Downloading or uploading waypoints, routes, tracks, or map data.

The process to complete both of these tasks is the same. (If you have a GPS receiver with a memory card, you don't need a cable to download or upload waypoints, routes, tracks, or map data because you'll be using the memory card and a card reader to do this. However, you'll still need a cable to capture your current location to use with a real-time mapping program.) Take a look at the general steps involved in transferring data with a cable:

1. **Connect the PC interface cable to your computer and to your GPS receiver.**

2. **Turn on your GPS receiver.**

   The GPS receiver doesn't need to have a satellite fix to transfer data unless you're using the receiver with a mapping program that's plotting your current location.

3. **Run the interface program.**

   4. **Ensure that the protocols and settings on both the GPS receiver and the computer are the same.**

      See the earlier section, "Understanding Ports and Protocols."

At this point you can

   ✔ Select the type of data (waypoints, routes, or tracks) and upload it to the GPS receiver from your computer or download it from the GPS receiver to your computer.

   ✔ Upload a map to the GPS receiver that was created with a GPS manufacturer's mapping program.

   ✔ Have the GPS receiver start providing location data to the interface program for real-time mapping.

G7ToWin and other utilities

G7ToWin is the Swiss Army knife of the GPS world. This free utility program works with most all brands of popular GPS receivers. With this Windows program, you can

✔ Upload waypoints, routes, and tracks to your GPS receiver.

✔ Download waypoints, routes, and tracks to your computer.

✔ Edit waypoint, route, and track data in a spreadsheet-style window.

✔ Create waypoints, routes, and tracks.

✔ Save waypoints, routes, and tracks in different file types. (Remember that GPS receiver and software manufacturers all use a number of different file formats for waypoints, routes, and tracks.)

✔ Save the image that appears onscreen of many Garmin GPS receivers.

G7ToWin is a must for the serious GPS receiver user. Its author, Ron Henderson, continues to add new features to the program. DOS and Pocket PC versions of the utility are also available. You can download G7ToWin at www.gpsinformation.org/ronh.

Other GPS utilities worth consideration include

✔ **EasyGPS:** A popular, free utility for creating, editing, and transferring waypoints and routes, available at www.easygps.com.

✔ **GPS Utility:** A popular freeware/shareware program that lets you manipulate and map waypoints, routes, and tracks and works with Geographic Information System (GIS) data. It's available at: www.gpsu.co.uk.

✔ **GPS TrackMaker:** A free utility that creates, edits, and deletes waypoints, routes, and tracks. It supports mapping features. You can download the program at www.gpstm.com.

✔ **GPSy:** For users who want to interface their receiver with a Mac. For more information, see www.gpsy.com.

Check the program's user manual or online help for specific instructions on transferring data between your GPS receiver and a PC. If the program can't connect to the GPS receiver, read through the "Troubleshooting Connection Problems" section, later in this chapter.

If you're transferring data to and from a memory card, refer to the GPS receiver's user manual or support Web site. With some receivers, you can simply drag data between the memory card and the hard drive via Windows Explorer. In other cases, you might need to use a utility program, such as G7ToWin or EasyGPS. (See the sidebar, "G7ToWin and other utilities.")

Troubleshooting Connection Problems

If you follow the instructions that come with the your software to connect your GPS receiver to a computer, usually getting the two devices talking is painless.

If you do run into problems, follow this set of steps, in this order, to help you identify a possible culprit for your connection troubles:

1. **Always make sure the cable is securely plugged in to both the GPS receiver and the computer.** While you're at it, check that the GPS receiver is turned on.

2. **Make sure that the baud rate and the protocol are the same in both the GPS receiver and the interface program.** Double-check this again if you can't establish a connection.

   Even if the baud rates match, they may be set too high — thus causing communication errors. When in doubt, lower the baud rate. You can either step-down a rate at a time or go directly to 4,800 or 9,600 baud. Although this is slow, this rate shouldn't generate errors.

3. **In the interface program, make sure that the correct COM port is specified.** If you can't get a connection, try different COM port numbers until you find one that works.

4. **Always check the program's user manual, online help, or support section of the vendor's Web site for specific information on interfacing with a GPS receiver.**

If you can't get your GPS receiver to talk to your computer and you happen to have a PDA, turn off the PDA synchronization program first. PDA synchronization software that's running in the background is a frequent culprit in causing GPS receiver interface problems.

Uploading Firmware Revisions to Your GPS Receiver

Just like software vendors, GPS manufacturers find bugs and add enhancements to their products. New versions of a GPS receiver's operating system can be upgraded through the receiver's *firmware* (the updateable, read-only software that's embedded in a hardware device).

Check that your GPS receiver's firmware is current every few months or so, especially if your receiver is a newly released model. GPS manufacturers offer free downloads of firmware upgrades on their Web sites, and these bug-fixes or new features can definitely make your GPS receiver perform better.

To upgrade your firmware

1. **Check the current version of your GPS receiver firmware.**

   Sometimes this is displayed when the GPS receiver is turned on, or it might be shown on an information page. Consult your user's guide or the manufacturer's Web site for specific instructions on how to get this information for your model.

2. **Visit the manufacturers's Web site and go to the software updates section.**

   Here are the URLs of the major GPS manufacturers:

   • **Garmin:** www.garmin.com

   If you have a Garmin GPS receiver, you can sign up for automatic e-mail notification of firmware upgrades at the Garmin Web site. I expect other GPS manufacturers to start offering this service.

   • **Lowrance:** www.lowrance.com

   • **Magellan:** www.magellangps.com

3. **Find your GPS receiver model and check its manufacturer's Web site for the latest firmware version.**

   If your firmware is older than the current version on the Web site, follow the online instructions to download the firmware installer. Usually, the higher the version number, the more recent the firmware version.

   Make sure that the firmware installer you download is for your GPS receiver model. If you upload firmware designed for a different model, plan on the GPS receiver not working until you load the proper firmware.

4. **Follow the installation instructions that come with the downloaded file.**

Usually firmware installation files come in two forms:

- ✔ **A standalone program** that runs on your computer, connects to the GPS receiver, and sends the upgraded firmware to the receiver. You need to have a PC interface cable attached to both the computer and the GPS receiver.

- ✔ **A special file** that you copy to a memory card. When the GPS receiver starts, it searches the card to see whether a firmware upgrade is present. If it is, the receiver uploads the upgrade. After the upgrade is successful, you can erase the firmware upgrade file from the memory card.

Upgrading a GPS receiver's firmware is pretty easy; not too much can go wrong. About the only thing that can get you in trouble is if the GPS receiver's batteries die midway through a firmware upload. A firmware upgrade usually only takes a few minutes to complete, but make sure that your batteries aren't running on empty before you start.

Some firmware update software works only on COM ports 1 through 4. If you're using a USB adapter, (which is usually set to COM port 5 or higher) and are having problems connecting to the GPS receiver, try reassigning the existing COM ports to numbers higher than the USB adapter's port; then set the adapter's port number to 1. Refer to online Windows help (choose Start➪ Help) and perform a search for *device manager* to get more information on changing device settings.

Chapter 10

Using GPS Manufacturer Mapping Software

In This Chapter

▶ Understanding how GPS manufacturer map software works

▶ Navigating through Magellan MapSend products

▶ Discovering Lowrance MapCreate products

▶ Exploring Garmin MapSource products

GPS receivers that support maps come with a basemap of the region the GPS receiver was sold in (such as North America or Europe) that shows city locations, highways, major roads, bodies of water, and other features. (For the lowdown on GPS receivers, see Chapter 5.) Precisely what the basemaps display varies by manufacturer and model. Although base-maps do provide general information, some GPS receiver users want more detailed maps that show city streets, topographic features, marine navigation aids, or places outside the United States.

The good news is you're not limited to the basemap that came with your GPS receiver: Most mapping GPS receivers allow you to upload more detailed maps. These GPS receivers either have a fixed amount of internal memory used to store the added maps, or they support external Secure Digital (SD) or MultiMediaCard (MMC) memory cards for map storage. (Check product marketing literature or the GPS receiver user manual for details on how many megabytes of map data a particular model can store. More is always better.)

Different types of maps are available from GPS receiver manufacturers and are sold on CD-ROMs, including street maps, topographic maps, fishing maps, and nautical charts. These map products have software that you run on your PC to install the maps, plan trips, and exchange data with your GPS receiver.

In this chapter, I discuss mapping software produced by the Big Three GPS receiver manufacturers (Magellan, Lowrance, and Garmin). I also show you the general features that all GPS map programs share as well as what kind of maps are available for the different GPS receiver brands.

Understanding Universal Principles of GPS Map Software

Take a look at some universal GPS map software principles that apply to all map software offered by GPS receiver manufacturers. I'll present the important rules that relate to GPS receivers that display maps and then discuss some common features all GPS receiver manufacturer software packages share.

Begin with the three rules of GPS receiver mapping software. If you're considering purchasing a GPS receiver or mapping software, pay attention to these rules to avoid hair-pulling frustration before or after shopping. Then I move on to show you common GPS map software features and how to upload a map to your GPS receiver.

Three rules of GPS mapping software

Consider these three basic tenets before you start to shop for GPS mapping software.

- ✔ **Not all GPS receivers can display maps.** Lower-cost models (typically under $150) or GPS receivers with very small screens usually don't support maps. If you already own a GPS receiver, make sure that it's compatible with the map software you're interested in using. Manufacturer Web sites are pretty good about listing product compatibility. The same holds true if you're shopping for a new GPS receiver.

- ✔ **You can use only *proprietary* products (made by the same company that manufactures your GPS receiver).** For example, you can't use Garmin maps on a Magellan GPS receiver. Likewise, you can't use third-party maps produced by DeLorme or Maptech on a Magellan GPS receiver. Repeat after me, "You can only use Magellan maps on a Magellan GPS receiver" (or whichever brand you happen to be using). Admittedly, I'm belaboring this point, but a fair number of novice GPS users think that they can load just about any map on their new GPS receiver, which isn't the case.

- ✔ **Don't expect the level of detail in a GPS map to match paper maps.** In order to maximize memory space, GPS receivers use *vector* maps (created with lines and shapes) instead of *raster* maps (scanned paper maps). And because a GPS receiver has a fairly small screen to display a map, don't expect the map on your GPS receiver to appear as an identical version of your favorite paper map. Until GPS receivers incorporate science-fiction-like, holographic projection systems where a map appears in midair (and I'm not holding my breath), viewing a paper map will always be easier and more effective than staring at a map on a GPS receiver.

Keeping these three rules in mind when you go map shopping, you can generally expect to pay anywhere from $100–$150 for a map software product from a GPS receiver manufacturer. You can easily avoid paying suggested retail for map software if you exploit the Internet for dealers offering better prices.

Even if your GPS receiver doesn't support maps, you can still use a manufacturer's map program with your receiver to download and upload waypoints, routes, and tracks, as well as access maps on your PC. However, I find that the third-party products I discuss in Chapters 12 and 13 that can interface with GPS receivers have more features and better maps when it comes to PC use.

Common GPS map software features

Here are some of the features that all GPS receiver map software have in common.

- ✔ **Upload maps to GPS receivers:** The main job of a mapping program on your computer is to upload maps to your GPS receiver. The maps appear the same on your computer and your GPS receiver screen although the GPS receiver displays smaller portions of the map than you can view on your computer screen. (And the map won't appear in color if your receiver has a monochrome display.) You use the mapping software to select the portions of the maps that you want to upload to your GPS receiver. (To read how to upload to your receiver, see the following section.)

- ✔ **Print from and use maps on your PC:** In addition to uploading maps to a GPS receiver, you can also use the map software on your PC to view and print maps, measure distances, and plan trips.

- ✔ **Download waypoints, routes, and tracks from GPS receivers:** With GPS mapping software, you can download information that you've recorded with your GPS receiver, such as waypoints, routes, and tracks. You can store this data on your PC's hard drive or display it as an overlay on the maps displayed on your PC. (Read how to create and use waypoints, routes, and tracks in Chapter 4.)

- ✔ **Upload waypoints, routes, and tracks to GPS receivers:** In addition to downloading GPS data, you can also upload waypoints, routes, and tracks from your PC to a GPS receiver. For example, you can plot several waypoint locations on the PC map and then transfer them to your GPS receiver.

- ✔ **View POIs:** Many software packages have Points of Interest (POIs), such as restaurants, gas stations, and geographic features shown on the maps that you view with your PC or GPS receiver.

Getting maps to GPS receivers

All GPS manufacturer map programs upload maps to your GPS receiver in similar ways. Although the user interfaces are different and the commands vary, you load a map onto a GPS receiver by using the same basic process.

1. **Run the map program and zoom in on the area that you want to upload to your GPS receiver.**

2. **Choose which parts of the map you want to upload to the GPS receiver.**

   This usually means selecting one or more rectangular areas on the map. Depending on the program, you either draw a rectangle that defines the areas that you want to upload, or you select grid squares that appear on the map that correspond to the areas you want to upload.

3. **Connect your GPS receiver to your PC.**

   You use a special cable for this data transfer connection. To read more on connecting your GPS receiver to a PC, go to Chapter 9.

   If the GPS receiver uses a memory card to store maps, you can skip this step.

4. **Set the communications parameters in the map program.**

   This comprises the COM port, baud rate, and other settings that are needed so that the GPS receiver can successfully communicate with your PC. (Read how to do this in Chapter 9.) This is usually a one-time setup, so you don't need to repeat this each time you want to upload a map.

   Again, you can skip this step if your GPS receiver uses a memory card.

5. **Upload the map to your GPS receiver.**

   The program extracts the information that it needs from the map data CD-ROM and builds a custom map of the area that you select. When this process finishes, the program either starts uploading the map to the GPS receiver or saves the map to your hard drive where you can copy it to a memory card (if applicable).

How long building a map takes depends on the size of the area that you select, how much map detail you want to include, and how fast your PC is. This can range from a minute or less for small areas (such as a metropolitan area) to five or ten minutes for a large map (such as one that includes many different states). For example, when using Lowrance's MapCreate, it takes a little under five minutes to create a 26MB map of the state of Oklahoma and the Texas panhandle on a typical PC that's been manufactured within the past several years.

How much time it takes to upload a map into a GPS receiver also depends on the size of the area you select and how the receiver stores maps. If you're uploading a large map from a PC via a serial cable, it can take hours to transfer the map between a PC and your GPS receiver. GPS receivers that support Universal Serial Bus (USB) communications are much faster. For GPS receivers that use SD or MMC memory for storage, after the map has been created and saved to the memory card, it's just a matter of inserting the card into the receiver.

After you purchase GPS receiver map software, be sure to check the manufacturer's Web site every now and then to see whether updated releases of the PC software are available. You may be able to download upgraded versions of the program with bug fixes and enhanced features. Keep in mind that when you download the program, updated map data doesn't come with it.

Some GPS receiver manufacturers use different methods for stemming software and map piracy. Both Garmin and Magellan use *unlock codes* on some of their map products that require you to visit a Web page and get a code to activate the program. Some map products (notably nautical charts) have multiple regions stored on CD-ROM, and you need to purchase an unlock code for each region you want to access. In addition, programs commonly link the serial number of a GPS receiver to a map, meaning that the map will work only with the GPS receiver that the map was originally uploaded to.

Reviewing GPS Manufacturer Software

GPS receiver manufacturers have a number of software products available for their models that support maps. So you have a better understanding of what types of maps are available, here are the different map software packages that the major GPS receiver manufacturers offer. Read on to discover what types of maps you can upload to the three main brands of GPS receivers. For more information and in-depth reviews of GPS receiver manufacturer map products, including screenshots, visit http://gpsinformation.net.

GPS receivers sold in different parts of the world typically have different basemaps. For example, a GPS receiver sold in Germany will have a more detailed basemap of Europe, compared with the same model of receiver sold in the United States.

I want to clarify a point that sometimes confuses current or prospective GPS receiver owners: Each of the major GPS receiver manufacturers has their own line of map products that all sound pretty similar. Here they are:

Magellan (www.magellangps.com) MapSend

Lowrance (www.lowrance.com)   MapCreate

Garmin (www.garmin.com)   MapSource

MapSend, MapCreate, and MapSource all refer to the respective PC *programs* that allow you to view maps on your PC, upload maps to your GPS receiver, and manage GPS waypoints, routes, and tracks. Magellan, Lowrance, and Garmin ship these programs with their respective map products. Just remember that MapSend, MapCreate, and MapSource are not maps nor map data but simply the programs that interface the map data.

In addition to map products, several GPS manufacturers sell waypoint and route management software. If you don't care about uploading maps but want to transfer and save waypoints, routes, and tracks, I recommend using the free G7ToWin program (which works with most all GPS receivers) that you can download at www.gpsinformation.org/ronh.

Some manufacturers offer GPS receivers bundled with map software and other accessories. These bundled products are usually cheaper than separately purchasing the GPS hardware and map software, so shop around.

Just like any other software line, GPS receiver manufacturers roll out new products, drop outdated ones, and add new features to existing products. Be sure to check the manufacturer's Web site to get the latest information on what map software is available for a particular model of GPS receiver.

Magellan MapSend

Magellan manufactures the popular Meridian and SporTrak GPS receiver lines. The Meridian receivers use memory cards for map storage, and the SporTrak models have a fixed amount of internal memory to store maps. (You can upload maps to all SporTraks with the exception of the basic model.)

Software products that you can use with Magellan mapping GPS receivers include the following. Information about all these products is available at the Magellan Web site.

> ✔ **MapSend DirectRoute:** This software package provides street maps, POIs, automated street routing, and turn-by-turn directions for most Meridian and SporTrak receivers. With automated street routing (also called *autorouting*), you can enter a starting and destination street address, and the GPS receiver will provide you with a route, including street directions. Most GPS receivers give you a straight-line route between two points, but Magellan upgraded the firmware on a number of their receivers to support both straight-line and street routes when MapSend DirectRoute maps are uploaded. Versions of the software are available for the United States, major cities in Canada, and Europe. The MapSend DirectRoute PC user interface is shown in Figure 10-1.

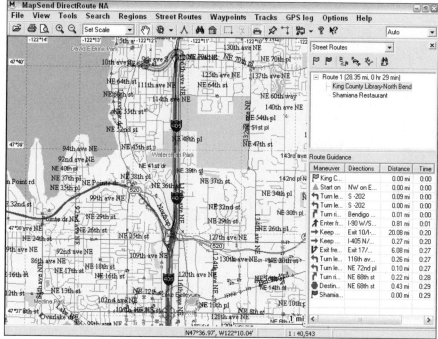

Figure 10-1:
Magellan
MapSend
DirectRoute
street map
software.

✔ **MapSend BlueNav charts:** These are nautical charts with detailed coverage areas and enhanced marine navigation information, such as currents, tides, and port services. Charts, available for a number of coastal areas in North America and Europe, can be purchased on CD-ROM or preloaded SD memory cards.

✔ **MapSend Topo:** The Topo product is designed for outdoor recreation use and features 1:100,000 scale topographic maps of the United States, including trails, roads, rivers, lakes, coastlines, and POIs. After you upload the maps, you can display elevation profiles on your GPS receiver for roads, trails, and user-created routes.

✔ **MapSend Streets & Destinations:** Magellan's original road map software package has versions available for the United States and Canada. If you're looking for street navigation software for your Magellan, I recommend MapSend DirectRoute because of its autorouting features and more current NAVTECH maps. Choose Streets & Destinations if you have an older GPS receiver that isn't compatible with DirectRoute or if you're on a tight budget. (Streets & Destinations is a bit cheaper than DirectRoute.)

✔ **MapSend Streets Europe:** Magellan also offers street-level maps of Europe for its GPS receivers. Like with Streets & Destinations (see the preceding bullet), if your GPS receiver is compatible with DirectRoute, I suggest going with the European version.

✔ **MapSend WorldWide Basemap:** This map software package expands your GPS receiver's built-in basemap coverage to other international regions. Each basemap region has basic map features such as cities, highways, waterways, railroads, national boundaries, and shorelines. Don't expect street-level detail, but there's enough information to help you get around.

Check periodically for current information about Magellan map products; go to www.magellangps.com.

Lowrance MapCreate

Lowrance was the first manufacturer to offer a GPS receiver with uploadable maps. (For you trivia buffs, it was the GlobalMap100, which first came out in April, 1998.) The company continues the electronic map tradition with its current line of iFINDER handheld GPS receivers; which use memory cards to store maps.

If you own a Lowrance GPS receiver or are considering purchasing one, here are the map products you can use:

✔ **MapCreate:** MapCreate is Lowrance's primary map program for creating GPS receiver maps of the United States. (See the MapCreate user interface in Figure 10-2.) In addition to street maps and points of interest, MapCreate also has an extensive database of navigation aids, wrecks, and obstructions for marine use. One nice feature of MapCreate is that you can select polygon map regions to upload, which maximizes map storage space. Although MapCreate currently doesn't offer autorouting and turn-by-turn directions, Lowrance does plan to offer this feature in the future.

Several versions of MapCreate are available. If you're using an iFINDER GPS receiver, be sure you get Version 6 or later.

✔ **FreedomMaps:** In addition to maps on CD-ROM, Lowrance also offers the FreedomMaps product line, comprising memory cards preloaded with maps of the United States, Europe, and Canada. Regional maps come on 128MB and 256MB memory cards that you just plug into your GPS receiver; no software or CD-ROMs are required.

✔ **Navionics charts:** Navionics (www.navionics.com) is one of the largest producers of electronic nautical charts. Navionics Gold and Classic charts and fishing HotMaps are all available on MMC memory cards and are also compatible with the iFINDER Pro GPS receiver.

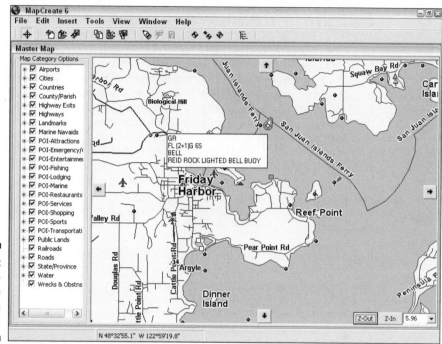

Figure 10-2:
Lowrance
MapCreate
street map
software.

Scout for current Lowrance map product information at `www.lowrance.com`.

Do-it-yourself maps

For the most part, GPS manufacturers have a lock on the market when it comes to maps that can be uploaded to their receivers. GPS receiver owners must use proprietary maps distributed by the manufacturers.

However, a small group of technically adept GPS and map enthusiasts have found ways around this map monopoly. They have created free tools such as GPSMapEdit and Mapdekode with which Garmin GPS receiver owners can create their own maps and upload them to their

receivers. Similar projects are under way for Magellan GPS receivers.

At the present, creating your own do-it-yourself GPS receiver maps is a somewhat complicated process, but a number of tutorials are available on the Internet. (Here's one for starters: `www.gpstm.com/eng/dekode_eng.htm`.) If you're really interested in this topic, check out the Yahoo! Group devoted to GPS map authoring at `groups.yahoo.com/group/map_authors`.

Garmin MapSource

Like the other GPS receiver manufacturers, Garmin offers a number of different types of maps for its products. Unlike Magellan and Lowrance, however, Garmin doesn't use memory cards in its current line of handheld GPS receivers. Any maps that you upload must be able to fit into whatever fixed memory the GPS receiver has available for storage. (The amount of fixed memory depends on the model, with high-end, handheld GPS receivers sporting between 56–115MB of memory.)

Although Garmin doesn't use commonly available SD or MMC memory cards in its GPS models, the company is using newer technology to make uploading maps quicker. Recent Garmin products feature USB connectivity, which is considerably faster than uploading a map to a GPS receiver through a PC serial port.

If you own a Garmin GPS receiver or are considering purchasing one, here are some of the mapping software packages that you can use. Detailed information about all is available from the Garmin Web site.

- ✔ **MapSource City Select:** City Select contains street maps and points of interest and is designed to work with Garmin GPS receivers that support *autorouting* (turn-by-turn street directions), such as the GPSMAP 196 and GPSMAP 60C/60CS. (If you own a GPS V or iQue 3600, this software came bundled with your GPS receiver.) The three versions of the product are available for North America, Europe, and South Africa.

- ✔ **MapSource MetroGuide:** MetroGuide is similar to City Select but is designed for Garmin GPS receivers that don't support autorouting (such as the eTrex Legend and Vista). Four versions of this product are available, providing street maps for the United States, Canada, Australia, and Europe.

- ✔ **MapSource WorldMap:** This software provides basic international maps that expand the default basemap coverage that comes with your GPS receiver.

  GPS receivers sold in different parts of the world typically have different basemaps.

- ✔ **MapSource BlueChart:** BlueChart products are Garmin's nautical charts and are available in regional versions that cover the Americas as well as the Atlantic and Pacific Oceans.

- ✔ **Fishing Hot Spots:** Fishing Hot Spots are maps of popular fishing areas in North America with depth contours, shoreline details, boat ramp information, and fishing tips. The maps are sold for multistate regions.

- ✔ **Minnesota LakeMaster ProMap:** Designed specifically for GPS receiver owners who fish in the Minnesota area, this map product has maps of popular lakes and includes three-foot contours with underwater structure detail, islands, reefs, points, bays, access points, and marinas.

- ✔ **MapSource U.S. TOPO:** The TOPO product contains 1:100,000 scale maps of the United States and shows terrain contours, elevation, trails, roads, and summits. It's designed for outdoor recreational use. (The MapSource TOPO user interface is shown in Figure 10-3.)

- ✔ **MapSource U.S. TOPO 24K:** 24K doesn't refer to gold but rather to 1:24,000 scale maps, which have significantly more detail than the maps found in MapSource TOPO. The maps provide detailed coverage of U.S. national parks and surrounding national forest lands. Points of interest and park amenities are also included. Two versions of the product are available: National Parks, East and National Parks, West.

Check for current information about Garmin map products at `www.garmin.com`.

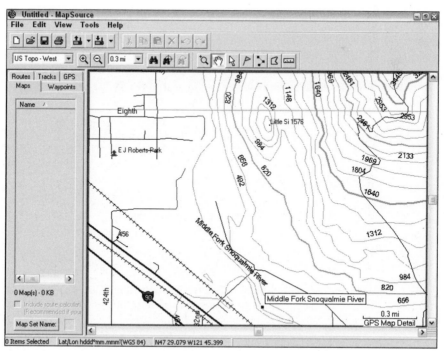

Figure 10-3: Garmin MapSource TOPO software.

MapSource on the Web

If you use a Garmin GPS receiver and are interested in seeing what maps from the different map products look like — or to check out the amount of detail and coverage for certain areas — visit www.garmin.com/cartography and check out the MapSource Map Viewer.

Choose any of Garmin's map products from a drop-down list, and the selected map is shown in your Web browser. After the map is displayed, you can move around the map and zoom in and out. What you see on your PC monitor is what you can generally expect to see on your GPS receiver if you upload that particular map product. Remember that your GPS receiver screen is smaller; and, if it doesn't support color, the map will be displayed in monochrome.

Even if you don't use a Garmin GPS receiver, this Web site is useful for getting a better idea of the types of maps that are available for GPS receivers, their general appearance, and what information they show.

Chapter 11

Finding Places and Coordinates

· ·

In This Chapter

▶ Using online gazetteers

▶ Converting coordinates

· ·

*W*hen you start using a GPS receiver, you'll soon discover that it's pretty numbers-oriented. There's time, speed, distance, altitude, and (of course) the location coordinates. But quite often you'll want names to go with those numbers. Or you might need to convert those coordinate numbers into another format. That's where this chapter comes in. Read here to discover how to locate places by their names and get their coordinates (and other information) and how to easily convert coordinates from one coordinate system to another.

Finding Your Way with Online Gazetteers

Sometimes you need a little bit more information about a location.

  ✔ You know a place name, but you don't know exactly where the place is located.

  ✔ You've heard about a place but don't know whether it's a mountain peak, a river, or a town.

  ✔ You generally know where a place is, but you need the exact latitude and longitude or Universal Transverse Mercator (UTM) coordinates.

In these cases, you can turn to a *gazetteer,* which is a collection of place names with such useful data as geographic coordinates, elevation, and feature type. Gazetteers are usually published as books, but digital versions are available. The U.S. government has two free online gazetteer services:

  ✔ **GNIS** provides information about places in the United States.

  ✔ **GNS** has information about locations all over the world.

Using the Geographic Names Information System (GNIS)

The Geographic Names Information System (GNIS) is the federal repository of geographic name information. The database contains information on nearly 2 million physical and cultural geographic features in the United States and its territories: a city, dam, island, school, or any other designated feature type. You can search for feature information at the GNIS Web site: http://geonames.usgs.gov.

The GNIS search page has a number of different data fields (as shown in Figure 11-1) that you can use to narrow down your search, including

✔ **Feature Name:** This is the name of the feature you're looking for. This can be either the whole name or a part of the name.

Feature name searches aren't case sensitive.

✔ **Query Variant Name?:** Some features have other names in addition to their primary name. If you select the Yes radio button, records with matched variant names are displayed.

✔ **State or Territory:** From this drop-down list, select the state or territory where the feature is located.

USGS GNIS (GNIS) - Mozilla Firebird

File   Edit   View   Go   Bookmarks   Tools   Help

http://geonames.usgs.gov/pls/gnis/web_query.gnis_web_query_f

USGS
National Mapping Information

Query Form For The United States And Its Territories

Feature Name: Query Variant Name? ○ Yes   ◉ No

State or Territory: ▼ *County Name:

Feature Type :   ▼   Elevation Range: -   (feet)

Topo Map Name:
(7.5'x7.5')

[Send Query] **or** [Erase Query]

Please Note: The elevation range search occasionally will not function. We are aware of the problem and working for a solution. If this happens, please try again at another time. Thank you for your patience.
Feature Name Wildcard: use % as the wildcard.

Done

Figure 11-1:
Search for geographic information by entering what you know about a place.

✔ **County Name:** If you click the County Name button, a drop-down list box shows all the counties in the currently selected state.

If you know the county where the feature is located, enter it to speed up your search.

✔ **Feature Type:** The Feature Type drop-down list box contains all the feature types, such as bridges, canals, lakes, and populated places. If you know what the feature is, select its type.

✔ **Elevation Range:** The Elevation Range text boxes let you search for features that occur at a certain height range; use feet when entering the range values.

✔ **Topo Map Name:** You can confine a search to features only found within a United States Geological Survey (USGS) 7.5 minute topographic map by entering the map's exact name.

Follow these steps to perform a basic search for a feature:

1. **Go to the GNIS Web site at** `http://geonames.usgs.gov`.

2. **Click the <u>Query GNIS: U.S. and Territories</u> link.**

3. **Enter the feature name that you want to search for in the Feature Name text box.**

4. **From the State or Territory drop-down list box, select the state where the feature is located.**

5. **Click the Send Query button.**

Finding street address coordinates

Commercial services can provide the information latitude and longitude of a particular street address, such as `www.geocode.com` (you can test drive their Eagle geocoding technology for free), but here's also another free and easy method:

1. **Go to the `www.terra-server-usa.com` site and enter a street address.**

2. **Select an aerial photo of the location.**

   An aerial photo displaying the street address of the location is displayed with a pushpin icon shown on top of the address.

3. **When the photo is displayed, click the Info link at the top of the page.**

   A grid appears over the aerial photo with the latitude and longitude coordinates of the address.

The accuracy of this information varies, but usually it puts you in the general vicinity of the address you want. If you really want precise information, visit the address with a GPS receiver and record the coordinates.

The more you narrow a search, the faster it is. For example, if you know the county where a feature is located, select it. If you don't know much information about the feature, be patient. The GNIS server can be pretty slow.

If GNIS finds any records that match your search criteria, it lists all the matching features. Figure 11-2 shows that a search for *Horse Butte* found three matches. Information about the features includes

- ✔ Feature name
- ✔ State
- ✔ County
- ✔ Feature type
- ✔ Latitude and longitude
- ✔ USGS 7.5 minute map that the feature appears on

If you aren't sure which result you need, use this information to narrow your search.

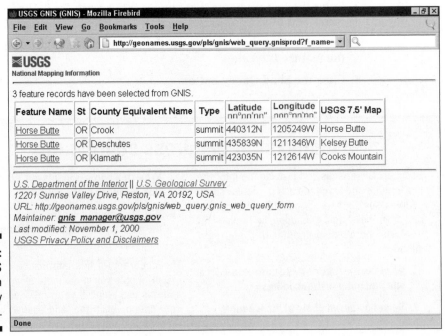

Figure 11-2: GNIS search display results.

After you pick a feature, click its Feature Name link to display more information. A new page (as shown in Figure 11-3) displays additional information including:

- ✔ **Elevation:** The elevation of the feature is displayed in feet.

- ✔ **TopoZone.com link:** Clicking this link goes to the TopoZone.com Web site and shows the feature location on a USGS topographic map.

- ✔ **FIPS55 Place Code:** Federal Information Processing Standard (FIPS) 55 contains codes for named populated places, primary county divisions, and other locations in the United States. Click this link to display the FIPS55 code for the location; unless you know that you need this, the code isn't very relevant for the average user.

- ✔ **Digital Raster Graphic (DRG) link:** Click this link to display the feature location on a digitized version of a USGS topographic map; supplied by www.terraserver-usa.com.

- ✔ **Digital Orthophoto Quadrangle (DOQ) link:** Click this link to display a black-and-white aerial photograph of the feature location, supplied by www.terraserver-usa.com.

- ✔ **Tiger Map Server:** Click this link to display a road map of the feature area prepared from U.S. Census Bureau data.

- ✔ **Watershed:** Click this link to visit U.S. Environmental Protection Agency (EPA) maps and information about the watershed where the feature is located.

You need an Internet connection to access the GNIS database. In addition to the online search capabilities at the GNIS Web site, you can download text files of all the features and associated information for each state. The files are quote- and comma-delimited and can be opened with your own databases and spreadsheets. The files come in compressed and uncompressed formats; if you have a slow Internet connection, download the Zip files.

Ever wanted to name a mountain or another land feature after yourself or a loved one? The U.S. Board on Geographic Names is responsible for naming and renaming features that appear on USGS maps. If there's an unnamed geographic feature, you can propose a new name for it (or suggest a name change for an existing feature). The Board even has an online form that you can fill out. Submitting the form doesn't guarantee you'll automatically get some peak named after Uncle Harry; this is a rather big deal. For instructions on filling out the online form see http://geonames.usgs.gov/dgnp/dgnp.html.

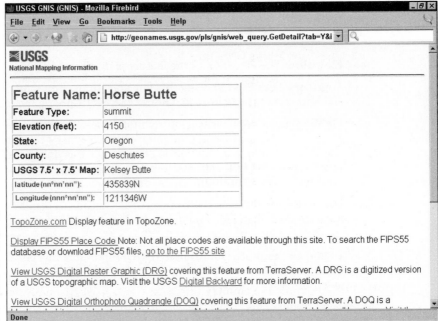

Figure 11-3:
Detailed
information
from the
GNIS
database.

Using the GEOnet Name Server (GNS)

The GEONet Name Server (GNS) searches for features around the world. GNS is located at `http://earth-info.nima.mil/gns/html/index.html`.

The database contains over 3.5 million features and over 5 million place names for locations outside of the United States. The military relies on GNS for its operations, so the database is updated every other week.

GNS is primarily designed for military use. Some of the search criteria and information in the database isn't very useful to the average civilian. At best expect to find these types of information for a given feature:

✔ Country

✔ Type

✔ Latitude and longitude

To perform a basic GNS search for a feature, follow these steps:

1. **Go to the GNS Web site at** `http://earth-info.nima.mil/gns/html`.

2. **Click the <u>Access GNS</u> link.**

3. **Click the <u>GNS Search</u> link in the GNS Main Menu at the left of the page.**

   The GNS search page is shown in Figure 11-4.

   You can enter search criteria by scrolling down the page.

4. **In the Name text box, enter the name of the feature you're looking for.**

   A drop-down list box to the right of the text box lets you narrow your search with these options:

   - Starts With
   - Is an Exact Match
   - Contains
   - Ends With

5. **If you know the country the feature is located in, select the country from the list.**

6. **Click the Search Database button.**

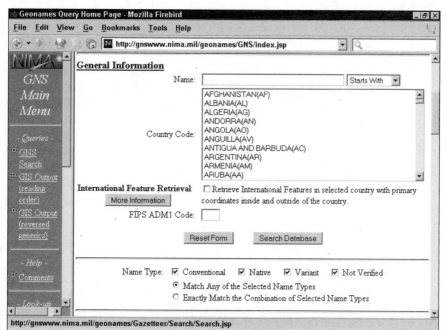

Figure 11-4:
The GNS search page.

Waypoint repositories

A number of Web sites provide waypoints that you can upload to your GPS receiver. (A *waypoint* is a set of coordinates for a location.) With these waypoint repositories, you can search a region or for a feature name for its waypoints in a database. If a waypoint has been logged in the site database, you can download the waypoint and then upload the coordinates to your GPS receiver. Some of the waypoint sites include

✔ http://wayhoo.com: This site converts GNIS and GNS feature information into waypoints. There are also coordinates for airports and a database where users can upload waypoints.

✔ www.travelbygps.com: This site holds a collection of waypoints for interesting places all over the world, including photos and descriptions. The site has an extensive collection of links to Web sites with special interest waypoints.

✔ www.trailregistry.com: This is a waypoint collection dedicated to hikers and backpackers.

✔ www.trailwaypoints.com: This is a GPS repository site that collects recreation-oriented waypoints from all over the world.

For GNS advanced searches, you can enter an extensive list of feature types as part of your search criteria. These include oil pipelines, refugee camps, and vegetation types. Other options limit searches by the latitude and longitude boundaries of a rectangle, use special character sets from foreign languages, and use government and military codes as part of the search. If you want to run these advanced searches, the GNS Web site has links with explanations.

If GNS finds records that match your search criteria, the features appear on a new page. A number of pieces of information are displayed (as shown in Figure 11-5). For the average civilian user, the most useful data includes

✔ **Name** of the feature.

✔ **Region** of the world where the feature is located. Click the link to get an explanation of the abbreviation.

✔ **Designation:** The feature type (such as populated locality, farm, or reservoir). Click the link to get the definition of the abbreviation.

✔ **Latitude and longitude** coordinates.

✔ **Area:** Country and state or province information for the feature. Click the link for the meaning of the code.

You can also download tab-delimited text files from the GNS Web site for any country that contain features and information. This data can easily be imported into spreadsheets and databases.

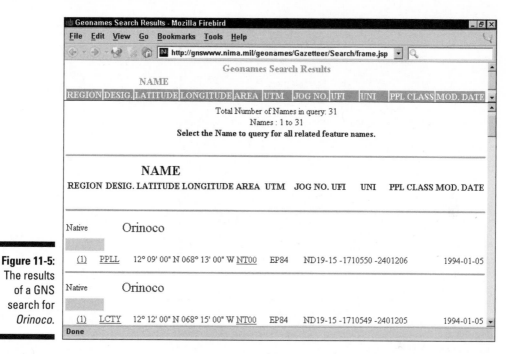

Figure 11-5:
The results
of a GNS
search for
Orinoco.

Converting Coordinates

Sometimes you might need to convert from one coordinate system to
another. For example, you might have coordinates in latitude and longitude
and a map with a UTM grid. Although there are many algorithms that you can
use to convert data, let conversion utilities do all the work for you.

Using GeoTrans

GeoTrans is a popular, free Windows program developed by the Department
of Defense (DoD). (GeoTrans is shown in Figure 11-6.) You can convert coordinates from many coordinate systems and datums. GeoTrans is available for
download at `http://earth-info.nima.mil/GandG/geotrans/geotrans.htm`.

Follow these steps to convert between coordinate systems with GeoTrans:

1. **Select the map datum used with the coordinates from the drop-down
   Datum list.**

2. **Select the coordinate system from the drop-down list below the
   datum.**

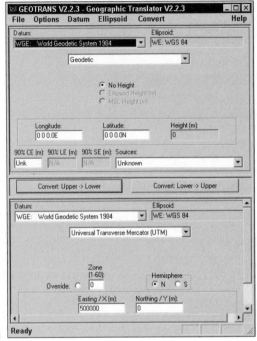

Figure 11-6:
GeoTrans
converts
coordinates
to another
format.

Use Geodetic if you're converting from latitude and longitude.

3. **Enter the coordinates in the appropriate text boxes.**

   • If you've converting from latitude and longitude, enter the coordinates.

   • If you're converting from UTM, enter the Zone, Hemisphere, Northing, and Easting.

4. **In the lower part of the window, select the datum and the coordinate system that you want to convert to.**

5. **Click the Convert Upper→Lower button.**

   The converted coordinates appear in the lower part of the window.

GeoTrans' Help file covers these advanced features if you need them:

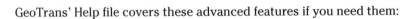

  ✔ Converting datums used in foreign countries

  ✔ Determining distance errors when converting between maps and scales

The Graphical Locator

The Environmental Statistics Group at Montana State University hosts a very powerful online tool called the Graphical Locator. It's a cross between a gazetteer and a coordinate utility converter. Some of its features are

✔ A map of the United States that shows coordinate information when you click a location. You can zoom in on regional and state maps. (The maps only show geographic features, not feature names.)

✔ Coordinate conversion utilities for latitude and longitude, UTM, and township, range, and section.

✔ Extensive information on selected locations, including latitude and longitude; township, range, and section; UTM; elevation; state

and country; nearest named features and distances; and USGS 7.5 minute topographic map name.

The Graphical Locater is designed to work with locations within the United States. It's fairly easy to use; its author, D.L. Gustafson, has extensive online documentation on the utility.

I use the Graphical Locator for quickly getting rough latitude and longitude coordinates of a location. Because there are no place names on the online maps, I consult a paper map with place names to zero in where I want to get location information if I'm unfamiliar with the terrain.

To check out the Graphical Locator, visit www.esg.montana.edu/gl.

Using online conversion utilities

If you don't need to convert coordinates on a regular basis, you can save some hard drive space by using a Web-based coordinate conversion utility instead of installing GeoTrans. Most conversion sites are pretty straightforward to use; just enter the coordinate values that you want to convert and click a button. These sites are a few of the most popular:

✔ For simple datum, latitude and longitude, and UTM coordinate conversions: http://jeeep.com/details/coord

✔ For latitude and longitude, UTM, and Township and Range conversions: www.esg.montana.edu/gl

✔ For advanced online and standalone conversion tools, visit the U.S. National Geodetic Survey: www.ngs.noaa.gov/TOOLS

Chapter 12

On the Road with DeLorme Street Atlas USA

*I*n the pre-PC days, taking a trip across town, a state, or the country to visit someplace you'd never been before often involved planning worthy of a major expedition. You'd have to carefully check maps, trying to figure out the shortest and fastest routes, guessing when and where you'd need to stop for gas, scribbling down notes, and highlighting roads on paper maps.

That's all changed with inexpensive and easy-to-use street navigation software. Just run a program on your PC and enter the address of your starting point and the final destination. Then, a few mouse clicks later, you've got both a map and exact turn-by-turn directions for how to get from Point A to Point B.

And as an added bonus, if you have a laptop and GPS receiver, you can take this software on the road with you, track your location in real-time, and get helpful hints in reaching your destination. (Most street navigation programs also have versions that run on PDAs for ultimate portability.) Several street navigation software packages are on the market that can keep you from getting lost. They all generally work the same, with the primary differences in the user interface and support of advanced features.

If you've never used a street navigation program before, this chapter gets you moving in the right direction. I focus on DeLorme's Street Atlas USA, showing you its basic features and how to use them.

Discovering Street Atlas USA Features

Like other street navigation software, Street Atlas USA displays road maps of the United States, finds addresses, and creates routes between two or more points. Check out a few other program features that are important to know about.

- ✔ **POIs:** All street navigation programs contain extensive databases of POIs. POIs refer to *Points of Interest*, not to Hawaiian side dishes made from taro root. POIs include restaurants (some of which might serve poi), hotels, parks, gas stations, and other locations you might be interested in while traveling. Street Atlas USA has a POI database that contains over four million businesses, services, and organizations.

- ✔ **Voice support:** If you're using a laptop and GPS receiver as part of a car navigation system, Street Atlas USA can give you voice instructions when you need to turn to reach your destination. You can also use a voice recognition feature to give Street Atlas USA commands instead of using a keyboard or mouse.

- ✔ **Routable roads:** A big issue that all map companies face is ensuring that their road data is accurate, which can be very challenging considering the number of new roads that are built every year. Street Atlas USA has a feature that allows you to draw in roads that are missing on a map. After you create a road, Street Atlas USA can use it when calculating routes.

- ✔ **Customizable maps:** Street Atlas USA has an extensive collection of drawing tools for customizing maps with symbols, shapes, and text annotations.

Street Atlas USA has many more features than I can cover in the space of this chapter (such as measuring distances and trip planning that takes fuel consumption as well as the number of hours spent driving into consideration). To find out more about all the program's features, visit www.delorme.com.

Street Atlas USA comes on two CD-ROMs: one with the installation program and files, and the other with map data files. By default, you need to insert the map data CD-ROM each time you use the program. If you have enough space, you can copy the map data files to your hard drive; see the online Help for instructions.

Navigating Street Atlas USA

The first thing that you notice about Street Atlas USA is that it doesn't use a familiar Windows, menu-based user interface. DeLorme uses a unique user interface with its mapping programs; after you get the hang of it, it's pretty easy to use. I walk you through the user interface and then show you how to move around inside a map.

Complete campgrounds

Street Atlas USA is popular with RV owners who travel across the United States. With a laptop and a GPS receiver, you've got your own personal navigation system for vacations and touring. And if you're a male (cough), you significantly reduce the chances of getting lost and being forced to ask for directions.

A POI database is a friendly traveling companion, but if you're an RV-er, you can supplement it with even more useful information.

The Discovery Motorcoach Owners Association Web site has an extensive list of U.S. and Canada campgrounds, including Wal-Mart and Costco locations, which you can import into Street Atlas USA and other mapping programs.

To download the free campground database and get complete instructions on how to load it into Street Atlas USA, go to www.discovery owners.com/cginfo.htm.

Be sure to quickly browse through the PDF help file that comes with Street Atlas USA, which you can access by clicking the HELP button at the top of the window. Street Atlas USA has a rich set of commands, often offering you several different ways to perform a single task or operation.

Exploring the Street Atlas USA interface

The Street Atlas USA user interface is made up of four different parts (as shown in Figure 12-1). They include the

- ✔ **Map:** The main map takes up most of the screen and is where all the action takes place. You'll find roads, bodies of water, parks, businesses and services, and other features displayed.

- ✔ **Control Panel:** The Control Panel, located to the right of the map, contains commands for moving around in the map and zooming in and out.

- ✔ **Tab functions and options:** Primary mapping commands and options are underneath the map in a series of tab items. For example, click the Find tab for searching commands and options.

  You can shrink the size of the Tab area to show more map area by clicking the down-arrow icon in the right corner of the Tab area. If the Tab area has been minimized, clicking any tab will automatically expand it.

- ✔ **Overview Map:** The Overview Map appears to the right of the Tab area and contains a small map with a larger overview of the main map that you're viewing.

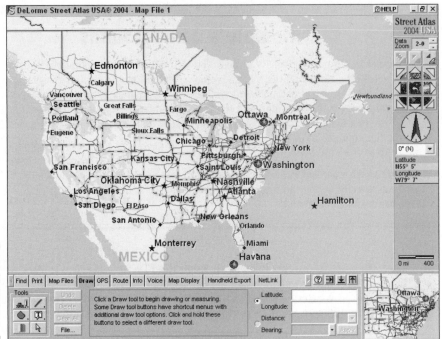

You can customize the Tab area by clicking the HELP button in the window title and selecting the Tab Manager menu item. Use the Tab Manager to show, hide, or reorder the tabs.

Zooming in and out

With Street Atlas USA, you can view the entire United States and then zoom in for street-level detail. As you zoom in, the Data Zoom level, which is displayed at the top of the Control Panel, increases. Data Zoom level 2–0 shows the entire U.S., and Data Zoom level 16–0 shows the maximum amount of detail for a location.

Beneath the Data Zoom are three buttons that control zooming. These buttons, each with red arrows and pictures of the Earth, are from left to right

   ✔ **Zoom out three levels:** Click the button with three arrows pointing away from Earth.

   ✔ **Zoom out:** Click the button with the red arrow pointing away from Earth.

   ✔ **Zoom in:** Click the button with the red arrow pointing toward Earth.

In addition to the zoom buttons, DeLorme also uses *Octave* controls, which are up and down arrows next to the Zoom Data level value, allowing you to have finer control over zooming in and out. Click the up arrow to zoom out; click the down arrow to zoom in.

When you click an Octave control, notice that the Zoom Data level number changes. The number to the right of the dash next to the Zoom Data level is the octave value. For example, if the current Zoom Data level were 12-3, clicking the Octave down arrow would zoom in and change the value to 12-4. (*Octaves* range between 0 and 7, just like a diatonic music scale.)

You can also zoom in on a specific area by holding down the left mouse button and dragging down and to the right. This draws a rectangle and will zoom in to that area when you release the mouse button. You can zoom out by holding down the left mouse button and dragging up and to the left.

Moving around in Street Atlas USA

Mouse around a little inside a Street Atlas USA map. Notice that as you move the cursor around, information appears on the lower edge of the map. Anytime you move the cursor over a map feature, whether it's a road, river, or even some open space, a line of text appears at the bottom of the map with a brief description of the feature.

The numbers in parentheses that appear before a street name description show the range of street addresses in the general vicinity of the cursor. This is handy for getting a quick idea of addresses on a particular street.

You're probably going to want to see more map than what appears on the screen, and Street Atlas USA has several ways to move the map, including

- **Centering:** Click a location to center the map over the cursor.
- **Dragging:** Whenever you move the cursor to the edge of the map, it turns into a hand icon. Hold the left mouse button down and drag the map to scroll.
- **Arrow keys:** You can use Alt+ the keyboard arrow keys to move the map in the direction of the arrow key you pressed.
- **Compass Rose:** In the Control Panel, beneath the zoom tools, is the Compass Rose. This is a series of nine buttons with yellow arrows. Click a button to scroll the map in the direction of the arrow.

If you click the middle button in the Compass Rose, the previously viewed map is displayed. You can view up to the last 256 previously displayed maps by clicking this button.

Getting POI information

Getting Point of Interest information from Street Atlas USA is a snap. Here's how.

When you zoom in to level 15, you start to see POIs on the map, such as restaurants, gas stations, theaters, hotels, and other businesses and services. At Zoom Data level 16, symbols appear that let show you what the POI is. For example, a plate with a fork and knife means a restaurant.

If you don't know what a symbol means, click the HELP button in the window title and choose Map Legend from the menu to display a list of all the map symbols and their meanings.

When you move the cursor over a POI, the business or service name, its phone number (if available), and the type of POI are shown at the bottom of the map. You can also get more information about a POI (or any map feature) by moving the cursor over the POI, right-clicking, and choosing Info from the pop-up menu. Information about the POI appears in the Tab area, which you can view by clicking the Info tab, as shown in Figure 12-2.

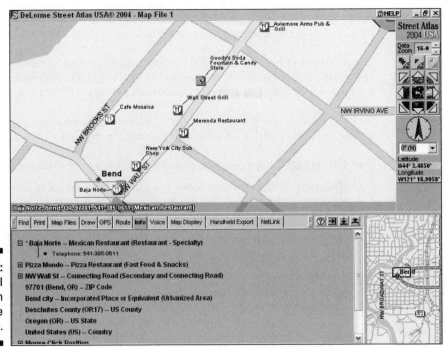

Figure 12-2:
Find POI
information
on the
Info tab.

Don't treat the POI database like an up-to-date phone directory. If you look up restaurants, gas stations, and other businesses in your city, you'll probably find a few listed that are out of business and others that are missing. DeLorme and other map companies try to keep POI data as current as possible, but because businesses come and go so often, it's difficult to keep up with all the changes.

Finding an Address with Street Atlas USA

Whenever I'm in San Francisco, I always try to visit Sam Wo's, my favorite authentic, Chinese noodle joint, located smack-dab in the middle of Chinatown. Anytime I hear about friends or acquaintances heading to San Francisco, I always tell them to head downtown and check out this famous Chinese fixture. It's been around for 100 years, Kerouac and Ginsberg hung out there, and it was home to arguably the rudest waiter in the world.

If you don't know San Francisco, finding this restaurant can be challenging. And even if you can get around the City by the Bay fairly well, giving precise directions to visitors can also be a little demanding. This is where street navigation programs like Street Atlas USA really shine. As an example of finding a location and creating a map to get to it, here's how to find Sam Wo's restaurant:

1. **Click the Find tab and then click the QuickSearch button.**

   You can perform several different types of searches, but this is a simple QuickSearch. (I talk about Advanced searches and Radar in a minute.) The Find tab options and commands are shown in Figure 12-3.

2. **In the Search For text box, enter the address you want to find.**

   Sam Wo's restaurant is located at 813 Washington Street, 94108. You can enter the city and state along with the address, but if you know the ZIP code, it's quicker and easier to use it instead.

3. **Click the Search button.**

   Street Atlas USA searches through map and street data; if the address is valid, a map of the location is displayed. In this case, Sam Wo's is exactly where I remembered it to be. See the resulting map in Figure 12-4.

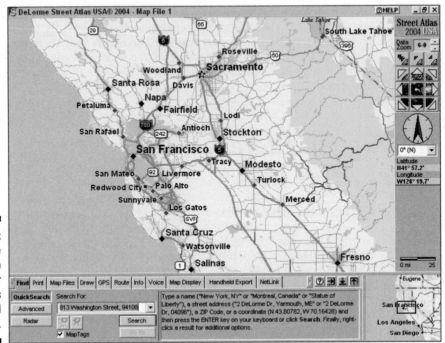

Figure 12-3:
Use the
Find tab to
search for
addresses
and
locations.

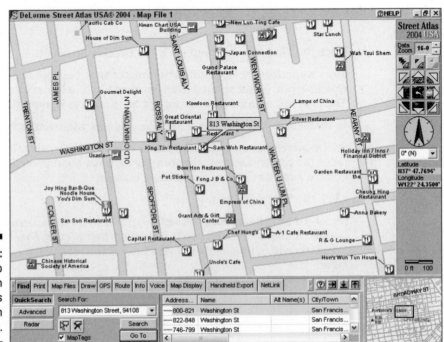

Figure 12-4:
A map
based on
the address
entered in
the Find tab.

In addition to a QuickSearch, which is great for basic searches involving places, addresses, ZIP codes, and coordinates, you'll find two other options in the Find tab:

- ✔ **Advanced searches:** As the name suggests, this option performs more detailed, advanced searches. You can search by categories (such as rest areas, schools, and parks) as well as specify searches take place within a certain area (such as a ZIP code, county, or the current displayed map).

- ✔ **Radar searches:** This is cool feature that lets you search for travel-related POIs within a certain distance of the current center of the map — or if you're using a GPS receiver with Street Atlas USA, from your current location. For example, you could request, "Find me all the restaurants within one mile," and a list of nearby restaurants would be displayed. When you click a restaurant in the list, Street Atlas USA draws a route on the map showing you how to get to the restaurant and tells you the address, how far away it is, and how long it will take to arrive.

Getting from Here to There with Street Atlas USA

Knowing the address of someplace and where it's located is a start, but getting there in a timely fashion without getting lost or frustrated is the true test of a driver (or his or her navigator).

One of the benefits of street navigation software is that it can automatically generate a route between two or more points. The software examines the roads between your starting point and destination, measuring distance and factoring in speed limits to select either the shortest or fastest route.

Street navigation software can give you only its best guess when it comes to a route. A program can't account for new roads that were built after the map data was compiled or local traffic patterns. You'll probably be able to find faster and more direct routes in cities based on your own local knowledge and experience. Although routes from software might not always be perfect, they're much more accurate than guessing or driving around aimlessly.

Street Atlas USA has a number of powerful options for creating routes. To give you a better idea of how route finding works, start off simple.

Creating a route

If you've followed the chapter to this point, you can use the example map created in the earlier section, "Finding an Address with Street Atlas USA." Suppose I want to give my friends this map of Chinatown, showing where Sam Wo's restaurant is located. Great, but that's not going to be much help if they've just arrived at the airport and are driving into the city. For their needs, I use Street Atlas USA to create a route for them to follow to noodle nirvana.

1. **Click the Route tab.**

2. **In the Start text box, enter your starting address.**

   I use a cool Street Atlas USA feature that lets you use the three-letter code of an airport. I enter **SFO**, which is the code for San Francisco International Airport.

3. **For the destination, enter the address in the Finish text box.**

   Here, I enter Sam Wo's address: **813 Washington Street, 94108**.

   When you enter a ZIP code as part of the search, Street Atlas USA removes the ZIP code from the Finish text box when the calculated route is displayed. The ZIP is required for the search but isn't shown with the route.

4. **Click the Calculate button.**

   Presto! A map appears with an outlined route from the airport to Sam Wo's, as shown in Figure 12-5. The route distance is shown as well as an estimate of how long it will take to get there.

Remember that your Calculate result is based on driving the speed limit with a normal amount of traffic. You can zoom in on the map to get more detail.

On all street navigation software, you'll find that the travel times for routes tend to be conservative estimates. Nine times out of ten, you end up taking less time to reach your destination.

Getting directions

Maps with highlighted routes are pretty cool, but sometimes it's nice to have a set of plain old *turn right on Main Street, then take a left at the light* directions. After you create a route (see the preceding section), Street Atlas USA can provide you with turn-by-turn directions to get to your destination.

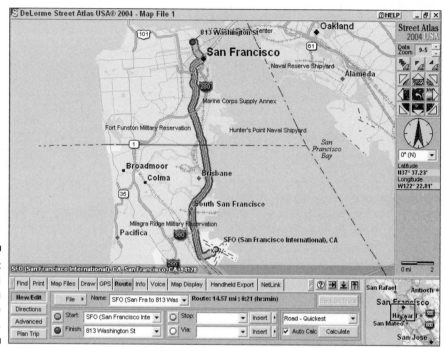

On the Route tab, click the Directions button. You'll get a list of turn-by-turn directions with street names, distances, and total times for each part of the route. The directions information is shown in Figure 12-6.

Printing and saving directions

After you have a map and driving directions (read earlier sections to follow me to Sam Wo's), you may need to make copies. Street Atlas USA has a number of options for getting the information off your computer screen and printing it to paper or saving it to a file.

To print or save maps and directions, click the Print tab. You see two buttons:

- ✔ Click the *Map* button for options to print or save the current map.
- ✔ Click the *Route* button for print and save options of the current route.

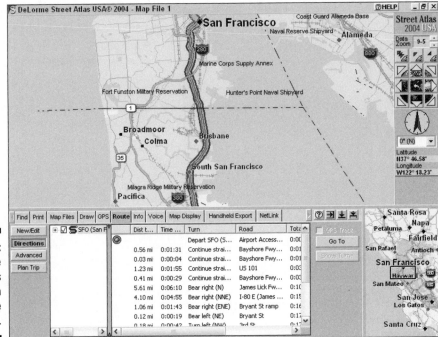

Figure 12-6:
Route
directions
display on
the Route
tab.

Saving and printing maps

All the Print and Save command buttons are next to the Overview Map on the
far right of the Print tab area. You have buttons for

- ✔ Printing the current map
- ✔ E-mailing the print area as an attachment
- ✔ Saving the print area to disk as a graphics file
- ✔ Copying the print area to the Clipboard

If you select the Print Preview check box, the map is reduced in scale, and a
rectangle is displayed around the print area.

Saving and printing routes

You can also save and print route information in a number of different formats,
including an overview map with directions, turn-by-turn details, and as *strip
maps* (detailed maps that follow a route with directions in the margins). Check
the type of directions you'd like to create, using the Save and Print command
buttons at the far end of the Tab area to output them. Figure 12-7 shows a
preview of a *Travel Package,* which is a format that prints the route map with
directions at the bottom of the page.

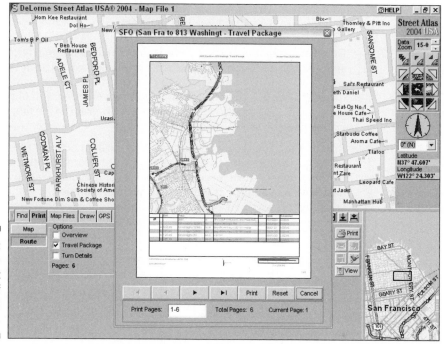

If you want only a text version of the route directions, click the Route button in the Print tab and then mark the Directions check box. You can then either save the directions as a text file or e-mail them to a friend.

If you end up in Chinatown, the entrance to Sam Wo's restaurant is through the street-level kitchen, so don't think you're in the wrong place. Head up the narrow stairs to the second floor and don't disturb the cooks on your way up. *Bon appétit!*

Moving Maps with Earthmate

In addition to its mapping software, DeLorme also offers the small Earthmate GPS receiver that's designed to work with Street Atlas USA and other map programs that use GPS data. (You can use other types of GPS receivers with Street Atlas USA, too, but the Earthmate is designed to work with the program with a minimal amount of setup.)

You can connect the Earthmate to a laptop via a Universal Serial Bus (USB) cable, serial cable, or a PowerPack that supports Bluetooth wireless communications. After you have the GPS receiver hooked up and Street Atlas is running, the two general modes of operation are

- **General navigation:** Street Atlas USA processes the received GPS data and displays your current position on the map with a series of dots that shows where you've traveled. As you move, the map automatically moves to show your position. In addition, your speed, direction of travel, and GPS satellite information is shown in the program's GPS tab, as seen in Figure 12-8.

- **Route:** After you create a route (see the earlier section, "Creating a route,") in addition to the general navigation features, Street Atlas USA displays turn-by-turn directions onscreen, informing you how far your destination is and the travel time to your destination. If you have the voice feature enabled, Street Atlas USA announces the directions; you can choose from several different types of voices.

GPS car navigation systems

Street navigation software coupled with a laptop and GPS receiver isn't your only option to stay found while driving through the asphalt jungle. GPS car navigation systems are starting to become popular as factory-installed options and third-party add-ons for cars and trucks. These systems are streamlined versions of street navigation programs, offering basic navigation features such as real-time map display, address searches, and route planning.

Car navigation systems range from portable, handheld GPS receivers that are equally at home on the trail or the road to systems permanently installed in a vehicle. Some of the more sophisticated products use gyroscopes, connections to the Vehicle Speed Sensor (car-speak for a *speedometer*), and three-axis accelerometers to provide speed and distance information when a GPS signal is temporarily lost; such as in tunnels or urban areas with tall buildings.

I have to admit I'm not a true road warrior and don't spend lots of time in my car. However, I did have a chance to try out a Magellan RoadMate GPS navigation system (www.magellangps.com) for a while and was pretty impressed. RoadMate mounts on your dashboard (as shown here) and is portable so you can easily transfer it from one car to another. The version I tested had an internal hard drive that was preloaded with street maps of the entire U.S., so you can just plug it into your cigarette lighter and go. This is perfect for a business traveler who just flew into a city he's never been to before and has to spend the next couple of days in a rental car trying to find his way around. Routes are calculated in a matter of seconds, and a large, high-resolution map screen keeps your progress updated. And with a touch screen, voice prompts, and a simple user interface, even my nontechnical friends and family members were able to figure out how to use it in no time.

Granted, the RoadMate is a single purpose device, costs about as much as a low-end laptop, and doesn't have all the features of a street navigation software package. However, if I were regularly spending a lot of time on the road or visiting cities I didn't know very well, I'd give some serious consideration to it or a similar GPS navigation system. My crystal ball tells me it won't be too many years into the future when in-car navigation systems start to become standard in most new cars and trucks.

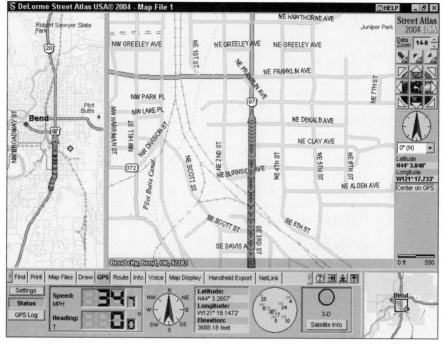

Figure 12-8:
Real-time
map display
with Street
Atlas USA
and an
Earthmate
GPS
receiver.

If you're driving by yourself, be careful when using the GPS features of Street Atlas USA with your laptop sitting next to you on the passenger seat. Fight the tendency to get distracted from your driving while you look at the screen and use the mouse and keyboard to enter commands. I recommend someone riding shotgun — that is, a navigator who's in charge of running Street Atlas USA. If you drive solo a lot, get a laptop-mounting bracket that places your computer in a more visible and easy-to-use location.

Other Street Navigation Software

In addition to Street Atlas USA, here are two other popular street navigation programs available for navigating the roads of America. I don't have enough space to fully describe them, but here's some general information in case you're shopping for software.

New versions of street navigation software are usually released annually with new street and POI data as well as new features. If you travel in an area that doesn't experience much growth or change, you probably don't need to upgrade every year. On the other hand, because all the street navigation software packages retail for under $50, it's not that expensive to stay current.

Microsoft Streets & Trips

Microsoft's Streets & Trips is a popular alternative to DeLorme's software. The program has all the basic street navigation features, including some advanced features such as saving a map as a Web page, downloading current road construction information from the Internet, and creating drive time zones (such as *show me all the places I can drive to from a certain location in under an hour*). The software is easy to use and comes bundled with Pocket Streets, the Pocket PC version of Streets & Trips. See Figure 12-9 for a screenshot of the user interface. To discover more about Streets & Trips, go to `www.microsoft.com/streets`.

Rand McNally StreetFinder & TripMaker Deluxe

Rand McNally, in the map business for over 130 years, is one of the main providers of U.S. paper street maps and road atlases. The StreetFinder & TripMaker Deluxe software package provides all the features you'd expect in a street navigation program, along with Mobile Travel Guide ratings for hotels and restaurants and suggested scenic tours and one-day driving trips. To read more about the product, go to `www.randmcnally.com`.

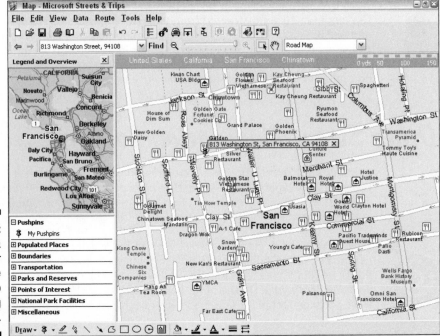

Figure 12-9: Streets & Trips user interface with a map displaying an address.

Chapter 13

On the Ground with Maptech Terrain Navigator

*I*f you spend a lot of time off the beaten path in the mountains, hills, deserts, and plains, you should consider using topographic mapping software. These programs come bundled with United States Geological Survey (USGS) digital maps and are a perfect companion for any outdoor enthusiast. Before you head off into the wilds, you can print a topographic map of an area you're interested in visiting and even plan your trip on your PC. If you have a GPS receiver, you can interface it with the map program to see exactly where you've been or upload waypoint and route information entered on the electronic map to your GPS receiver.

Commercial topographic software packages are easy to use, convenient (you don't need to find and download maps to use them), and economical. Most of the map products on the market cost under $100 and give you 1:24,000 scale map coverage of a state or region; for the same price, other software provides less-detailed 1:100,000 scale maps of the entire U.S. This is a bargain considering that a paper version of a USGS topographic map costs around $7, and you might have to buy up to a thousand maps to fully cover a single state.

In this chapter, I discuss commercial software packages that offer topographic maps of the U.S. I focus primarily on Maptech's Terrain Navigator to illustrate these programs. Although they sport different user interfaces, most commercial topographic map programs share the same basic capabilities and features. At the end of this chapter, I briefly review some other popular topographic map programs.

Discovering Terrain Navigator

Maptech's Terrain Navigator (www.maptech.com) was one of the first commercial, Windows topographic map programs. (In the old days it was known as *TopoScout.*) Over the years, Terrain Navigator has evolved into a sophisticated, powerful, electronic mapping tool.

You can purchase different versions of Terrain Navigator. The program that accesses map data is the same, but the maps that come bundled on CD-ROMs are different. Different versions of Terrain Navigator provide topographic maps for individual states and different regions of the U.S. (in this chapter I use Oregon state maps). The majority of commercial map programs are also sold this way. Plan on spending around a hundred dollars for a complete set of Terrain Navigator digital maps for a single state.

You use Terrain Navigator's main features — which most other topographic map products share — to help you

✔ Quickly find locations by name or coordinates.

✔ Accurately measure distance and area.

✔ Display terrain three-dimensionally.

✔ Show elevation profiles of routes of travel.

✔ Customize maps with labels, markers, and routes.

✔ Interface maps with GPS receivers to upload and download waypoints, routes, and tracks or use for real-time tracking.

Read on to take a look at some of Terrain Navigator's basic features and see how to use them. Whether you put on your boots and backpack is completely up to you.

Maptech has a free demo version of Terrain Navigator that comes with a single map of a wilderness area in Colorado. You can download the demo at www.mpatech.com/support/downloads.cfm. Be sure to read through the online help and tutorial because it describes a number of program features that I don't have space to cover in this chapter.

Displaying Maps and Finding Places

When Terrain Navigator starts up, a map of the state or region that you've installed on your PC is displayed. Figure 13-1 shows a state map: in this case, the state of Oregon. Here are the basic rules of engagement:

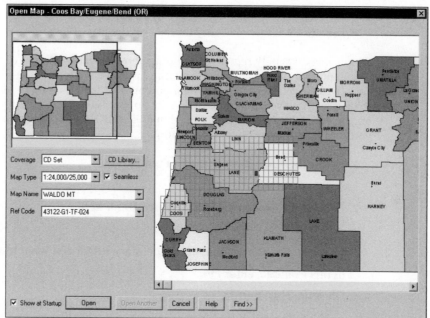

Figure 13-1:
Terrain
Navigator
state start-
up map.

✔ If you know the general area you'd like to view, click there on the map. A grid appears in the vicinity of where you click. Each of the rectangles in the grid represents a 1:24,000 USGS topographic map.

✔ Moving the cursor over the grid displays the map name at the top of the window that's associated with a rectangle.

✔ Double-click a rectangle to display a map.

✔ If you know the USGS map name, you can select it from the Map Name drop-down list, which displays all the map names associated with the currently selected grid.

If you click different parts of the state map, you'll notice that grids appear and disappear. When a grid is displayed, it shows all the maps that are on one of the CDs that came with Terrain Navigator; the name of the CD appears in the window title. This helps you know which disc you need to insert into your CD-ROM drive to display maps for different areas.

Double-clicking a grid rectangle is one way to display a map, but here are quicker and more precise ways to view a specific location. You can display a map by searching for

✔ City or town name

✔ ZIP code

✔ Coordinates

🟩 ✔ Place names

🟩 ✔ Features you've previously marked on the map

Suppose you vaguely remember hearing about a real cool hike to the top of a mountain that has an amazing view. You know it's somewhere around Waldo Lake, Oregon, but the name of the mountain just isn't coming to mind. You think it might have something to do with apples: Gala, Granny Smith, Braeburn, maybe Fuji. Even with fuzzy information like this, Terrain Navigator can help you zero in on the location. Here's how:

1. **Under the state map, click the Find button.**

   A pop-up menu appears.

2. **Choose the Search All Place Names menu item.**

   The Search All Place Names dialog box opens.

3. **In the Keyword text box, enter the place name you want to search for.**

   In this example, enter **Fuji**.

4. **Click the Find button.**

   A list of places that match your search text is displayed, as shown in Figure 13-2. Ah, ha! There's Fuji Mountain. That rings a bell.

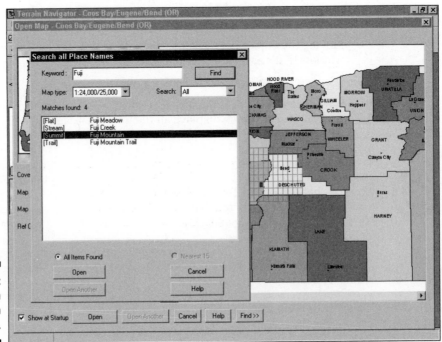

Figure 13-2:
Zero in on a location from here.

5. Double-click the place name that you want to view.

For this example, double-click Fuji Mountain.

The map that corresponds to the place name is displayed with the location circled — in this case, exactly the place you were looking for, Fuji Mountain, a couple of miles southwest of Waldo Lake.

After the search map is displayed, you can search for other place names or coordinates by clicking the Find Place button (with the binoculars icon) on the toolbar.

Navigating a Terrain Navigator Map

After you have a map displayed, as shown in Figure 13-3, you can do a lot more than just look at it onscreen and print it out. One of biggest advantages to a digital map is you can interact with the map more than if it were a paper map. Stick with me here to find out how to move around in a map and change its size.

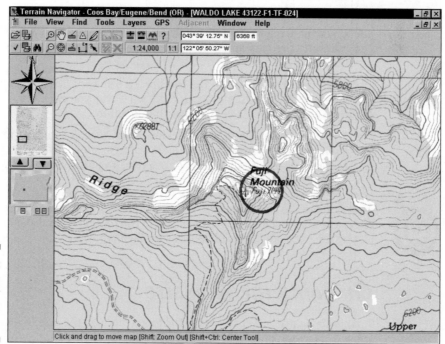

Figure 13-3:
Terrain
Navigator
map of Fuji
Mountain.

Shifty tips

Don't overlook the keyboard and mouse short-cuts in Terrain Navigator that can speed things up as you move around the map. They include

✔ **Shift+click:** Zooms out and centers the map at the location you clicked — unless the zoom-out (magnifying glass icon with a minus sign) tool is selected, in which case you'll zoom in.

✔ **Shift+Ctrl+click:** Centers the map wherever you click.

✔ **Ctrl:** Changes the cursor to the Drag tool and allows you to scroll the map.

✔ **Right-click:** Displays a pop-up menu with zoom and other options.

Moving around in a map

More than likely, you'll want to move around the map and check out the countryside that currently isn't being displayed onscreen. Here's how:

✔ **Move the cursor to one of the edges of the map.** The cursor turns into an arrow; click to scroll the map in the direction that the arrow points.

✔ **Click the Drag tool on the toolbar.** (It's shaped like a hand.) Move the cursor to the map and hold down the left mouse button; then scroll the map by dragging.

✔ **Click the Center tool on the toolbar.** (It's shaped like a bull's-eye with crosshairs.) With this tool selected, wherever you click the map, the map is drawn so it's centered at that location.

✔ **Move the rectangle in the overview map.** A small overview map appears to the left of the main map. A blue rectangle shows what part of the map is currently displayed onscreen. You can drag the overview map rectangle to show a new location onscreen.

As you move the cursor around the map, the coordinates and the elevation under the cursor location are displayed in the toolbar. This is useful for determining the exact locations of features on the map.

Changing the map size

Terrain Navigator offers two ways for you to change the size of a map and show more detail or area.

✔ **Zooming:** The toolbar has two icons bearing a magnifying glass: one with a plus sign and the other with a minus sign. When the plus sign magnifying glass is selected, you zoom in when you click the map. When the minus sign magnifying glass is selected, clicking zooms you out.

✔ **Changing the scale:** Maps can be displayed in either 1:24,000 (more detail, smaller area) or 1:100,000 scale (less detail, larger area). Note the map scale command in the toolbar that displays a menu for selecting the scale of your choice.

Planning a Trip with Terrain Navigator

If you've followed this chapter to this point, you've located a map of Fuji Mountain. Keep your imagination flowing and plan a hiking trip there. Suppose that your friends gave you some vague directions about taking a series of logging roads to get to the trailhead. The trail wasn't very well marked, but when they found it, it climbed steeply for a couple of miles to the summit. However, the last time you listened to your friends, the short pleasant hike that they described turned into an eight-hour death march through thick underbrush and straight up a rock face. This time, you decide to use Terrain Navigator to get a better picture of this little outing.

1. **Look on the map for a trail.**

   You want the one that goes to the summit of Fuji Mountain. (Only one trail goes to the top.) As you follow it down, you see that it intersects with an unimproved road — probably the logging road your friends told you about.

   The symbol for a trail on USGS maps is a single dashed line. Lines with two sets of dashes indicate an unimproved road.

2. **Click the Marker tool on the toolbar, move the cursor to where the road intersects the trail, and click to create a waypoint for the *trailhead* (the beginning of the trail).**

   The Marker tool looks like a pyramid.

   This creates a GPS waypoint at that location named Mrk1. Click the name and rename it Fuji Trailhead.

3. **Use the Marker tool to create another GPS waypoint at the end of the trail.**

   This marks a waypoint at the summit of Fuji Mountain. Rename this one Fuji Mountain (see how in Step 2).

With these two GPS waypoints set, you now know where the trail starts and ends. If you're using a GPS receiver, the first waypoint will help you find the trailhead, and the second waypoint will help you reach your final destination. You can manually enter the waypoints in your GPS receiver or have Terrain Navigator upload them for you.

Be sure that the map datum matches the datum your GPS receiver is using (head over to Chapter 4 for information about what happens when datums don't match). You can set the map datum in Terrain Navigator by choosing File➪Preferences➪General.

4. **Click the Track tool on the toolbar to draw your planned course of travel on the map.**

The Track tool, which looks like a pencil, works by drawing a line from the last place you clicked. However, it doesn't allow you to freehand draw like with a real pencil.

5. **Follow the trail by clicking the mouse (like playing connect-the-dots).**

Trace the trail that heads up Fuji Mountain, starting at the road intersection. After you click, the current length (in feet or miles) of the track is displayed in the status bar below the map.

6. **When you're finished, right-click and choose Finish Track from the pop-up menu.**

7. **Edit the track, giving it a name and changing its color if you like.**

Move the cursor on the track that you just created, right-click, and choose Edit from the pop-up menu. You can now name the track (use **Fuji**) and change its color if you like.

The finished map with the waypoints and the track is shown in Figure 13-4. You can upload the waypoints and track data to your GPS receiver before you leave on the hike to help with your navigation.

Use Terrain Navigator to turn a track into a route. A *route* is a course of travel that's broken up into a series of waypoints that define segments of your trip. You navigate between the route waypoints to reach your final destination. Typically the number of track points is reduced when you convert a track to a route. Thus, there's not as much detail, and you end up with straight lines instead of curves. If you want to upload a course of travel to your GPS receiver, it's more efficient to use a route than a track. To convert a route, right-click a track and choose Create Route from the pop-up menu.

Even if you don't have a GPS receiver to which you can upload waypoint, route, or track data, you can use Terrain Navigator to find a trail, print a map of that trail to take with you, and determine the distance of your hike. Just remember to bring your compass!

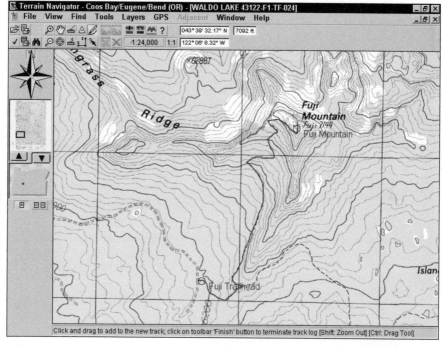

Figure 13-4:
A trail
map with
waypoints
and track
can be sent
to your GPS
receiver.

You can upload data from topographic map programs to your GPS receiver or download waypoints, routes, and tracks from your GPS receiver to the map program. For example, you could overlay a track you recorded with your GPS receiver on the electronic map to see where you had been. Check the map program documentation or online help to find out how to interface your GPS receiver. Chapter 9 has a number of hints and tips for connecting GPS receivers to PCs.

Understanding Terrain Elevation

Unless you've had some experience reading topographic maps, trying to figure out terrain elevation based on contour lines can be challenging. (Contour lines are a way of representing height on a map.) Terrain Navigator has two features — 3-D View and the Terrain Profile tool — that help you better visualize where the land starts to get steep or flatten. You can use the map from earlier sections of this chapter to see just how much of a climb you're in for.

Other Maptech products

In addition to Terrain Navigator, Maptech has several other topographic map products that you might find useful, including

- ✔ **Terrain Navigator Pro** is Maptech's high-end version of Terrain Navigator targeted toward professional map users and is priced around $300 per state. Use its enhanced features to

- ✔ Display aerial photographs downloaded from the Maptech's Internet servers.

- ✔ Locate street addresses.

- ✔ Link digital photos, spreadsheets, and other files with locations on maps.

- ✔ Export maps for use with Geographic Information System (GIS) programs such as ArcGIS and AutoCAD.

- ✔ **National Park Digital Guide** has topographic maps of all the National Parks in the United States, including photos and information about sights and services both inside and outside the parks. The guide costs around $50.

- ✔ **Appalachian, Continental Divide, and Pacific Crest Trail** products contain topographic maps for the areas around each one of these classic trails and cost under $100. The Appalachian Trail software, priced around $50, has extensive guidebook information along with maps.

- ✔ **Outdoor Navigator** is a mapping program for Pocket PCs and Palm PDAs that lets you load detailed topographic maps on your PDA. The product is priced around $100.

You can find more about these products and their features by visiting: www.map tech.com

Using a 3-D map image

Use Terrain Navigator to display 3-D, shaded relief images of a map to help you better understand the terrain. To show a 3-D image of the map that's currently displayed onscreen, click the 3-D View button on the toolbar. (It looks like mountains with a small bar underneath.)

The topographic map of Fuji Mountain (including the markers and track added in the earlier section, "Planning a Trip with Terrain Navigator") is displayed in 3-D, as shown in Figure 13-5.

A red rectangle appears on the overview map, showing you the general location of the terrain, based on the current 3-D view of the map.

To control the view of the 3-D map

✔ Click and drag the cursor on the map to rotate the image.

✔ Use the trackball control to the left of the map to rotate up, down, left, and right. You can also use the keyboard navigation arrow keys.

✔ Use the Elevation slider bar control (it has a picture of a truck, a helicopter, and an airplane) to adjust the height you're viewing the map from.

✔ Use the zoom arrows above the Elevation slider bar to control how close forward or backward your view of the terrain is.

✔ Use the Vertical Exaggeration buttons beneath the trackball control to increase and decrease the vertical scale so elevation differences are easy to distinguish.

To toggle back to a 2-D version of the map, click the 3-D View toolbar button.

If you want a true 3-D experience, Terrain Navigator comes with a special pair of red-and-blue-lens, stereoscopic glasses. If you click the 3-D Glasses icon, the map is colored so it appears to have three-dimensional depth when you're wearing the glasses.

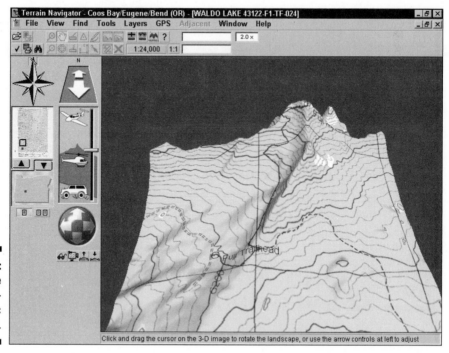

Figure 13-5:
Manipulate a topo-graphic map in 3-D.

Charting elevation profiles

Although the 3-D map view gives you a visual sense of how steep your hike is, you can get even more detailed information by using the Terrain Profile tool. This feature shows you the elevation gain/loss of your hike in pictures and numbers. Here's how to use this tool:

1. **Make sure that the map is displayed in 2-D.**

   See the preceding section for how to do this.

2. **Click the Information tool on the toolbar (an arrow with a question mark).**

3. **Right-click the track and select Profile from the pop-up menu.**

   A Profile dialog box opens, as shown in Figure 13-6, that displays an elevation chart of the trail as well as how many feet you'll be climbing and descending over the course of the trip.

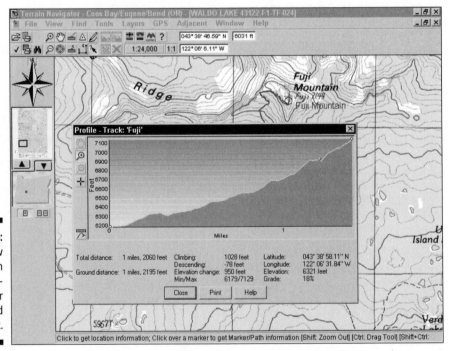

Figure 13-6: Show elevation profile information for a selected track.

Vertical profiles may have a lot of vertical exaggeration to show relative steepness. This can make terrain appear steeper than it actually is.

Reviewing Other Topographic Map Software

In addition to Maptech and its topographic mapping programs, DeLorme and National Geographic also offer software that's suited for off-road use. As previously mentioned, most topographic map programs have the same basic features; the biggest difference is their user interface. Because I don't have the time to cover the other mapping programs in detail, this section provides a brief description of a few popular programs, shows some screenshots to give you an idea of what the user interface is like, and provides manufacturer Web sites to get more product information. When it comes to choosing a topographic map program, you really can't go wrong with any of the programs mentioned in this chapter.

You can't upload detailed maps to your GPS receiver from any of the programs discussed in this chapter. GPS receivers that display maps can use only *proprietary* maps (sold by the GPS manufacturer), and these tend to show considerably less detail than maps you can display on your PC. Several topographic map software companies do offer products that you can use with a Pocket PC/Palm PDA and GPS receivers that can display detailed topographic maps just as they appear on a PC screen.

DeLorme mapping products

DeLorme, well known for its Street Atlas USA road navigation software, also makes two topographic mapping programs: Topo USA and 3-D TopoQuads. DeLorme uses the same user interface for its entire line of consumer mapping products, so if you're a happy user of Street Atlas USA and are looking for a map program for off-road use, it makes sense to keep things in the DeLorme family.

DeLorme was one of the first vendors to offer customers a choice of map data on CDs or DVDs. If you have a DVD player on your PC, DVDs are far more convenient because you don't have as many discs to keep track of, and you don't have to swap discs as often to view maps of different areas.

DeLorme topographic mapping products can interface with GPS receivers, display 3-D maps, search for locations, provide elevation profiles, and plan for trips just like other map programs. These two unique features in the program are especially useful:

- ✔ **Satellite imagery:** DeLorme sells 10-meter resolution color satellite data for each state. When you use the images with DeLorme mapping products, you can view the satellite photos side by side with topographic maps in 2-D or 3-D. (See an example produced by Topo USA in Figure 13-7.)

- ✔ **Mural printing:** If you need to produce a large map for a presentation, the programs support printing mural maps that are up to three pages high by three pages wide that you can join to make a large map.

To read more about DeLorme's mapping programs, visit `www.delorme.com`.

Topo USA

Topo USA provides 1:100,000 scale topographic maps of the entire United States (for around the same price as a collection of 1:24,000 scale digital maps for a single state). Remember, you don't get as much detail as you would with a 1:24,000 scale map, but there's enough detail for rudimentary navigation and to use as a general reference.

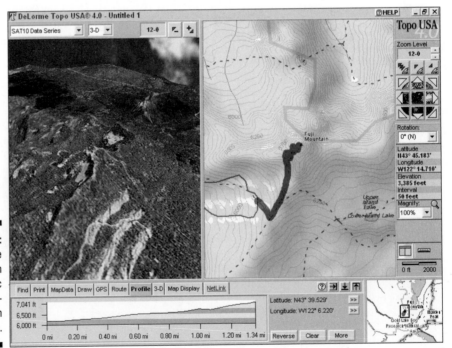

Figure 13-7:
3-D satellite image with topographic map displayed in Topo USA.

The Topo USA maps are *vector-based* (drawn with lines and shapes), so they don't have the crisp appearance of a USGS digital raster map. However, DeLorme vector maps tend to have more updated road information because some of the scanned raster maps are based on data from maps made over 20 years ago.

3-D TopoQuads

3-D TopoQuads provides more detailed maps that are sold by state or region. The maps are displayed as vector maps until you zoom in far enough, and then they become 1:24,000 scale USGS scanned digital raster maps. (See an example of a map, including 2-D and 3-D views, in Figure 13-8.)

National Geographic mapping products

Many children got their first introduction to maps from *National Geographic* magazines. Each month, a carefully folded paper map of somewhere foreign and exotic came nestled inside the magazine. National Geographic is still in the map business, now producing several topographic map programs.

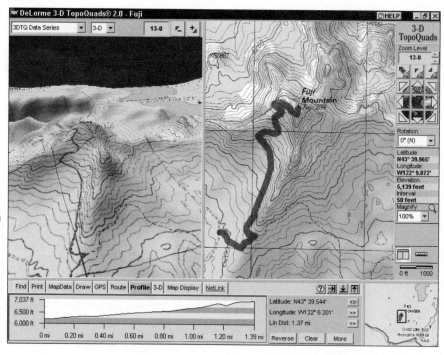

Figure 13-8: 2-D and 3-D display of 1:24,000 topographic maps in 3-D TopoQuads.

I was one of those kids that got hooked on National Geographic maps when I was growing up, and I still like them today. The company's map software is easy to use and strikes a nice balance of having just the right number and types of features, without having too many whistles and bells.

National Geographic software has all the same basic features as other mapping programs, such as GPS support, route planning, printing maps, and searching for locations. The only exception is that National Geographic programs currently use only relief shading to show elevation and don't render 3-D map images.

National Geographic has a number of paper and electronic map products available; visit www.nationalgeographic.com/maps. The two digital map products that you'll find the most practical for backcountry use are Back Roads Explorer and TOPO!

Back Roads Explorer

Back Roads Explorer contains 1:100,000 scale topographic maps and larger overview maps of the entire United States. In addition to terrain data, the software also has road and street data that you can overlay on top of a map, including paved and unpaved roads. (An example is shown in Figure 13-9.)

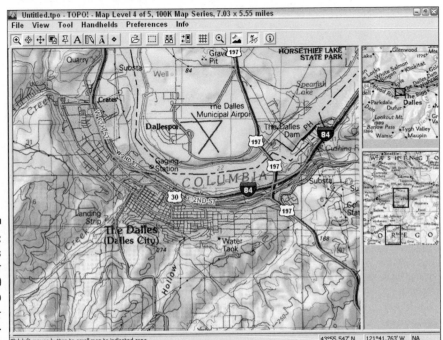

Figure 13-9: Back Roads Explorer 1:100,000 scale map with overlaid roads.

Unlike DeLorme's Topo USA, Back Roads Explorer uses *raster maps* (scanned versions of paper maps), which contain more detail. If you prefer more of a traditional looking map to one that looks like it was computer-generated, you'll like Back Roads Explorer.

Raster maps take up more disk space than vector maps because they're scanned images of paper maps. Vector maps are smaller because they're composed of lines and shapes. For example, the raster map data for the entire United States that comes with Back Roads Explorer fits on 17 CDs, but the same vector data in Topo USA comes on 6 CDs.

With the option of overlaying up-to-date roads over topographic maps, Back Roads Explorer is ideal for basic navigation and is especially well suited for 4 x 4 enthusiasts who use a laptop and GPS receiver.

TOPO!

National Geographic's TOPO! line of software provides 1:24,000 maps for each of the states and is comparable with Maptech's Terrain Navigator and DeLorme's 3-D TopoQuads products. (A screenshot of a TOPO! 1:24,000 scale map is shown in Figure 13-10.)

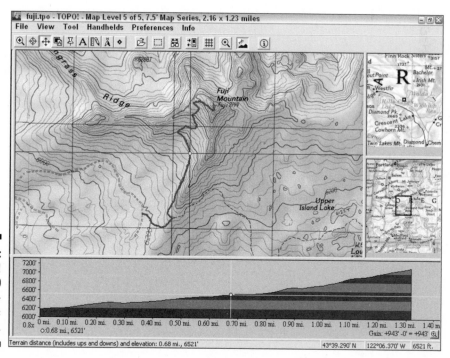

Figure 13-10: TOPO! 1:24,000 scale topographic map.

One feature that I especially like in the TOPO! products is mapXchange. You can visit the National Geographic Web site and select the state you have TOPO! maps for. A list of hikes and other outdoor activities is displayed with descriptions, and you can freely download files that contain waypoints and routes you can use with TOPO! If you like, you can also upload your own files of places you've been to share with other outdoor enthusiasts.

Chapter 14

From the Air with USAPhotoMaps

*A*erial photos complement other types of maps because they give you a snapshot of reality. Programs that display *aerials* (map-speak shorthand for aerial photos) are both inexpensive and easy to use. In this chapter, I review mapping programs that can exploit aerial photos, primarily focusing on the popular shareware application, USAPhotoMaps.

To better illustrate the capabilities and functions of this program, I walk you through downloading an aerial photo, scrolling and zooming, interfacing the program with a GPS receiver, and saving map data.

To get the most from this chapter, download and install USAPhotoMaps (`http://jdmcox.com`) and then use the program to work through the examples in the following pages. Unlike some shareware programs, USAPhotoMaps isn't crippled; that is, all its features work when you download the program. If you find the program useful, you can make a donation to the author's PayPal account.

Enhancing TerraServer-USA with USAPhotoMaps

TerraServer-USA is a popular Web site that displays free aerial photographs and topographic maps of the U.S. that are produced by the United States Geological Survey (USGS). (Read more about TerraServer-USA in Chapter 20.) And although TerraServer-USA is a great Web-hosted mapping service, it has several limitations:

✔ Only a relatively small geographic area can be displayed.

✔ You can't edit downloaded photos and maps.

✔ GPS receiver data can't be used with the photos and maps.

You can read more about TerraServer-USA in the sidebar, "TerraServer-USA limitations."

To address these issues, several developers have created programs that download TerraServer-USA aerial photos and maps so you can put the data to more versatile use. Instead of relying on a Web browser, you use these standalone programs — like USAPhotoMaps — to create scrollable, aerial photos of just about anywhere in the United States that can be customized and saved and optionally overlaid with GPS data.

Discovering USAPhotoMaps Features

USAPhotoMaps is an aerial photo and map program written by Doug Cox, who is a retired airline pilot turned Windows programmer. USAPhotoMaps is elegantly small and simple to use, with a number of powerful features. Use it to

✔ Display USGS aerial photographs and topographic maps.

✔ Zoom in and out on map features.

✔ Support user-defined text labels.

✔ Save user-selected areas as JPG format files.

✔ Interface with a GPS receiver for real-time tracking.

✔ Import and export GPS waypoints, routes, and tracks.

USAPhotoMaps has an extensive online help file.

Downloading Aerial Photographs

The first time you run USAPhotoMaps, a dialog box appears that prompts you to create a new map. You need to enter the following:

✔ **What you want to name the map.**

✔ **The coordinates of the area you're interested in viewing.** The coordinates can be in either

  • Latitude and longitude

  • Universal Transverse Mercator (UTM)

TerraServer-USA limitations

The first time you see USAPhotoMaps display TerraServer-USA aerial photos, you're probably going to say, "Wow! This is like having my own personal spy satellite." Well, sort of, but there are a few catches:

✔ **Yanks only:** TerraServer-USA provides aerial photos and maps of United States locations only. And although the aerial photo database is fairly complete, some areas in the U.S. don't have photo data.

✔ **Not always current:** TerraServer-USA aerial photographs tend to be not very current. In fact, they can be up to ten years old because

the USGS produces new sets of aerial photos only as often as needs and budgets allow.

✔ **No color:** Only black-and-white photos are currently available. TerraServer-USA does plan to carry more recent, high-resolution, color aerial photographs that the USGS has produced for selected urban areas, but it will be many years until color aerial photographs are available of most of the United States.

✔ **Data transfer hiccups:** Network outages and server upgrades can disrupt TerraServer-USA data transfers.

Read more about UTM, latitude, and longitude in Chapter 2. If you don't know the latitude and longitude coordinates of the location you're interested in seeing, quickly skip over to Chapter 11 to read how to find coordinates of place names.

As an example, create an aerial photomap of Seattle, Washington.

1. **Enter the name, latitude, and longitude in the New Map dialog box. (See Figure 14-1.)**

   • Name: Seattle

   • Latitude: 47.61431

   • Longitude: 122.32898

2. **Click OK.**

   A series of gray squares appear onscreen.

3. **Download aerial photos from TerraServer-USA for the area that you specified (with the latitude and longitude coordinates). Make sure that you're connected to the Internet and then press the F key.**

   A mosaic of aerial photograph images replaces the gray squares as the screen is filled with data from TerraServer-USA. The final result is shown in Figure 14-2.

If you're using a firewall, your computer might complain when USAPhotoMaps tries to connect to TerraServer-USA. Because the program is just downloading map data, you can give permission for USAPhotoMaps to access the Internet.

New Map

USAPhotoMaps downloads USGS aerial photos from
http://terraserver-usa.com/
and creates a scrollable, zoomable, GPS-enabled map.

First enter a name for your map: Seattle

Then enter the initial latitude & longitude for your map:
    (decimals, minutes, and seconds are optional)
Lat   Deg N: 47.61431   Min: Sec:
Lon   Deg W: 122.32898   Min: Sec:
or: UTM Easting: Northing: Zone:

You can get latitudes/longitudes from the above Internet address:
1. On that Web page, enter a city name in Search Terraserver.
2. On the next page, under the Available Image column,
   click on the Aerial Photo for that city.
3. On the next page, use the Navigate box (on the left side)
   to scroll and zoom to find your area of interest.
4. Click on Info (above the photo) to see the page with
   latitude/longitude, UTM information, and photo date.

Cancel   OK

Figure 14-1:
Create a
new map
here.

Figure 14-2:
USAPhoto-
Maps aerial
photo
mosaic of
Seattle,
Washington.

If you plan to use USAPhotoMaps to build an extensive aerial photo collection, a high-speed Internet connection will make your life much easier. Each individual aerial photo or topographic map image in the displayed mosaic is roughly 50–200K in size. (The actual size depends on how much unique terrain is shown in the image.) At 2 meters-per-pixel resolution, it takes 70 images to fill the screen of a 1024 x 768 monitor; that's anywhere from 7–17MB of data to download.

Getting the Most from Aerial Photos

After you have an aerial photo displayed, navigate inside the image. (Read the preceding section for how to download and display an aerial photo.) USAPhotoMaps has a number of different commands to view and manipulate the photo.

The datum used for all TerraServer-USA maps is NAD 83. This is nearly identical to the WGS 84 datum used as a default by GPS receivers. If you plan on using your GPS receiver with USAPhotoMaps, be sure that the datum settings match. (Read more about datums in Chapter 2.)

The first thing you'll notice is that when you move the mouse cursor around the screen, map coordinates appear in the window title bar. This feature allows you to move the cursor over a feature that's shown on the aerial photo and get its precise coordinates.

You can change how you want the coordinates displayed from the View menu. Choose the Lat/Lon item and then specify whether you want the coordinates shown in decimal degrees, degrees and decimal minutes, degrees/minutes/seconds, or UTM formats.

Press the X key to display a dialog box with the coordinates that the cursor is currently over. You can copy the coordinates from this dialog box and paste them into another program.

Switching between aerial photos and topographic maps

After you know where you are in a photo (see the preceding section), look at the commands that you can use to move around. As I mention earlier, TerraServer-USA provides both aerial photos and USGS topographic maps, and USAPhotoMaps lets you switch between the two types of images. (Figure 14-3 shows a topographic map.) This is useful because you can look at a topographic map and then immediately see what the same location looks like as an aerial photo. This is a big advantage because aerial photos often show more feature detail than topographic maps.

Here are the two ways (in USAPhotoMaps) to display a topographic map version of an aerial photo you're viewing:

 ✔ From the View menu, choose Map Type⇨Topo.
 ✔ Press the T key.

If gray squares appear onscreen, you haven't downloaded map data for that area yet. To download the map, press the F key.

To switch back to an aerial photo view of the location

 ✔ From the View menu, choose Map Type⇨Photo.
 ✔ Press the P key.

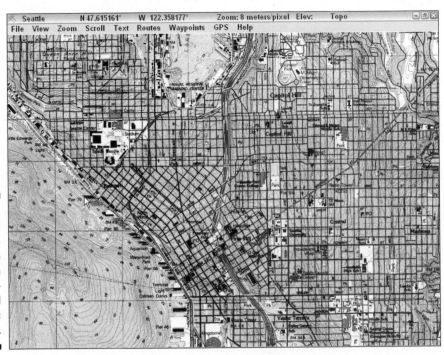

Figure 14-3:
Use
USAPhoto-
Maps to
display both
aerial photo-
graphs and
topographic
maps.

Moving around the map

You've probably noticed that USAPhotoMaps doesn't use scroll bars like other Windows programs. Not to worry; you can still move around in a photo or map by using the keyboard navigational arrow keys:

If you see gray squares while you're scrolling, map data has yet to be downloaded for that particular area. Figure 14-4 shows gray squares with aerial photo data that hasn't been downloaded. Here are two ways to fill the squares with map or photo data:

✔ From the File menu, choose Download Map Data➪Fill Screen.

✔ Press the F key.

USAPhotoMaps connects to TerraServer-USA and downloads the map data for that area.

Instead of scrolling, you can also go directly to a location that you know the coordinates of. Just choose the Go To Lat/Lon item in the View menu and enter the coordinates.

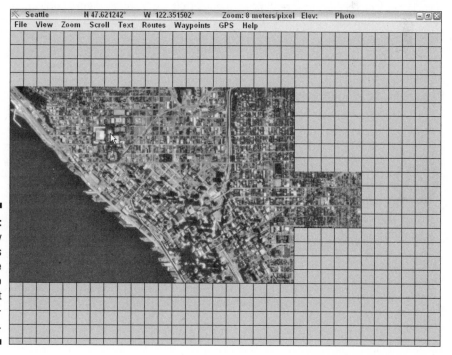

Figure 14-4:
The gray squares indicate where map data hasn't been downloaded.

USAPhotoMaps has two display modes: aerial photo and topographic map. When you download data to fill in the gray squares, only data for the particular mode that you're in is downloaded. For example, if you're viewing an aerial photo, only new aerial photo data is downloaded.

Zooming in and out

You can zoom in and out on an aerial photo or map to see more detail or get a larger, big picture view. For zooming, use these keys:

- ✔ **Zoom in:** Press Page Down or the plus (+) key.
- ✔ **Zoom out:** Press Page Up or the minus/dash (–) key.

The current zoom level appears in the window title bar, so you always know how far you've zoomed in or out.

The zoom level on the window title bar displays the resolution of the image. If the resolution is 4 meters-per-pixel, each *pixel* (picture element) onscreen represents an object 4 meters in size. (Remember that a *meter* is roughly a yard.) Smaller numbers mean higher resolution and greater detail. For example, 1 meter-per-pixel resolution means that you can distinguish objects on the ground that are one meter in size. Figure 14-5 shows a 2 meter-per-pixel aerial photo.

How far you can zoom in and out on an image depends on what type of map you're viewing.

- ✔ **Topographic maps:** 4, 8, 16, or 32 meters-per-pixel
- ✔ **Aerial photos:** 1, 2, 4, 8, 16, 32, or 64 meters-per-pixel

If you're switching back and forth between aerial photos and topographic maps, use either a 4 or an 8 meters-per-pixel zoom level. This will give you close to a one-to-one size representation of features on the aerial photo and the topographic map.

Enhancing contrast

One of the things you'll notice as you start to view aerial photos is that the contrast might be lighter or darker with certain images. This has to do with the amount of sunlight when the photo was taken and the background color of the terrain.

Figure 14-5:
The aerial photograph of Seattle viewed at 2 meter-per-pixel resolution.

To enhance less-than-optimal contrast, USAPhotoMaps has a nifty feature that lets you adjust the contrast of the photos displayed onscreen by either lightening or darkening them. This can really enhance detail in a photo.

You can control the contrast of a photo by using these keys:

- ✔ **Lighten:** Press the B key.
- ✔ **Darken:** Press the D key.

You can also set contrast by selecting Brightness from the View menu, including restoring the contrast back to its default setting.

Entering text

After you have an aerial photo displayed, you can add text labels to different features when the image is displayed at the 1- or 2-meter zoom levels. To enter a text label

1. **Move the mouse cursor to the location where you want the text to start.**

2. **Hold down the Shift key.**

3. **Move the cursor in the direction you want the text to be aligned.**

   A line is temporarily drawn as you move the cursor. For example, if you draw a line at a 45-degree angle, the text will flow at a 45-degree angle.

4. **Release the Shift key.**

5. **In the dialog box that appears, type in the text label and click OK.**

   A list of all the text labels is displayed.

   Text in a label is limited to 60 characters and can be edited or deleted by choosing Text⇨List.

You can set the text color by choosing File⇨Preferences⇨Colors. The Color Preference dialog box, which isn't all that intuitive, uses a series of radio buttons that correspond to red, green, and blue values. Your best bet for choosing a color you'd like is to enter some text and then display the Color Preference dialog box. When you select different combinations of color radio buttons, the text you entered changes color.

Creating and Using Multiple Map Files

USAPhotoMaps uses a *map file* to name areas that have downloaded aerial photo or map data. A map file is a bookmark for a general vicinity or location. For example, you might have downloaded aerial photos for the entire Grand Canyon. Instead of scrolling to view photos at each end, you could create two map files, one called North Grand Canyon and the other South Grand Canyon.

To create a map file bookmark

1. **From the File menu, choose New Map File.**

2. **In the New Map dialog box that appears, enter the name of the map file and the coordinates that you'd like to bookmark.**

   Refer to Figure 14-1.

3. **Click OK.**

After you create a map file, select it, and USAPhotoMaps displays the aerial photo or map associated with that area.

To select and display a new map file

1. **From the File menu, choose Open Map File.**
2. **Select the name of the map file to load.**
3. **Click OK.**

The area that you bookmarked is now displayed onscreen.

Map file bookmarks are used to identify a general location. They shouldn't be used for marking a very specific set of coordinates, such as a GPS waypoint.

Saving Aerial Photos

After you have an aerial photo or map displayed onscreen, you can save the image to use with other programs:

✔ **From the File menu:** Choose Copy to Screen.jpg. This saves a copy of the aerial photo or map currently displayed onscreen to a file named `Screen.jpg` in the same folder that USAPhotoMaps is installed in.

✔ **Print Screen:** Press the Print Screen key to save the current image to the Clipboard. If you want to save only a portion of the map or aerial photo that appears onscreen, read Chapter 17 for practical tips on saving and editing images.

✔ **BigJpeg:** Use the BigJpeg utility. Doug Cox has a free utility that creates a single, 1-meter resolution, JPG format graphics file from a photo or map. You define the boundaries of an area you want to save in USAPhotoMaps and then run BigJpeg to create the graphics file. You can download BigJpeg, with complete instructions, at `http://jdmcox.com`.

Saving strategies

After an aerial photo or map is displayed on-screen, that data now resides on your hard drive. USAPhotoMaps doesn't discard old data files as new data is downloaded. If you've already downloaded a series of photos and maps for a geographic area, you don't need to connect to TerraServer-USA again to access that data. The only limitation to the amount of photo and map data you can have is the size of your hard drive.

USAPhotoMaps writes all the data it gets from TerraServer-USA to a single folder, so you can copy that folder and its data to a CD or DVD. This is an excellent way to access aerial photos and maps on a number of different computers that might not have an Internet connection (such as laptops in the field). The USAPhotoMaps online help has instructions on how to do this.

Interfacing with a GPS receiver

Downloading and viewing free aerial photos and maps is pretty cool, but if you have a GPS receiver, USAPhotoMaps has even more features that you can put to use, including

- ✔ **Downloading waypoints, routes, and tracks** from a GPS receiver to overlay on aerial photos and maps. (See Figure 14-6 for an example of an aerial photo with overlaid track data.)

- ✔ **Uploading waypoints and routes** that you've created with USAPhotoMaps to your GPS receiver.

- ✔ **Interfacing USAPhotoMaps to a GPS receiver** for real-time updates of your current position shown on an aerial photo or topographic map.

USAPhotoMaps has a separate help file that covers only GPS-related topics. You'll find comprehensive information on interfacing your GPS receiver to the program and descriptions of GPS-related features. To display the help file, choose Help from the GPS menu.

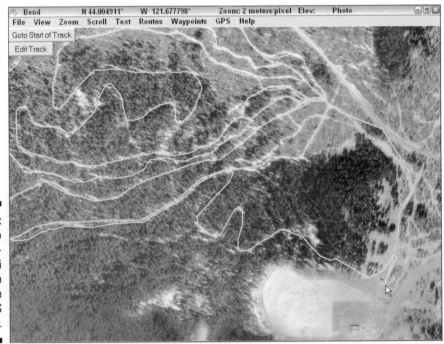

Figure 14-6:
Aerial photo of a cross-country ski area with tracks from a GPS receiver.

Importing tracks

USAPhotoMaps can interface directly with your GPS receiver and download current track data. However, if you want to import existing GPS track logs into USAPhotoMaps, the data needs to be in a comma-delimited text file in the following order:

Track name, UTM zone, Northing, Easting, Hour, Minute, Second, Month, Date, Year, Altitude (in meters)

The first line of the file contains the field information and should exactly read as follows:

```
Track,UTM Zone,UTM Northing,UTM Easting,Hour,Min,Sec,Month,Date,Year,
Alt(Meters)
```

The second line of the file starts listing the track data. An example line of data looks like this:

```
SKI,10,4873291,605991,17,56,30,11,29,2003,1935.27
```

Each line of data must have ten commas and end with a carriage return. The minimum amount of track data required is the UTM zone, Northing, and Easting.

Probably the easiest way to manipulate previously saved track data is to load a comma-delimited file containing the tracks into a spreadsheet and then arrange the columns of data.

Click the mouse to add a waypoint wherever the cursor is currently positioned. You'll be prompted to enter a description and a name (to identify the waypoint if you upload it to a GPS receiver). The waypoint will be displayed as a dot on the aerial photo or the map. Right-click the mouse button to display a list of waypoints.

Reviewing Other Aerial Photo Software

USAPhotoMaps isn't the only program that uses TerraServer-USA data to display aerial photos and maps. Other mapping utilities have the same basic functionality with additional features. These programs are inexpensive, ranging from free to around $60. If you like USAPhotoMaps, take the time to download and try a few of these programs to see whether they meet your mapping needs.

TerraClient

Bill Friedrich's TerraClient is a free, easy-to-use Windows program that displays TerraServer-USA aerial photos and maps. It doesn't interface with GPS receivers or use GPS data, but it does have two features that make it ideal for beginning map users:

- ✔ **Easy location lookup:** Instead of knowing the exact coordinates of the area you want to view, enter a place name and watch TerraClient return a list of possible matches. To view the aerial photo, click the one you're interested in.

- ✔ **Superimposed maps:** This is a very slick feature that allows you to superimpose a topographic map on top of an aerial photo (see Figure 14-7 for an example). You can control the transparency of the overlay so that only a faded, ghostlike image of the map appears on top of the aerial photograph. This is very useful for quickly identifying features on aerial photos.

TerraClient has an extremely user-friendly interface, and you can be up and running the program in a matter of minutes. You can download TerraClient at `http://billfriedrich.tripod.com`.

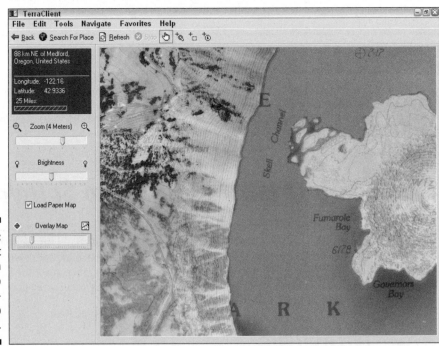

Figure 14-7:
TerraClient showing an aerial photo with topographic map overlay.

TopoFusion

Scott and Alan Morris, brothers and computer science graduate students, weren't satisfied with the various Windows mapping programs on the market, so they wrote their own. Both are avid mountain bikers, GPS users, and outdoor recreationists; the features in their program reflect this. Some of TopoFusion's features include

- ✔ Optimized graphics routines for fast map display
- ✔ Terrain profiles of GPS tracks
- ✔ Multiple track file support for constructing trail networks
- ✔ Map digital photo support by determining the location where a photo was taken by correlating the photo time-stamps with those of the track points
- ✔ Trip playback mode that replays your travel route and provides statistics
- ✔ Combining aerial photos with topographic maps for composite images

The Morris brothers are constantly adding new and useful features to the program and have an online support forum. If you're using a GPS receiver as part of a trail-mapping project or you are a serious outdoor enthusiast, the advanced features of TopoFusion should put it high on your list.

To download a free demo version of TopoFusion and get more information about the program, go to www.topofusion.com. (See the demo version in Figure 14-8.)

ExpertGPS

TopoGrafix is a software company that produces GPS and mapping programs. ExpertGPS is an extensive waypoint, route, and track management system with mapping capabilities grafted on top of it. (See Figure 14-9 for ExpertGPS displaying a waypoint list and overlaying waypoints and routes on an aerial photo.)

ExpertGPS has a large number of features. In fact, at first glance, the extensive features and user interface can be a little intimidating. However, if you're a GPS power user with a large collection of waypoints and route data, it's definitely worth spending some time working with the program to see whether it meets your needs.

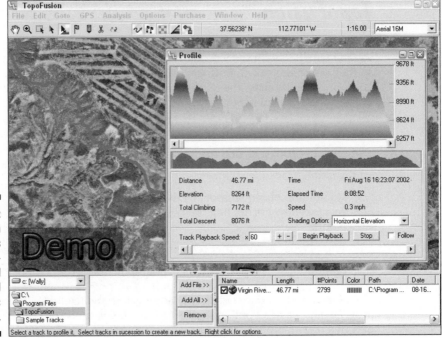

Figure 14-8:
TopoFusion
displays
TerraServer-
USA aerial
photos and
topographic
maps.

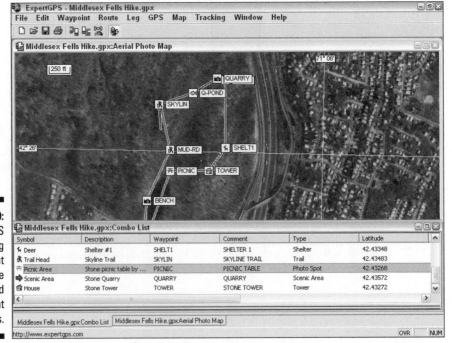

Figure 14-9:
ExpertGPS
showing
waypoint
database
and overlaid
waypoint
and routes.

To download a fully functional, 31-day trial version of ExpertGPS, go to www. expertgps.com.

QuakeMap

QuakeMap is written by Sergei Grichine and was originally designed to download worldwide earthquake data from various Internet sources and display the information on maps. The program has since evolved into a general purpose, mapping utility that uses TerraServer-USA data. You can use GPS data with QuakeMap, and if you're a geocacher (see Chapter 7), the program has several specialized features designed for the sport.

To download a demo version of QuakeMap (see Figure 14-10 for a screenshot of QuakeMap displaying the location of an earthquake on an aerial photo) visit www.earthquakemap.com.

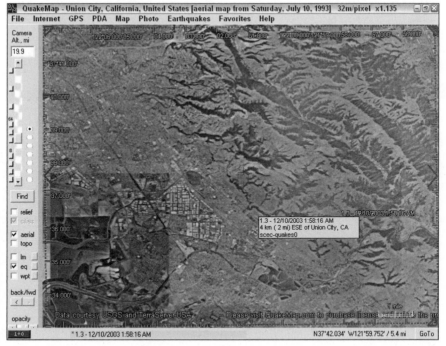

Figure 14-10: QuakeMap showing an aerial photo of a recent California earthquake.

Chapter 15

Creating and Using Digital Maps with OziExplorer

OziExplorer is a popular, Windows shareware program that you can use to create your own digital maps. OziExplorer is widely used by recreationists, land managers, and public safety agencies. The program doesn't come bundled with a set of maps per se; instead, you can use it to view maps that are commercially or freely available on the Internet in a number of different data formats, from which you can create your own do-it-yourself, digital maps. In this chapter, I describe some of OziExplorer's features and then I walk you through the process of creating digital maps from scanned paper maps.

Discovering OziExplorer Features

OziExplorer is a powerful and versatile mapping program developed by Des Newman. (Newman hails from Australia, and *Ozi* is slang for *Australia* — get it?). Newman originally wrote the program for personal use during four-wheel-drive trips in the Australian outback. He released OziExplorer as shareware, which has evolved into a sophisticated mapping tool that's constantly updated. Some of the program's key features are that it

▸ **Interfaces with GPS receivers:** OziExplorer can communicate with just about every GPS receiver on the market, allowing you to upload and download waypoints, routes, and tracks to and from GPS receivers and PCs. (For more on waypoints, routes, and tracks, see Chapter 4.)

✔ **Works in many languages:** Localized versions of OziExplorer are available in a number of different languages, including English, German, French, Spanish, and Italian.

✔ **Provides real-time tracking:** If you have a laptop connected to a GPS receiver, OziExplorer displays a *moving map* with your real-time, current position and other travel information. (For more on using a laptop in tandem with a GPS receiver, see Chapter 9.)

✔ **Is easy to use:** OziExplorer boasts a large number of features, such as annotating maps and extensive import and export capabilities, all of which are easy to use. Figure 15-1 shows a demo map that comes with OziExplorer and the program's toolbar and menu-based user interface.

✔ **Supports an extensive number of map formats:** OziExplorer can access many popular digital map data formats (such as *DRG,* a Digital Raster Graphics map) and can associate georeferenced data with common graphics file types. For example, you can take a file that you created in Paint or some other graphic program and turn it into a *smart map* (a map where geographic coordinates are associated with individual pixels). Loading graphics files and calibrating the data to create digital maps are discussed in upcoming sections of this chapter.

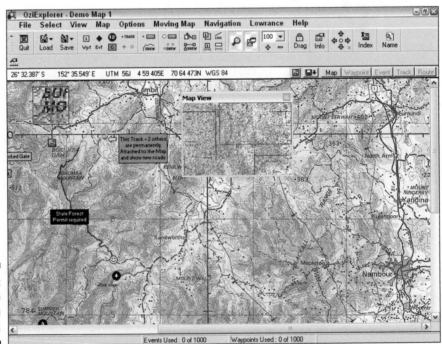

Figure 15-1:
A demo
map in
OziExplorer.

The best way to find out about OziExplorer's features is to download the program and try it. (OziExplorer works with PCs capable of running Windows 95 through XP.). You can find it at www.oziexplorer.com. Two versions of the program come in the install package:

- ✔ **Trial:** The trial version is a limited version of OziExplorer that has all the program features enabled, except the program can't

    - Communicate with GPS receivers

    - Save or load waypoints, routes, or tracks

    - Save maps as image files

    - Run for more than an hour at a time

- ✔ **Shareware:** The shareware version has a number of features disabled and has the following limitations:

    - Only bitmap (BMP) images can be imported as maps (as opposed to many graphics file types in the registered version).

    - Only two points can be used to calibrate a map, reducing the potential accuracy. (Up to nine points are available in the registered version.)

    - Limited support is available for map projections, grid systems, and datums (compared with extensive support in the full version).

Between these two programs available in the install package, you'll be able to get a feel for all OziExplorer's capabilities. And when you register the shareware version, the full monty of features is enabled. The $85 registration fee is a nominal investment considering the many features that the full version of OziExplorer offers.

If you're looking for a street and road navigation program, OziExplorer isn't the best choice. Ozi is more suited for adventures off the beaten path. If you need a program that helps you find the best route between two addresses on streets and highways, you're much better off using some of the commercial mapping programs that I describe in Chapter 12.

For more practical information on OziExplorer, including troubleshooting tips, check out the popular Yahoo! Groups e-mail list and forum devoted to the program at groups.yahoo.com/group/OziUsers-L.

In addition to OziExplorer, Des Newman also has two other related mapping programs:

✔ **OziExplorer3D:** This program is used in conjunction with OziExplorer to display maps in three dimensions. OziExplorer writes elevation data to a file, which OziExplorer3D uses to display a 3-D representation of the map. OziExplorer3D is priced at $30.

✔ **OziExplorerCE:** OziExplorerCE is moving-map software for Pocket PC (formerly known as Windows CE) PDAs. You create maps and plan trips with OziExplorer on your PC and then download the map data to your PDA to use with OziExplorerCE. When you connect your PDA to a GPS receiver, the program retrieves GPS data and displays your current location on a map. The PDA version of Ozi costs $30.

To discover more about the features of these two programs and download demonstration versions, go to www.oziexplorer.com.

Moving from Paper to Digital Maps

OziExplorer supports a number of different digital map types that use *georeferenced data* (information that allows a program to precisely identify locations and coordinates on a map). But one of the program's most powerful features is its ability to turn your own graphics files into georeferenced maps. This means if you have a paper map, you can scan it, load it into OziExplorer, and effectively make it an electronic (digital) map. This is a three-step process:

1. **Scan the map.**

   Use a scanner to create a digital image of the paper map. Stitch individual map pieces, if necessary.

2. **Edit the map.**

   Make changes to the scanned map before it's used.

3. **Calibrate the map.**

   Load the edited map into OziExplorer and associate georeferenced data with the map image.

The following sections explore the above three steps in further detail.

Scanning and calibrating your own maps can be fairly time consuming and sometimes frustrating if you can't seem to get the map coordinates to match up with reality. Some maps are definitely easier to calibrate than others. If you're not technically inclined or are somewhat impatient, you'll probably want to stick to importing maps that are already georeferenced, such as freely available United States Geological Survey (USGS) DRG topographic maps. (See Chapter 21 for places on the Internet you can download free maps.)

Step 1: Scan the map

The first step when converting a paper map to a digital map is to scan the map and turn it into a graphics file. You don't need an expensive, high-end scanner to accomplish this task; most any color scanner will work.

If you want to scan a large map — say, anything bigger than a legal size piece of paper — consider literally cutting it up into pieces that will fit on your scanner. (8.5 x 11 inches works well.) Instead of using a pair of scissors, use a paper cutter, such as those found at copy centers, to ensure that you end up with straight cuts. The straight cuts are important for accurately aligning the map on your scanner. Although you can scan a large map one portion at a time without cutting it, it's more of a challenge to get the edges lined up when you stitch them together as I discuss next.

Here are some tips to improve your map scanning:

- **Use medium dpi:** Scanning the map between 125–200 dots per inch (dpi) is good enough; you don't need to scan at higher resolutions typically used for reproducing photos.

- **Use color photo scanning:** Most scanning software has different settings for different types of documents you want to scan, such as text, line drawings, and photographs. Select the color photograph option to retain the most detail. However, remember that most maps don't have millions of colors like photographs, so if your scanning software supports it, use a 256-color setting.

- **Watch edge alignment:** Place the to-be-scanned map directly on the scanner, ensuring that the edges are aligned directly against the scanner bed with no gaps. You need to keep the paper map as square as possible to reduce distortion during a scan.

- **Prevent edge distortion:** To help keep the map edges pressed flat, leave the scanner cover open and use a book or something heavy to set on top of the map. The edges are typically where the most distortion occurs during scanning because they tend to lift up.

- **Experiment with settings:** Try a couple of experimental scans first, changing the brightness and contrast settings. If you're going to be scanning a number of maps over a period of time, write down the settings that gave you the best output so you can use them next time.

- **Save the final scan as BMP:** When you're ready to produce a final scan of the map, initially save it as bitmap (BMP) format file. This produces an image that's as close to the original map as possible; bitmap files aren't compressed like JPG and other graphics file formats. Bitmap files do take up a lot of memory and disk space, but after you edit a file, you can save it as another graphics format that's smaller in size.

OziExplorer and World War I

The 1980s movie *Gallipoli* recounted the Australian experience of fighting the Turks during World War I. Although long before the time of computers and mapping software, WWI also has a link to OziExplorer.

Howard Anderson wrote a fascinating article on using OziExplorer to locate old World War I trench lines in France and Belgium. The remains of the trenches are long gone, but by using old maps from the period, scanning them, and adding georeferenced data, Anderson was able to clearly determine where the trenches were dug during the early 1900s.

After he had scanned and georeferenced the old military maps, Anderson used OziExplorer to draw GPS tracks on personally created digital

maps to trace the outlines of the trenches. He also used waypoints to identify military and land features. Anderson then took the tracks and waypoints and overlaid them on a modern map in OziExplorer. This revealed where the long-ago war emplacements once stood. Anderson's last step was to visit France with a GPS receiver and his old and modern maps. He found that, with relative accuracy, he could stand on the site of a trench where his grandfather had fought over 85 years ago.

To read Anderson's complete account, which has historical insights as well as his experiences in using OziExplorer, visit the Western Front Association's Web site at www.western frontassociation.com/thegreatwar/articles/trenchmaps/stand.htm.

If you have a map that's made up of multiple image files, such as a large map cut up into a series of smaller maps, you'll need to *stitch* them and a single, large image. Commercial graphics program such as Adobe Photoshop and Jasc Paint Shop Pro have commands for combining files. You can also manually stitch together images with Microsoft Paint by using the Paste From command of the Edit menu. Here's a link to a great tutorial on stitching together scanned images: www.sibleyfineart.com/index.htm?tutorial—join-scans.htm.

Step 2: Edit the map

After you successfully scan the map, make any last-minute changes to the image. This could include

- ✔ Adjusting the brightness and contrast to make the map more readable.
- ✔ Adding symbols or text information.
- ✔ Removing the white space (or *collar* as it's known in map-speak) that surrounds the map.

Use your favorite graphics program to make any final edits to the map image. After you're through, save the map as a TIFF, PNG, or JPG file to reduce how much disk and memory space the image takes up. (These compressed file formats are more space-efficient and memory-efficient.)

The shareware version of OziExplorer can load only BMP images. Because bitmaps aren't compressed, the entire file must be loaded into memory, which can slow down the performance of computers that don't have much RAM.

Step 3: Calibrate the map

After you scan, edit, and save your map, one more step is left before you can start using the map with OziExplorer. At this point, your map is simply a graphics file. You can use Microsoft Paint or any another graphics program to view, edit, and print the map, but you want to turn the image into a *smart map* to take advantage of OziExplorer's features.

This involves calibrating the map, which involves linking georeferenced data with the map image so that each pixel in the map has a geographic coordinate associated with it. When a map has georeferenced data, you can

- ✔ Move the cursor on the map, and OziExplorer will accurately report the coordinates of the cursor in latitude and longitude or UTM (Universal Transverse Mercator; read more about these in Chapter 2).

- ✔ Draw lines on the map to measure distance.

- ✔ Calculate the size of areas.

- ✔ Track and display your current position on the map when the computer is connected to a GPS receiver.

- ✔ Transfer GPS waypoints, routes, and tracks between the map and a GPS receiver.

When you calibrate a map with OziExplorer, the georeferenced data isn't embedded directly inside the image file. OziExplorer creates a separate MAP file (.map) that contains the following information:

- ✔ The location of the map image file
- ✔ The map datum
- ✔ The map projection
- ✔ Map calibration data

Inside a MAP file, the file is in text format and can be viewed with any word processor.

Calibration requires you to identify a series of points on the map with known coordinates. Depending on the number of points that you select, as well as the map datum and projection, OziExplorer performs different mathematical calculations to link coordinate information with the map image.

To demonstrate the process of calibrating a map with OziExplorer, use a scanned copy of a 1:100,000 scale USGS topographic map. (Check out Chapter 21 for sources of free maps.)

FUGAWI

FUGAWI is a popular Windows mapping program with some of the same basic features as OziExplorer.

Like OziExplorer, FUGAWI can read a number of different map formats with georeferenced data as well as use do-it-yourself, calibrated, scanned image maps. The program can also interface with a GPS receiver and handle waypoints, routes, and tracks. See a FUGAWI map in the figure here.

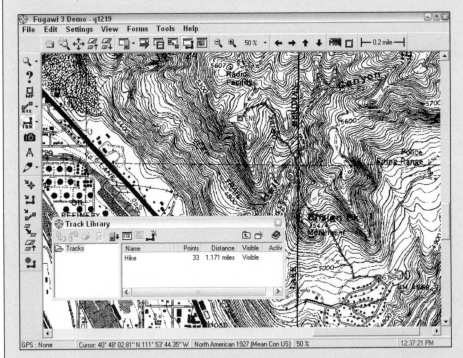

Comparing FUGAWI with OziExplorer, you'll see that FUGAWI isn't shareware, it's priced a little higher, and it comes bundled with a base set of maps.

FUGAWI and OziExplorer both have extremely loyal user bases. If you check around the Internet, you'll see some strong feelings expressed about why one product is better than the other. (I think OziExplorer has a better user interface and supports a few more advanced features.) If you're considering FUGAWI or OziExplorer, download the free demo versions of each program and see which one you prefer.

For more information about FUGAWI and to download the demo version of the software, visit www.fugawi.com.

Some digital maps have georeferenced data embedded directly into the map image as tags or come with associated files that contain the reference data. (A common example is a DRG map.) OziExplorer can use these maps without going through the calibration process that I describe next. Check the OziExplorer Web site or the program's online help for a full list of these supported map types.

Choosing calibration points

To associate georeferenced data with your scanned map, you'll need to find a series of points on the map with coordinates you know. If you can't assign a latitude and longitude (or UTM) position to a few features on the map, you won't be able to calibrate the map.

Here are some ways in which you can pick calibration points:

- ✔ If the scanned map has a collar with coordinates printed on the edge, use the coordinate marks. USGS topographic maps are easy to calibrate because each corner is marked with the latitude and longitude.

- ✔ Use another mapping program (such as those described in Chapter 14) to get the coordinates of a feature on a map that you want to calibrate. This can be a man-made feature (such as a building or a bridge) or a natural feature (such as a mountain peak).

- ✔ If you're in the United States, you can use National Geodetic Survey datasheets to identify points on the ground that have known coordinates associated with them. Visit www.ngs.noaa.gov/cgi-bin/datasheet.prl to access datasheets for your area.

- ✔ Visit a location that's clearly identifiable on the map, and use your GPS receiver to record the coordinates for that location. Road intersections make good calibration points. (Just watch out for traffic!)

The number of points that you select for calibration depends on the map and how much accuracy you want. Use the following guidelines to determine how many points you should use:

- ✔ **Two points:** If you're limited to two calibration points, select two points at opposite corners of the map. (This is the only calibration method available in the shareware version of OziExplorer.)

  If you have a registered version of OziExplorer, always choose at least three calibration points, such as three corners of a map.

- ✔ **Three or four points:** Selecting three or four points (such as the map corners) provides better map accuracy and should be all you need for calibrating most maps.

- ✔ **Five or more points:** If the latitude and longitude lines are curved, if the paper map has been folded, or if the scan of the map is distorted, use more than four points. OziExplorer supports up to nine calibration points; generally, the more points you choose, the better the accuracy with any map that might have distortions that could impact accuracy.

Try to spread your calibration points out over as much of the map as possible. If you clump the points together in a small area, the accuracy won't be as precise.

After you look at the map and determine which calibration points you're going to use, write down the coordinates and then double-check that they're correct. Entering calibration points with incorrect coordinates is a common cause of map accuracy troubles.

In Figure 15-2, the example USGS topographic map was scanned in pieces, stitched, and then saved as a JPG file. The original paper map had the latitude and longitude coordinates in all four corners, so I use these coordinates as the calibration points. (This map is too large to reproduce here, so note that you can see the coordinates only in the upper-left corner.)

Figure 15-2:
Corner coordinates on a map make good calibration points.

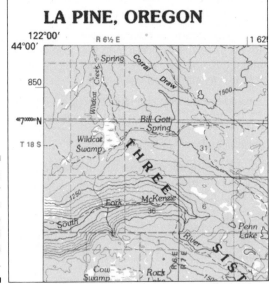

Setting calibration points

After you decide which points you'll use to calibrate the map, load the map image file into OziExplorer and do some georeferencing. Here are the steps to take:

1. **Select Load and Calibrate Map Image from the File menu; a file dialog box is displayed.**

2. **Select the location of the map image file and click Open.**

   The map appears in a setup window, as shown in Figure 15-3.

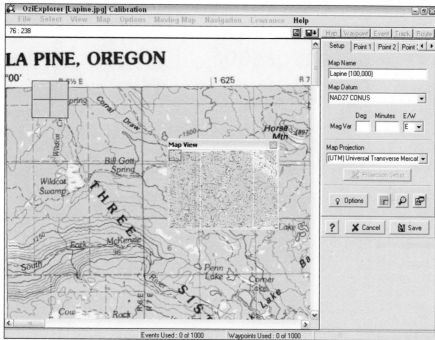

Figure 15-3:
The
OziExplorer
setup win-
dow with a
loaded map.

3. Enter the map's name, datum, and projection.

Information provided on the example paper map says the datum is
NAD 27 and the projection is Universal Transverse Mercator. Enter
those values. (To read about map datums and projections, check out
Chapter 2.)

If you don't know the map datum, make an educated guess or use WGS
84. If you don't know the map projection, try using Latitude/Longitude.
Both of these settings can be changed later if they end up incorrect.

Entering the wrong map datum and projection can severely affect the
accuracy of your map. If you don't know the datum and projection,
your best bet when calibrating the map is to match coordinates that
you recorded with your GPS receiver to features that you can clearly
identify on the map; then use the WGS 84 datum and Latitude/Longitude
projection.

4. For each calibration point (up to nine points), repeat the following steps:

a. *Click the point's tab in the setup window.*

Figure 15-4 shows Point 1.

b. *Move the cursor on the map over the point.*

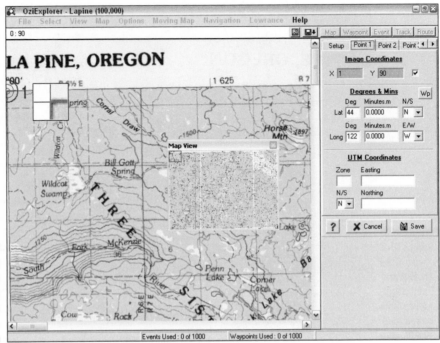

Figure 15-4:
The first calibration point setup window.

The cursor turns into a cross-hair icon with the number 1 next to it. A zoom window shows a magnified image of the cursor location allowing you to precisely place the cursor over the calibration point.

c. *Click the left mouse button to select the calibration point.*

A bull's-eye appears over the calibration point.

After the bull's-eye appears onscreen, you can move the calibration point to a new location by holding down the Shift key and using the navigational arrow keys. This gives you a fine level of control over placing the calibration point.

d. *Enter either the latitude and longitude or the UTM coordinates for the calibration point.*

OziExplorer expects the latitude and longitude coordinates to be expressed in degrees and decimal minutes. If your coordinates are in another latitude and longitude format, you can quickly convert them at this Web site: http://jeeep.com/details/coord.

5. **When you're finished, click Save.**

OziExplorer prompts you for a name and where to save the MAP file. You're now ready to start using your imported map. The example scanned-and-calibrated map being used with tracks and waypoints is show in Figure 15-5.

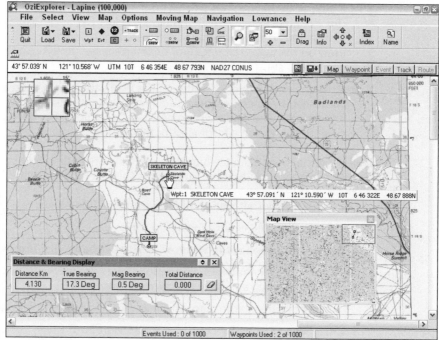

Figure 15-5:
A scanned
and
calibrated
OziExplorer
map with
waypoints
and tracks.

Maps that are made for general information purposes (such as park visitor maps or maps in textbooks) are usually difficult to calibrate correctly because they don't have the level of accuracy as navigation or survey maps do. (In fact, they're more of diagrams — not maps — because they don't have projections.) The actual locations of features shown on the map might not be correct, and distances and proportions might not be accurate.

Checking your work

After you load and calibrate a scanned map, always check to make sure that your calibration was correct. Here are some ways to do this:

✔ Select Grid Line Setup from the Map menu. This allows you to overlay latitude and longitude grid lines over the map. The overlaid grid lines should match with the grid lines on the map or the coordinate marks on the map edges.

On USGS topographic maps, don't get latitude and longitude lines confused with the more predominant Township and Range lines. (To find out the difference between latitude and longitude and Township and Range, read Chapter 2.)

✔ If your scanned map has a ruler printed on the map that shows distance (for example, in one-mile increments), select Distance Display from the View menu. This allows you to measure the distance of a line that you draw on the map. The length of the map's ruler should match whatever distance is shown when you measure it.

✔ Move the cursor over a feature on the map with known coordinates. (The coordinates can come from a GPS receiver, another mapping program, or a gazetteer.) The cursor coordinates in OziExplorer should be relatively close to the known coordinates of the feature.

If any coordinate or distance numbers seem significantly off, there's likely a problem with your calibration. To address this, do the following:

1. **Choose Check Calibration of Map from the File menu.**

   This displays the calibration setup window.

2. **In the calibration setup window, verify or change calibration data.**

   • Make sure that your calibration points are in the proper location on the map and have the correct coordinates.

   • Try changing the map datum and/or projection to different values.

3. **Click Save to save the results to a different MAP file.**

   The newly calibrated map is loaded and is displayed onscreen.

4. **Check whether the calibration is more accurate.**

   If the calibration isn't sufficiently accurate, repeat these steps.

Chapter 16

Going Three Dimensional with 3DEM

*T*he freeware program *3DEM* is a popular 3-D mapping program for Windows. In this chapter, I show you how easy it is to make 3-D maps of your own with 3DEM's features and freely available Digital Elevation Model (DEM) data. You'll discover how to create basic 3-D elevation maps, navigate inside the maps, and overlay topographic maps on top of the 3-D images to create some pretty stunning, professional-looking maps. At the end of the chapter, I review several other 3-D mapping programs that are similar to 3DEM.

Comparing 2-D and 3-D Maps

A 2-D digital map can give you a pretty good sense of place (see Chapters 13 and 19 for examples of what 2-D contour maps look like), but a 3-D map can really help you understand your surroundings. You can clearly see where mountains rise up from the flats and canyons sink down from plateaus. 3-D mapping programs display terrain features by either

▶ **Using shading** to show elevation changes (also known as *shaded relief*)

▶ **Creating layered models** of the terrain, just like a layer cake, with each layer representing a different elevation

With a 3-D map, instead of relying on contour lines to understand the terrain, the land features jump out at you and are immediately obvious. Professional map users such as surveyors, land managers, and public safety officials use 3-D maps in addition to 2-D maps because they provide a different perspective when looking at landforms. With a 3-D map, it's also much easier to show what the terrain is really like to someone who's unfamiliar with reading contour maps.

Discovering 3DEM Capabilities

3DEM allows you to visualize terrain in three dimensions. Its name is a play on words, referring to *three-dimensional* as well as *Digital Elevation Model* (DEM), which is the data the program uses to create maps. With 3DEM, you can

✔ Create and save 3-D maps based on elevation data.

✔ Change the view and perspective of 3-D maps.

✔ Overlay topographic maps on top of 3-D images.

✔ Identify coordinates on maps.

Developer Richard Horne made the program straightforward and easy to use. It's fast because it uses the SGI/Microsoft OpenGL libraries for image rendering.

Time to put 3DEM to work. In the following sections, I use 3DEM to create some three-dimensional maps. If you want to follow along with the examples, point your Web browser to www.visualizationsoftware.com/3dem.html and download 3DEM.

You might be wondering why the program icon associated with 3DEM is a pair of sunglasses with one red lens and one blue lens. 3DEM has an option to display images that look even more three-dimensional if you're wearing special 3-D glasses with red and blue lenses. (Yup, just like cheesy movies such as that 50s horror classic, *House of Wax,* where you wear the same kind of glasses, and it looks like Vincent Price is jumping out of the screen at you.) If you don't have a pair of 3-D glasses lying around the office, visit www.3dglassesonline.com where you can get a pair for the price of a self-addressed envelope and postage.

Using DEM Data to Create a Map

The first step in using 3DEM is to load a DEM file. *DEM* (Digital Elevation Model) is a file format that contains elevation data. DEM files are produced by the United States Geological Survey (USGS) and cover most all land areas in the U.S. Frugal mapmakers can retrieve free DEM files from many sites on the Internet.

Chapter 21 covers Web sites where you can download DEM files and other free map data. The 3DEM online Help also has several sources for no-cost DEM data. In your search for DEM data, be aware that elevation data can often be found in Spatial Data Transfer Standard (SDTS) format files. You'll need the free utility SDTS2DEM to convert SDTS data into DEM files that can be used with the programs discussed in this chapter. You can download SDTS2DEM at www.cs.arizona.edu/topovista/sdts2dem.

For this example, I use a DEM associated with the area around Mount St. Helens, the volcano in Washington State that erupted in 1980. Mount St. Helens is interesting because instead of blowing straight up, it blew out the side. This (and a small dome in the center of the crater) makes the still active volcano a good candidate to view three-dimensionally.

To follow along as I create a 3-D map, download the DEM file used in this example from the University of Washington's Department of Geology Web site. Here's how:

1. **Go to** http://duff.geology.washington.edu/data/watiles/index.html.

2. **Click the Hoquiam grid.**

3. **Click the 10-meter DEMs link.**

   Just a quick note about DEMs. You'll often see references to 10-meter DEMs and 30-meter DEMs. These numbers refer to the elevation data resolution: The smaller the number, the higher the resolution. For example, with a 10-meter DEM, the ground spacing between elevation points is 10 meters.

4. **Click the Mount Saint Helens grid on the map (in the lower-right corner).**

   A Zip file (f2323.zip) downloads to your computer. The file is a bit over 2MB and contains a compressed version of the DEM file for Mount St. Helens.

5. **Uncompress the Zip file to access the DEM file.**

   If you're using Windows XP, double-click the Zip file to open it, and then copy the f2323.dem file and paste it in a folder to uncompress and save it.

   If you're not using Windows XP, you need a utility to uncompress the Zip file and extract the DEM data. I like the free file archiver 7-Zip, which is available at www.7-zip.org.

After you have a DEM file to work with, load it into 3DEM. This is simple:

1. **Run 3DEM.**

2. **Choose Load Terrain Model from the File menu.**

3. **In the DEM File Type dialog box, make sure that USGS DEM is selected and then click OK.**

4. **Select the DEM file you want to use (in this case, the** f2323.dem **file from the preceding steps) and then click Open.**

3DEM displays a message that the DEM file is loading. After a few seconds (or minutes if you have a slow computer), a shaded image of the DEM file is displayed, which looks like you're viewing the location from directly overhead.

The image created with the Mount St. Helens DEM file is shown in Figure 16-1. The volcano crater is clearly visible, with the side of the mountain gone from the eruption. You can clearly see the landforms that surround the volcano, and shading is used to show terrain relief.

The DEM data is *georeferenced*. When you move the cursor around the map, 3DEM displays the latitude, longitude, and elevation of the spot beneath the cursor.

Click the right mouse button and hold it down while drawing a line on the map. When you release the mouse button, an elevation profile window is displayed that shows a chart with the elevation profile of the line you drew.

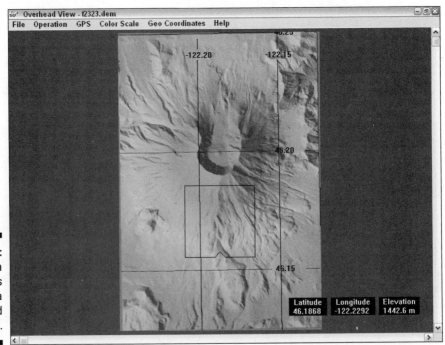

Figure 16-1:
DEM data
converts
into a
shaded
relief map.

Creating a 3-D Map

When you have the DEM data loaded into 3DEM, you can create three-dimensional scenes of the area that's displayed. It's dangerous (and illegal) to venture inside the Mount St. Helens crater in real life, but with 3DEM, you can get a better idea of what the crater looks like from inside.

Defining the display area

To define the area to display in 3-D, first look on the map for a square with a notch in the bottom of it. This is the View tool.

✔ The notch represents the direction you're looking.

✔ The square is the area to render in 3-D.

To use the View tool, follow these steps:

1. **Move the cursor to where you'd like the view to originate; then click.**

   This moves the view square to that location.

2. **Move the cursor to one of the corners of the view square, and then click and hold down the left mouse button.**

   You can resize the square and rotate its position by moving the cursor.

3. **Release the mouse button after you define the view area.**

3-D display troubleshooting

If you get an error message, the system crashes, or the 3-D image isn't rendered correctly, you probably have an issue with your graphics card.

✔ Check for any updated drivers for the card on the manufacturer's Web site. If you find updated drivers, install them.

✔ If that doesn't solve the problem, turn off any *accelerator options* on the graphics card in the Windows Display dialog box. The graphics card might conflict with OpenGL 3-D rendering libraries that come with the program.

See the 3DEM online Help for additional details on troubleshooting drawing problems.

Creating a 3-D scene

After selecting the area, you're now ready to create a 3-D scene:

1. **Choose 3-D Scene from the Operation menu.**

2. **In the Terrain Projection Parameters dialog box that opens (as shown in Figure 16-2), enter options to change the appearance of the 3-D image.**

   For this example, use the default settings.

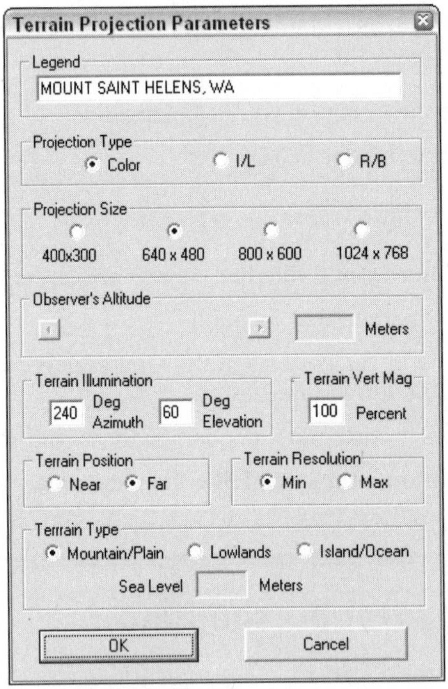

Figure 16-2: Change the 3-D image appearance here.

3. **Click OK.**

   The Terrain Colors dialog box opens (as shown in Figure 16-3). The settings in this dialog box allow you to change the colors of the 3-D image, such as associating different colors with different elevations. For this example, use the default settings.

4. **Click OK.**

   3DEM opens a separate window, displaying a smoothed, 3-D image of the view that you selected. In this example, Figure 16-4 shows the view inside the Mount St. Helens crater.

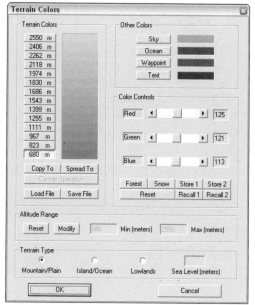

Figure 16-3:
Change the
3-D image
color set-
tings here.

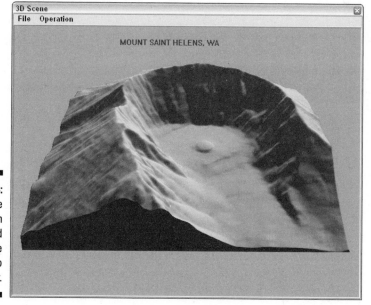

Figure 16-4:
A 3-D image
created from
the selected
view, inside
the volcano
crater.

Manipulating the 3-D Scene Window

After you create a 3-D map in 3DEM, you can move around the scene to change your view. With this way-cool feature, you can look at a location from a number of different perspectives. To move around the scene, do the following:

1. **Choose Change Position from the Operation menu.**

   The Rotate or Shift Scene dialog box opens (see Figure 16-5), in which you can rotate or shift the scene.

2. **Click the control buttons to move the 3-D scene until you are satisfied with the image.**

   Control buttons are described after these instructions.

3. **Finish up by either**

   • Clicking OK when you're done.

   • Clicking Reset to restore the scene to its original appearance.

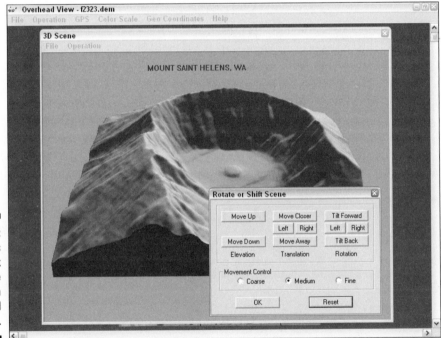

Figure 16-5:
Use this dialog box to move around a 3DEM scene.

Using the scene control buttons isn't that intuitive from just looking at the dialog box. Here's a brief description of what each of the buttons does:

✔ **Elevation:** These buttons control where the image appears in the scene window.

  • **Move Up:** Moves the image toward the top of the window

  • **Move Down:** Moves the image toward the bottom of the window

✔ **Translation:** The Translation buttons zoom in and out and move the image to the sides.

  • **Move Closer:** Zooms in on the image

  • **Left:** Moves the image to the left of the window

  • **Right:** Moves the image to the right of the window

  • **Move Away:** Zooms out from the image

✔ **Rotation:** The Rotation buttons control the angle from which you view the image.

  • **Tilt Forward:** Moves the image so you look at it from more of an overhead view.

  • **Left:** Rotates the image to the left.

  • **Right:** Rotates the image to the right.

  • **Tilt Back:** Moves the image so you look at it from more of a direct, on-the-ground view. You can also use this button to look at the underside of the image.

✔ **Movement Control:** These radio buttons determine how much movement occurs when you click the control buttons. Movement can be Coarse, Medium, or Fine.

Saving and Printing a 3DEM Scene

After you have the appearance of a 3DEM scene just how you want it, you can save the image to disk or print it. The several different options for saving and printing are all found in the File menu, including

✔ **Save Scene Image:** Saves the image in one of nine different graphics formats, including BMP, JPG, and TIFF.

✔ **Save Large Format Image:** Saves the image as a large format graphics file, up to 6,000 pixels wide; you select the size. If you're creating a map for publication purposes, this option is useful for saving a large image that can be reduced in size yet still retains detail.

✔ **Print Scene Image:** Prints the image.

✔ **Save Rotation Animation:** Rotates the 3-D image 360 degrees and saves the output as an AVI file that can be replayed as a movie with Windows Media Player or other multimedia software.

Overlaying Digital Raster Graphics Data

Using DEM data to create a three-dimensional map is pretty cool, but 3DEM allows you take one step beyond simple terrain modeling. You can also take a USGS topographic map and overlay it on top of the DEM data to create a 3-D topographic map.

To do this, you need a topographic map in Digital Raster Graphics (DRG) format, which is another map data type produced by the USGS. A *DRG file* is a scanned version of a topographic map that has georeferenced data associated with it. DRG maps typically come in the TIFF graphics format.

Downloading a sample DRG

If you've read this chapter to this point, continue with the running example. Download the DRG that's associated with the Mount St. Helens DEM file already loaded into 3DEM. (See the earlier section, "Using DEM Data to Create a Map.") To download the DRG

1. **Go to** `http://duff.geology.washington.edu/data/watiles/index.html`.

2. **Click the Hoquiam grid.**

3. **Click the clipped Digital Raster Graphics link.**

The other link at the Web site, Digital Raster Graphics, contains the complete (unclipped) 7.5 minute topographic map, including the *collar* (the white space border that surrounds the map). 3DEM can remove a DRG file's collar so it isn't displayed in your map; if a clipped version is available, it saves a bit of processing time.

4. **Click the Mount Saint Helens grid on the map (in the lower-right corner).**

The file `046122b2.zip` downloads to your computer. The file is a bit over 3MB and contains a compressed version of the DRG for Mount St. Helens.

5. **Uncompress the Zip file to access the DRG data.**

Three files are inside the Zip file:

- 046122b2.tfw: Each DRG has an accompanying World file that contains georeferenced information. The World file has the same filename as the DRG but typically ends with a .tfw extension.

- 046122b2.tfw83: Another georeferenced data file, this one contains information for using the NAD 83 datum with the map (which is close to WGS 84) instead of the NAD 27 datum typically used with USGS topographic maps. (See Chapter 2 to read about the differences between different map datums.)

- 046122b2.tif: This is the actual DRG map image file.

3DEM uses just the TIFF map image file; you don't need to worry about the other two files.

The TFW files that come with DRGs usually contain redundant georeference information; the same data is embedded in the map image file as a GeoTIFF tag. Depending on the software you're using, the data in the TFW file might take precedence over the embedded data in the image file for georeferencing the map image.

Loading the DRG as an overlay

After you uncompress the DRG file, you can load it into 3DEM. Make sure you have the DEM data loaded first, and then do the following:

1. **Choose Apply Map Overlay from the Operation menu.**

   The Apply Map Overlay dialog box is displayed.

2. **Click the Load button.**

   A file Open dialog box appears.

3. **Select the DRG file you want to overlay (in this case, 046122b2.tif), and then click Open.**

   A message appears asking you to wait while the data is loaded and is prepared for overlaying. When the process is finished, the message Geo Reference Complete appears.

4. **Click the Accept button.**

   3DEM renders the overlay image; a status message appears during overlay generation telling you how many lines are left to process.

   When 3DEM is finished, the overlay map is displayed.

   Instead of showing only a relatively boring terrain elevation map, the topographic map is merged with the DEM data to create a shaded relief map that shows labeled features, contour lines, map grids, and a graphic representation of elevation (as shown in Figure 16-6).

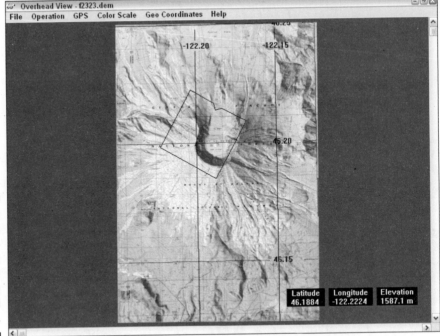

-122.20   -122.15

46.20

46.15

| Latitude | Longitude | Elevation |
| 46.1884 | -122.2224 | 1587.1 m |

Figure 16-6:
Topographic map combined with DEM data showing features and elevation.

You can change the size of the map by choosing Resize Overhead View from the Operation menu. This brings up the Map Scale dialog box, where you can use the slider bar to change the image size. Entering a **1** for the Map Scale value displays the map at a 1:1 ratio. You can move around the map with scroll bars if it's too big to fit in the window.

DRG filenames

So what's with the numbers in the DRG filename? Why couldn't the USGS just have named it after the name of the topographic map (Mount St. Helens) to make things easier? There's actually some logic behind the file-naming convention of DRG map files (called the *o-code,* short for *Ohio-code).* Carve the o46122b2 filename to see what it means:

✔ **46:** 46 degrees of latitude.

✔ **122:** 122 degrees of longitude.

✔ **b:** A row within that latitude and longitude square. (Rows run south to north and are labeled a–h.)

✔ **2:** A column within the latitude and longitude square. (Columns run east to west and are numbered 1–8.)

That makes a little more sense. All USGS DRGs use this standard, which makes it easy for programs to figure out which data files should be used for displaying adjacent maps.

Working with overlay maps

After you create an overlay map, you can print, save, and create 3-D scenes just like with the map made from the DEM data in the preceding section.

In Figure 16-7, you can see a 3-D scene of inside the Mount St. Helens crater with overlaid DRG data. Most of the menu and dialog box commands that I describe in earlier sections of this chapter work the same.

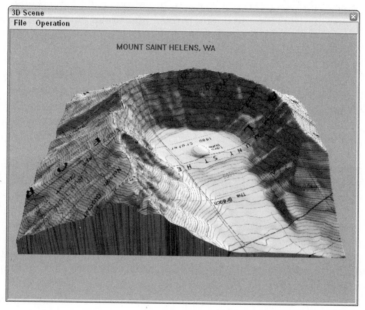

Figure 16-7:
A section of an overlay map displayed as a detailed 3-D scene.

One command that's unique to working with overlay maps displays the topographic map without any relief shading (just like the paper version of the map would appear). To view the overlay map with no relief shading

1. **Use the View tool to define the area you want to view. (Move and resize the view square to choose the area.)**

2. **Choose Map Overlay View from the Operation menu.**

    3DEM displays the selected area as a topographic map without shading. To navigate around the map, use the window scroll bars.

3. **To return to the shaded relief overlay map, choose Overhead View from the Operation menu.**

Reviewing Other 3DEM Features

3DEM has a number of other features worth mentioning:

- **Multiple DEM file support:** Instead of loading only a single DEM file at a time, 3DEM can merge DEMs to create 3-D models of large areas.

- **GPS support:** Waypoints, routes, and tracks can be downloaded from a GPS receiver and displayed on maps created by 3DEM.

- **Aerial photo overlays:** Aerial photographs can be overlaid on DEM data, just like DRG files, to create three-dimensional photos. (You need to geo-reference the photos first, which consists of identifying the coordinates of several known points on the photo.)

- **Flyby animation:** 3DEM can create animation movies of flying over a three-dimensional scene.

- **Additional data sources:** 3DEM isn't limited to using only DEM and DRG data. 3DEM can create maps based on elevation data gathered by satellites, the Space Shuttle, and even Mars exploration probes.

After you master the basics of working with 3DEM, spend some time experimenting with other program features. 3DEM has an extensive online Help system that you can use to find out more about all aspects of the program.

If creating 3-D maps interests you, be sure to check out the Virtual Terrain Project at http://vterrain.org. This Web site is a clearinghouse for 3-D terrain modeling information. You'll find a number of links to resources and tools for creating three-dimensional maps of land forms and both natural and man-made features.

Other 3-D Mapping Software

3DEM isn't the only kid on the block when it comes to creating 3-D maps. Several other free or inexpensive Windows programs are available that you can use for three-dimensional terrain modeling.

Global Mapper

Global Mapper is an easy-to-use, reasonably priced, and powerful mapping program that has some of the same features as 3DEM for processing DEM and DRG data. Global Mapper also has some options typically only found in expensive Geographic Information System (GIS) programs, including

✔ **Extensive map data support:** You can view and export a large number of raster, vector, and elevation map data types.

✔ **Multiple data layers:** 3DEM works with only two layers (the elevation data and the overlay image), but Global Mapper can use multiple layers of data.

✔ **Relief shading:** Like 3DEM, Global Mapper can create relief-shaded maps to show elevation. (Global Mapper doesn't produce layered 3-D images or animations.)

✔ **Vector editing:** Data in existing vector maps such as areas, lines, and points can be edited, and new data can be created.

✔ **Contour generation:** Contour lines maps can be generated by using elevation data.

✔ **Line-of-sight tools:** Global Mapper has a series of tools for determining line-of-sight between two points and displaying *view sheds* (areas of terrain that can be seen from a certain vantage point). These tools are especially useful for placing radio transmitters.

A trial version of Global Mapper (with limited features) is available. Folks interested in digital maps should have this in their tool collection; it can display just about every digital map data type that's commonly used. If you get serious about making maps, consider purchasing the registered version because of its ability to export data, *rectify* images (make image data conform to a map projection system), and support multiple data layers.

You can find more about Global Mapper and download a free trial version of the program (a single license registration costs $179) at `www.global mapper.com`.

The USGS (`www.usgs.gov`) distributes the free program dlgv32 Pro for using DEM and DRG data. This is the same program as the unregistered version of Global Mapper. Global Mapper is based on the publicly available source code of an earlier USGS program called dlgv32; DLG stands for *Digital Line Graph,* which is a vector map data format.

TerraBase II

The U.S. Army Engineer School at Fort Leonard Wood (`www.wood.army.mil/tvc`) has a version of MICRODEM: TerraBase II. It's the same program as MICRODEM but was developed to train soldiers on terrain analysis and using digital maps. The school's Web site has an extensive collection of screen capture, how-to videos devoted to using MICRODEM. Although the AVI videos are more oriented to military users, they're still very helpful in finding how to get the most out of MICRODEM for civilian purposes.

MICRODEM

MICRODEM is a free Windows mapping program written by Peter Guth of the U.S. Naval Academy, Department of Oceanography. The program uses DEM data to create terrain maps, contour maps, topographic profiles, and 3-D scenes. The software can also overlay raster and vector data.

MICRODEM contains an impressive collection of features, including powerful options for manipulating and analyzing geographic data. It also supports many different map data types. These features can be a little overwhelming to a new user, and you really should spend some time reading the documentation to understand its capabilities before using the program. MICRODEM is well suited for the advanced digital map user.

You can download MICRODEM (the full install package is over 30MB) from `www.usna.edu/Users/oceano/pguth/website/microdem.htm`.

Bundled map programs

If you're not that excited about finding and downloading DEM and DRG files for making your own 3-D maps, you can purchase a commercial software package that comes with map data and supports three-dimensional terrain views. These commercial programs don't have as many options for creating custom 3-D images compared with 3DEM, Global Mapper, and MICRODEM, but they're very easy to use. Some programs to consider include

✔ Maptech Terrain Navigator

✔ DeLorme Topo USA and 3-D TopoQuads

✔ National Geographic TOPO!

I discuss these map products in more detail in Chapter 13.

Part IV
Using Web-hosted Mapping Services

The 5th Wave   By Rich Tennant

I located the bear and began testing the GPS tracking collar over a week ago, but he seems to have left the cave and now I can't locate him or the collar anywhere.

In this part . . .

The deal with this part is there are a whole lot of mapping resources on the Web that are free. You know all of those commercial programs in Part III that you have to shell out bucks for? In many cases you can get the same basic functionality (that means without the advanced features found in commercial programs) for free, simply by knowing the right place to point your Web browser. This part discusses how to access and use online street maps, topographic maps, aerial photos, and slick U.S. government-produced maps. You'll also learn how to save and edit all of those wonderful, free Web-hosted maps.

Chapter 17

Saving and Editing Street Maps

· ·

In This Chapter

▶ Saving Web maps

▶ Using fonts

▶ Adding symbols

▶ Selecting file formats

· ·

*W*hen you need to tell someone how to get somewhere, Web-hosted mapping services are a great resource for creating maps, especially if you're artistically challenged. You get a professional looking map by typing some text and clicking a few buttons.

However, a Web map might not exactly meet your needs. Maybe it's missing a street name, or you want to add a few colored arrows to show a route through a confusing set of streets. Most map Web sites don't have many options to customize a map.

This chapter has everything you need to customize a basic Web map. You'll also find tips and hints on how to make your own maps, using a Web map as the foundation. After you edit the map, you can

✔ Attach it to an e-mail.

✔ Paste it into a word processing document.

✔ Post it on a Web site.

✔ Print it on party invitations.

You're not going to become a world-class cartographer overnight, but you can produce some pretty good-looking maps.

The techniques in this chapter apply to any digital map. If you're using a mapping program, you can use the same methods to copy and save parts of any map that's onscreen.

Saving Maps

Most Web-hosted mapping services don't have an option for saving a map to your hard drive. You can print the map, e-mail it, or maybe save a part of it so you can upload to a personal digital assistant (PDA), but there's no command to save the map as a file.

Here are three paths around this roadblock:

✔ Right-click the map and choose Save Picture As.

✔ Use the Print Screen key.

✔ Use a screen capture program.

Save Picture As

After you display a map on a Web site, some Web sites let you save the map to disk with a little-known browser command. Follow these steps:

1. **Make the map the size that you want it in your Web browser.**

   When a screen capture is stored on the Clipboard, it's saved in bitmap (.bmp) format. Bitmaps don't scale very well, so you end up with jagged lines or a blurry image if you shrink or enlarge the map in your graphics program.

2. **Right-click the map.**

3. **Choose Save Picture As (or Save Image As, depending on your browser).**

4. **Select the file directory location to save the image.**

   The map picture is saved as a file to the directory location that you select.

Captured: Screen capture programs

Lots of screen capture programs are available on the Internet. Most are either shareware or freeware. Two of my favorites are

✔ **SnagIt:** A commercial screen capture utility that's been around since the first versions of Windows. It has a number of powerful features. It's available at `www.techsmith.`

`com/products/snagit/default.asp`.

✔ **MWSnap:** If you're on a budget, this is an excellent freeware screen capture utility with lots of features. It's easy on system resources, too. It's available at `www.mirekw.com/winfreeware/mwsnap.html`.

Using the Print Screen key

Before Windows appeared on personal computers, the Print Screen key on a PC keyboard sent a copy of the monitor screen to the local printer. When Windows was introduced, things changed. Here's what happens now:

- ✔ **Press Print Screen only.** The entire screen is copied to the Clipboard.
- ✔ **Press Print Screen while you hold down Alt.** The active window is copied to the Clipboard.

Using the Print Screen options are handy if a Web site has disabled the Save Picture As menu command or if the Web map isn't being stored as a graphics file that can be easily saved.

Pressing Print Screen or Alt+Print Screen sometimes copies parts of the screen that don't have anything to do with the map, such as menus, title bars, and buttons. If you don't want these on your map, you can either use a screen capture program instead of Print Screen or manually edit the map in a graphics program. This chapter explains both.

Different keyboards label the Print Screen key different ways. It might be Print Screen, PrintScreen, PrtSc, or something else, but you should be able to spot it. The key usually is to the right of the F12 function key.

Follow these steps to save a Web page map with Print Screen:

1. **Display the map in the size you want to save.**

   Map Web sites usually can show maps in several sizes.

2. **Press Alt+Print Screen to save the active window to the Clipboard.**

   This is more efficient than capturing the entire screen with just the Print Screen key.

After the map is on the Clipboard

1. **Run a graphics program such as Paint.**
2. **Use the Paste menu command to insert the Clipboard image into a new file.**
3. **Save the file.**

Using screen capture programs

Screen capture programs provide more options and flexibility than the Print Screen key. For example, you can select part of the screen and copy it. You just save the map without editing all the clutter around it.

Although screen capture programs have different user interfaces, they generally work like this:

1. **Run the screen capture program.**

2. **Assign a *hot key* (usually either a function key or a combination of control keys) that starts the screen capture.**

3. **Make the map the size you want it in your Web browser.**

4. **Press the hot key.**

5. **Click and draw a rectangle over the region of the screen that you want to capture.**

6. **Use the capture command to copy the screen region to the Clipboard.**

   This command will vary depending on the screen capture program you're using. Depending on the screen capture program used, a copy of that piece of the screen is either placed on the Clipboard or directly saved to a file that you name.

Figure 17-1 shows a Web map selected with the MWSnap screen capture program to place in the Clipboard.

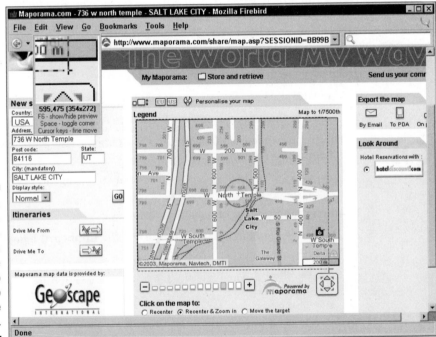

Figure 17-1: Using the MWSnap screen capture program to copy a map to the Clipboard.

Editing a Map

Editing a saved map is just a matter of opening the saved file with a graphics program. The graphics program can be as basic as the Paint accessory program that comes with Windows or as sophisticated as a commercial, high-end design program.

A simple graphics program like Paint is fine if you're not making a lot of changes.

If you've got an itch to be a cartographer and want to go beyond using general graphics programs, check out Map Maker, a popular commercial desktop mapping program. You can get a free, limited-feature version called Map Maker *Gratis* at www.mapmaker.com.

Almost all Web maps have text at the bottom with copyright information and where the map came from. Leave it intact to respect the copyright and to credit the company that provided the map.

Opening a file

If you used Print Screen or a screen capture program, you need to get the map into the graphics program so that you can edit it. Follow these steps to load a map so you can edit it:

1. **Run the graphics program.**
2. **If one isn't already onscreen, open a new file.**
3. **In the Edit menu, select the Paste command. Or, if you've previously saved the map to a file, use the Open command in the File menu to open it.**

   The map image is loaded, and you're ready to change it.

Cropping

If your map file has more than just your map (such as unrelated windows, icons, or dialog boxes), one of the first things that you need to do when the captured screen is loaded in the graphics program is to *crop* (trim) the image so only the map is shown.

Automatic cropping

Automatic cropping is fast and easy if your graphics program has a crop command. The command automatically removes everything outside of a selected rectangle, leaving only the image within the rectangle intact.

Manual cropping

If your graphics program doesn't have a crop command, you can crop a map manually by copying and pasting what you want. Follow these steps:

1. **Use the selection tool to select the map.**

2. **In the Edit menu, choose the Copy command.**

3. **Open a new file.**

4. **In the Edit menu, choose the Paste command to place the map into the new file.**

Using colors and fonts

The colors and fonts that you use in a map can make a big difference in appearance and readability.

Colors

Colors let a user quickly differentiate features on a map. A black-and-white map might convey the same information as a color map, but hues and shades can make a map easier to read.

Pixels for free

Although a number of commercial graphics programs are on the market, I'm a big fan of free software. Here are some free graphics programs I find useful for creating my own maps:

✔ **DrawPlus 4** (simple to use with lots of professional features): www.freeserif software.com/serif/dp/dp4/index. asp.

✔ **EVE** (a very small, vector graphics program perfect for drawing diagrams and maps): www.goosee.com.

✔ **OpenOffice-Draw** (part of the OpenOffice suite, which means you also get a word processor, spreadsheet, and presentation software in addition to a graphics program): www.openoffice.org.

✔ **Zoner Draw 3** (fast with support for lots of graphics file types): www.zoner.com/ draw3/default.asp.

All these programs are more powerful than Paint, and have object-oriented (vector) drawing capabilities. Plus, you can't beat the price.

Here are some of the most important rules when it comes to dealing with color:

✔ **Use the same general color scheme as the Web map you're editing.**

Any text or features that you add to the map should be the same color as the text and features shown on the Web map.

✔ **Use contrast between background and text.**

- On a light background, use dark text. Black text is usually best.

- On a dark background, use light text.

✔ **Use bright colors to draw attention to a feature such as a location or route of travel.**

Use red to identify a location the user is searching for.

Fonts

Text labels play an important role in maps; here are some well-founded guidelines for using fonts and typeface styles with maps. These tips will make your digital maps easy on the eyes:

✔ **When adding new labels, use the same typeface as Web map text (or as close to the typeface as possible).**

✔ **Feature names should be in a normal typeface.** Don't bold or italicize them.

✔ **Feature names should only have the first letter capitalized.**

Capitalizing an entire name on a map makes it harder to read.

✔ **Text in a straight line is easier to read and find than curved text (such as a street name that curves around a corner).**

✔ **Sans serif fonts are easier to scan on a computer screen.**

You're reading a serif font right now. Sans serif fonts, such as Arial, have letters without *serifs* (small lines on the top and bottom of some characters).

If you must use a serif font, Georgia is more legible than Times New Roman.

✔ **Don't mix fonts and font size when labeling map features unless you have a really good reason.**

Adding symbols

Symbols convey information without using words. For example, a tent means a campground, a skier indicates a ski trail, and an airplane means an airport.

Most Web maps don't show many symbols. Adding your own symbols is a quick and easy way to improve a map's readability. For example, if you make a map where the route passes a restaurant, you can add the usual round plate with a knife and fork in the center to show the restaurant on the map.

If you're adding a symbol to a map, make sure that users will understand what it means. You may think a picnic table clearly represents a park, but someone else may have no idea what the symbol is and wonder why there was a smudged blob on the map.

Finding symbols

Here are two ways you can get symbols for a map:

- ✔ **Create your own.** Making your own symbol involves using your graphics program to design a small, icon-sized image.

    If you're not artistically inclined, this will result in something that looks like a smudged blob.

- ✔ **Use a symbol from a font.** Many fonts contain symbols that you can use on your map. Some fonts are composed solely of mapping symbols. Using a font symbol is quick and easy, and you don't need a graphics art degree to make one.

    A number of fonts that contain map symbols are freely available on the Internet. Here are two Web sources that I turn to when I'm looking for symbols to include on a map:

    - • Luc Devroye's Map/Travel dingbats Web site has a large number of links to symbol fonts suitable for maps. Go to `http://cgm.cs.mcgill.ca/~luc/travel.html`.

    - • Mapsymbols.com contains a number of symbols formatted for use with the commercial ArcInfo and ArcView Geographic Information System (GIS) programs. A number of symbol fonts are also listed. Check out `www.mapsymbols.com/symbols2.html`.

Commercial GIS software companies offer free programs that can view GIS files created by their full-featured programs. Many of these programs install a collection of symbol fonts into the Windows Font folder. (Some demonstration versions of mapping programs do this, too.) Even though you might not use the viewer or demo program, sometimes it's worthwhile installing just to use the fonts.

Inserting symbols

Follow these steps to add a symbol from a font to a map in your graphics program:

1. **Install the symbol font.**

   This process depends on your Windows version. Your Windows online Help system or user guide has instructions for installing fonts.

2. **Run the Character Map program by following one of these two steps:**

   • Choose Start➪Programs➪Accessories➪System Tools➪ Character Map.

   • Choose Start➪Run, and then type **charmap** in the Run dialog box.

3. **Select the font you want from the Font drop-down list.**

4. **Click the symbol you want to use.**

5. **Click the Select button; then click the Copy button to copy the symbol to the Clipboard.**

   Figure 17-2 shows the Character Map user interface.

6. **Select the text tool in your graphics program.**

7. **Move the cursor to where you want the symbol to appear and then click.**

8. **Paste the symbol from the Clipboard into the map.**

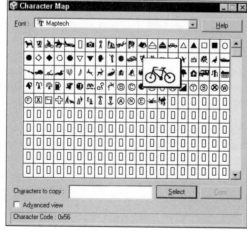

Figure 17-2:
Use
Character
Map to
copy a map
symbol
to the
Clipboard.

Missing Character Map?

If Character Map doesn't show up in the System Tools menu, choose Start⇨Select Programs and Accessories; some versions of Windows store the command here instead of in System Tools. If you still can't find the program, you need to install it. This is easy and usually doesn't require inserting any floppy disks or CDs. Follow these steps to install Character Map:

1. **Choose Start⇨Settings⇨Control Panel.**

2. **Double-click the Add/Remove Programs icon.**

3. **Click the Windows Setup tab and enable either the System Tools or the Accessories option, depending on your Windows version.**

4. **Click the Details button.**

5. **Enable the Character Map option.**

6. **Click Apply.**

Moving symbols

If you want to move the symbol after you've placed it, follow these steps:

1. **Click the graphics program's selection tool.**

2. **Select the symbol.**

3. **Drag the symbol to a new location on the map.**

Selecting the right file format

When the map is exactly how you want it, the last step is to save the file. It's important to select the file format that best suits your needs.

If you're sending a map to someone as an e-mail attachment or posting it on a Web page, be considerate of those who will view the map. Keep the file size as small as possible while making the map retain enough detail to be easily read.

A map on a Web site should take less than ten seconds to download over a dialup Internet connection — that means roughly less than a 70K graphics file.

BMP

A *bitmap* (BMP) file is a bit-for-bit representation of how an image appears on a computer monitor. Bitmap files can contain millions of colors.

Don't save your map as a bitmap file if you're using it in e-mail or placing it on a Web site. Files in this format tend to be pretty large because images aren't compressed.

JPG

A *JPG* (or JPEG; pronounced *JAY-peg*) file is designed for saving photographs and other complex images. JPG stands for Joint Photographic Experts Group, the people who came up with this file format.

It supports millions of colors. JPG images are compressed, so they're smaller than BMP files. The JPG format should be used for photographic quality images where most pixels are different colors.

GIF

GIF (pronounced *jif* or *gif)* should be your first file format choice for saving your edited maps.

GIF stands for Graphics Interchange Format. GIF files are compressed but are limited to a palette of 256 colors. This format is widely used for Web maps or any image that has large regions of the same color.

PNG

PNG (Portable Network Graphics) is designed to support millions of colors for Internet use. It's slowly replacing the GIF format. Because it produces relatively small files, you should consider using it for maps that will be sent in e-mail or associated with a Web site.

Designing maps for the Web

Successfully designing maps that are displayed on a Web site isn't just a matter of randomly selecting fonts, colors, and lines and combining them.

If you're serious about creating maps for the Web, check out these three excellent resources:

- *Map Content and Design for the Web: A Guide to Optimizing Cartographic Images on the Web.* A Canadian government site with detailed information on Web map design principles.

  `http://atlas.gc.ca/site/english/learning_resources/carto/content.html`

- *Web Cartography* edited by Menno-Jan Kraak and Allan Brown. London: Taylor & Francis. A good reference book on how maps are used on the Internet. The book has a companion Web site:

  `http://kartoweb.itc.nl/webcartography/webbook/index1.htm`

- *Web Style Guide: Basic Design Principles for Creating Web Sites* by Patrick J. Lynch and Sarah Horton. Not map-specific, but important style design guidelines for developing any Web site. There's an online version of this guide:

  `http://info.med.yale.edu/caim/manual/contents.html`

Chapter 18

Navigating Web Road Maps

· ·

In This Chapter

▶ Exploring street map Web sites

▶ Reviewing common features

▶ Choosing between Web and PC street maps

▶ Taking a tour of street map Web sites

· ·

As surprising as it sounds, the Internet has actually made a big difference in helping people in cars not get lost. Free Web services that provide street maps and driving directions consistently generate some of the highest amounts of 'Net traffic. As an example, at the end of 2003, the popular MapQuest Web site produced over 10 million maps and sets of driving directions per day with 30 million visitors each month. That's a lot of maps and a lot of people who are looking for maps.

In this chapter, I explore the world of online street maps. Here you discover the basic features that street map Web sites offer, some advantages and disadvantages to using the services, and some popular street map Web sites in action.

If you've never used a street map Web site before, use this chapter to get on the road using them. And even if you're a veteran online map user, you'll probably discover some tips as well as other street map sites you might not have known.

Using Street Map Web Sites

A *street map Web site* is simply an easy-to-use front end to a large database that contains location and map information. When you visit a site and want to view a map associated with a specific street address, the server retrieves the appropriate data from a database and displays a map in your Web browser. You can then scroll and zoom in and out on the map to change views and also get other information (such as driving directions) by using your keyboard or mouse.

Map sites use *geocoding* to locate addresses, which means that latitude and longitude coordinates are assigned a street address. These coordinates are then passed to the map database to retrieve a map or driving directions.

Listing common street map Web site features

You can find quite a few street map Web sites on the Internet, and they generally all have the same features in common, including

- ✔ **Map display:** Obviously, street map sites have street maps. Streets and roads are displayed in *vector* maps (created with lines and shapes) instead of *raster* maps (scanned versions of paper maps). Vector maps are faster and efficient to display. You can zoom in and out on the maps to view them in different scales.

- ✔ **Address searches:** To display a map, you enter a street address, city, state, or ZIP code. The map Web site checks the location information that you entered to see whether it's valid; if it is, the map is displayed.

- ✔ **Route creation:** In addition to showing a map of a single location, street map Web sites can also create routes that show you how to get from Point A to Point B. Just enter a starting and ending address, and the Web site will display a map of how to get to your destination.

- ✔ **Route directions:** Street map Web sites also can provide you with driving directions for getting to a location. The directions list streets, turns, and estimated times and distances for traveling between different parts of the route.

- ✔ **Printing:** All street map Web sites can output maps and driving directions to your printer, which is usually easier than lugging your PC with you on a trip.

Street map Web site companies usually don't make their own maps but rely on map data licensed from one or more third-party map companies such as Geographic Data Technology (GDT), NAVTECH, and TeleAtlas. Although map Web sites might use the same data, their maps can look different depending on how they display and use the data.

Web versus PC software street maps

If you've read Chapter 12 (all about PC street-navigation programs), you might be wondering whether you should use a Web-hosted street map or a program that comes bundled with a street map CD-ROM. Both can find addresses, display street maps, and create routes. To answer your question, look at the advantages and disadvantages to using street map Web sites compared with their PC program cousins.

Map accuracy

On Christmas Day, 1998, a German driver out for a spin in a GPS-equipped BMW drove his car into a river as he dutifully followed the directions of his in-car navigation system. Despite the stop signs, he continued down a ferry ramp and drove into the Havel River, slowly sinking in about 12 feet of water. Fortunately, the driver and his passenger were not injured. The digital map displayed in his dashboard showed a bridge when it actually should have been marked as a ferry crossing — and the driver trusted his BMW more than his common sense.

This is a rather extreme case, but it does illustrate an important point: Street maps will always have some errors in them, and you can't expect 100 percent accuracy. Software companies, Web sites, and map data vendors do try their best to keep maps current and up-to-date. (Most map Web sites even have ways to report errors in maps and driving directions.) However, when you consider the 3.95+ million miles of public roads in the United States — with constant, ongoing construction — keeping maps accurate can be a daunting challenge. So try not to get too frustrated if a map Web site occasionally makes a boo-boo. And watch out for ferry crossings.

Street map Web site advantages

Some of the advantages that street map Web sites offer are that they're

✔ **Free:** Street map Web sites are one of those valuable resources that you can still get for free on the Internet. The companies that host these map sites stay in business by selling advertising, offering other mapping products and services to corporate customers, or charging for premium services.

✔ **Easy to use:** Street map Web sites are very simple to use. They offer basic mapping features and easy-to-understand user interfaces.

✔ **Available almost anywhere:** If you have an Internet connection and a Web browser, you can find street addresses and create maps from just about anywhere you can access the 'Net.

✔ **More frequently updated:** One of the big selling points to maps on Web sites is they can be updated more frequently than maps that come with PC software; which tend to be updated annually. (However, I've yet to see a map site provide details on how often and which maps have been updated.)

Street map Web site disadvantages

Some of the drawbacks to using street map Web sites include

✔ **Limited POIs:** PC street map software packages have a large number of Points of Interests (POIs) on maps such as gas stations, restaurants, and other businesses and services. Most street map Web sites don't show

POIs or only display a limited number, such as selected hotels or other advertisement-based services

✔ **Limited route capabilities:** Many street map Web sites can create routes only between two locations. PC map programs allow you to build routes with multiple legs, change routes on-the-fly while you're driving, and specify locations to travel through on your way to a destination.

✔ **No trip-planning features:** PC street map programs support calculating trip costs, determining gas stops, setting typical driving speeds, and other advanced trip-planning features. Map Web sites don't have all these options.

✔ **No customization options:** Unlike PC map software, street map Web sites don't have drawing tools for customizing maps with added text or symbols.

If you want to add text or symbols to a map created with a Web site, you'll need to apply some of the techniques that I describe in Chapter 17 and use a graphics program to edit your map.

✔ **Lack of GPS compatibility:** Unlike a laptop or PDA that's running street-navigation software and is connected to a GPS receiver, Web sites don't provide you with real-time GPS tracking capabilities.

✔ **Advertisements:** If you use a street map Web site, be prepared for lots of ads. Although the ads pay for the mapping service (which allows the service to continue to be free to you), ads can take up to two-thirds of the screen, leaving only a small portion available to display a map.

Choosing between Web-hosted and PC software street maps

If you can't make up your mind whether to use Web-hosted or PC software street maps, here are few guidelines:

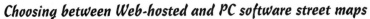

✔ **Infrequent use:** If you need to look up an address only every now and then and periodically plan trips, you'll probably be served perfectly well using a street map Web site.

✔ **Frequent use:** If you travel quite a bit, you'll likely want the additional features that I mention earlier in this chapter that are found in PC street-navigation programs. The enhanced features make life easier for the frequent traveler.

✔ **Customizable:** If you want to customize your maps such as adding text labels to them, PC map software offers many more features and options for creating custom maps.

✔ **Speed:** Even if you have PC map software, street map Web sites can be faster to use if you need to quickly look up a street address, especially if you have a broadband Internet connection.

Reviewing Street Map Web Sites

In this part of the chapter, I review several popular street map Web sites, talk about their features, and show what their maps look like.

Map companies are always trying to improve the usability of their maps. You might find some differences in the appearance of the maps that you see displayed on a Web site and the ones in this chapter.

To start with, all street map Web sites work the same when it comes to displaying maps and driving directions. Their user interfaces might be slightly different, but if you're familiar with using one street map Web site, you'll be able to easily use others. By mastering these basic skills, using just about any street map Web site should be a snap:

✔ **To display a map for a specific location,** you enter an address, city, state (or country), and optional ZIP (or postal) code and then click a search button. See an example of the MapQuest address search page in Figure 18-1.

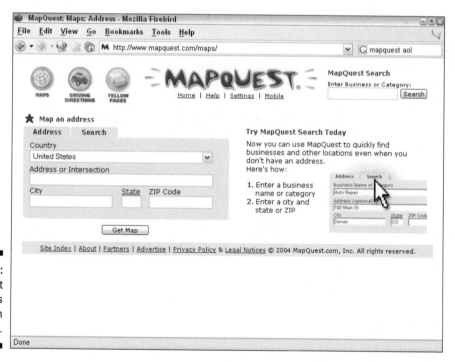

Figure 18-1:
MapQuest
address
search
page.

You can also just enter a city and state or a ZIP code to display an overview map of an area.

✔ **To display a driving route between two points,** either in the form of a map or turn-by-turn directions, you click a directions button or link, and then enter the address, city, state (or country), and optional ZIP (or postal) code for the starting point and destination. As an example, the MapQuest driving directions search page is shown in Figure 18-2.

After a map is displayed, you can zoom in and out to show more detail or a larger area, respectively. Most maps feature a zoom scale with a series of boxes with a plus and minus sign at each end. Clicking a box nearer to the plus sign zooms in, and clicking a box closer to the minus sign zooms out.

You can move around the map by clicking arrows or compass points that border the map; the map scrolls in the direction of the arrow or compass point.

All map Web sites provide an online help link. Even if you've used a street map Web site for a while, it's worth your time to read the help information. There's a good chance that you'll discover something new that might save you some time.

Take a quick look at some street map Web sites.

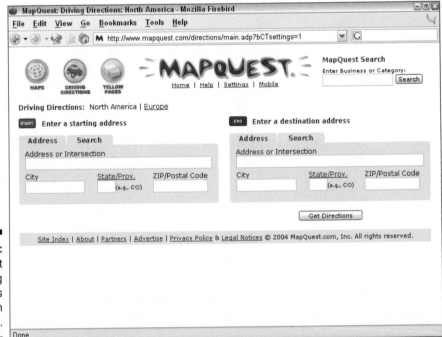

Figure 18-2:
MapQuest
driving
directions
search
page.

MapQuest

MapQuest (www.mapquest.com) is the largest and most popular map Web site on the Internet and provides street maps of North America and Europe. (You can also view less-detailed, worldwide, city, and country maps.) The site was first launched in 1996, and its corporate roots extend back to the 1960s, when its original parent company started making paper road maps that were distributed by gas stations. America Online currently owns MapQuest, and the site generates millions of maps each day and consistently ranks in top ten of the most-popular Web site lists.

After you search for an address and display a map, as shown in Figure 18-3, you can print it, e-mail the map as an attachment, or download it to a PDA that's running AvantGo (www.avantgo.com) software.

MapQuest can provide specially formatted maps and driving directions for wireless PDAs and cellphones with Internet connectivity. Check out the link to Mobile MapQuest (look for <u>Mobile</u>) on the MapQuest home page for information on using different types of wireless devices.

Like all street map sites, MapQuest provides route maps (an example is shown in Figure 18-4) and driving directions. In addition to addresses, you can also search for businesses by name or type even if you don't know their address.

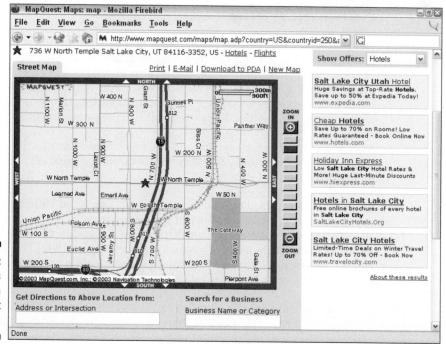

Figure 18-3: An address search MapQuest map.

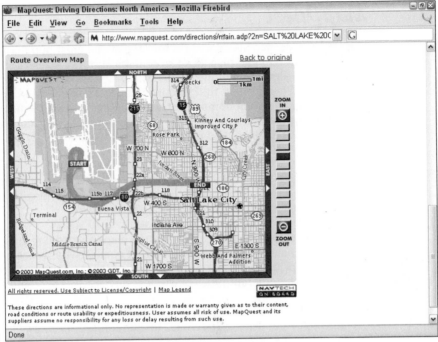

Figure 18-4:
A route
MapQuest
map.

Rand McNally

Rand McNally (www.randmcnally.com), in the map business since 1856, now produces both paper and electronic street maps for the United States. Its Web site offers some of the cleanest, easiest-to-read online maps that are available on the Internet; an example is shown in Figure 18-5. If you're used to maps with jagged lines that look computer-generated, the second-generation digital maps that Rand McNally produces will pleasantly surprise you.

After you display a map, you can change its size, print it, e-mail it, or save it online if you've previously registered with a free or paid Road Explorers membership.

In addition to standard route mapping capabilities, Rand McNally has options such as selecting fastest or shortest routes, whether to use a greater or lesser number of route steps, and displaying driving directions in several different formats. (A simple route map is shown in Figure 18-6.) The site is also one of the best places on the Web for planning vacation road trips. Rand McNally has taken a large amount of content from its popular paper travel guides and put it online to help you find attractions and activities on your trips. The only major issue that I've found with this site is its servers seem to get bogged down every now and then, tending to be slower displaying maps and generating routes compared with other sites.

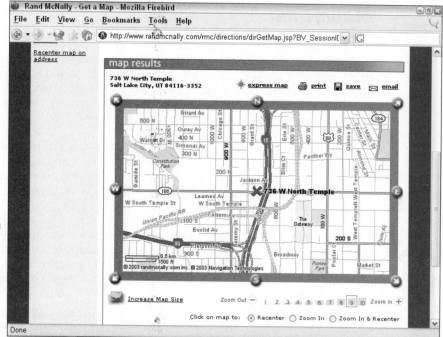

Figure 18-5:
An address
search
Rand
McNally
street map.

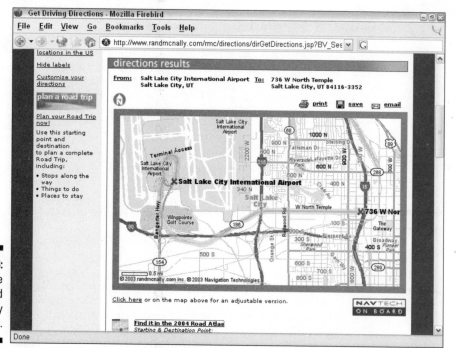

Figure 18-6:
A route
Rand
McNally
map.

Maporama

When I'm going to travel outside the United States, one of my first stops is Maporama (`www.maporama.com`), the French company that maintains a free street map Web site to showcase its mapping products and services. At Maporama, you can look up street maps from all over the world. The level of detail varies depending on how industrialized a country is; for example, you get better maps for Switzerland than you will for Swaziland.

Street maps such as the one displayed in Figure 18-7, can be printed, e-mailed, or downloaded to a PDA. Maporama is one of the few mapping sites that lets you select exactly what size to display the map and what colors you want the map shown in. For example, a grayscale color style is available for using maps on monochrome screen PDAs.

If you ever need latitude and longitude coordinates for an address, Maporama displays the coordinates (beneath the map) of an address you've searched for. The latitude and longitude might not be as precise as standing outside the location with a GPS receiver in hand, but they'll be close.

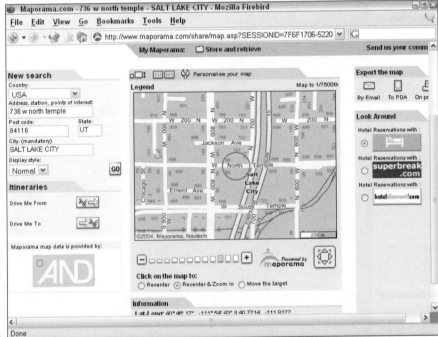

Figure 18-7:
A
Maporama
street map.

Maporama also displays routes and driving directions, but I find that the route maps often don't show as much detail as route maps created by other Web sites. (A sample map is shown in Figure 18-8.) Detailed turn-by-turn directions are displayed below the route map, though, steering you in the right direction to reach your destination. Maporama also has some nice features usually not found on map sites such as

✔ You can select routes depending on your mode of transportation: by car, foot, or foot and subway (more suited for Europe than the U.S.).

✔ Zoomed-in maps show numbered address ranges on street blocks.

✔ Symbols show transportation and other points of interest.

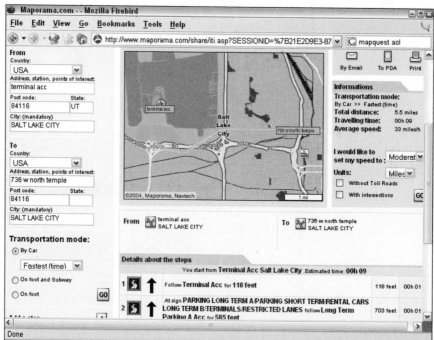

Figure 18-8:
A route
Maporama
map.

More online street map sites

Use these alternative street map Web sites on the 'Net to find your way around. Here are several other popular ones, with the geographic areas that they cover, and their Web addresses:

✔ **Map24**: Europe; www.map24.com

✔ **Maps On Us**: United States; http://mapsonus.com

✔ **ViaMichelin**: Europe; www.viamichelin.com

✔ **Multimap**: Europe, United States, and Australia; www.multimap.com

✔ **MSN maps and directions**: North America and Europe; http://mappoint.msn.com

✔ **Yahoo! maps**: North America; http://maps.yahoo.com

Chapter 19

Exploring Web Topographic Maps

Web-hosted street maps are handy for finding your way around in cities, but what if your travels take you off-road, on less-beaten paths in forests, mountains, and deserts? You're in luck because a number of Web sites provide free or inexpensive topographic maps of the United States that you can view, print, and take with you on your next adventure.

In this chapter, I discuss some of the differences between topographic maps offered on the Web and dedicated topographic mapping programs that run on your computer. I also present some popular topographic map Web sites as well as basic instructions on using them to display maps.

Using Web-hosted Topographic Maps

Web-hosted topographic sites are fast and easy to use. If you've already read Chapter 13 (which covers topographic map software for PCs), you might be wondering whether you should buy a mapping program or rely on free or low-cost Web map services. Look at some of the advantages and disadvantages to using topographic map Web sites.

Advantages of topographic Web sites

Topographic map Web sites are pretty handy. Just visit a Web site and *voilà!* — instant map. These maps have several advantages:

✔ **Available anywhere:** If you can access a computer with an Internet connection — say at home, the office, a library, or an Internet café — topographic maps are but a few mouse clicks away.

✔ **Easy to use:** If you're intimidated by the many options and commands in most PC mapping software products, Web-hosted map sites usually have a basic set of features and commands that are easy to master and use.

✔ **Inexpensive:** If you're on a budget, these Web sites are either free or charge nominal subscription fees to access their maps.

Disadvantages of topographic Web sites

Web-based topographic mapping sites have a few limitations:

✔ **Small map size:** Most sites display only relatively small-sized (onscreen, that is) maps.

✔ **Internet accessibility issues:** Sometimes you might not have access to an Internet connection, the mapping Web site could be down, or your Internet connection could be very slow.

✔ **Time investment:** Saving a Web-displayed map (whether you're using screenshots and other techniques described in Chapter 17 or downloading a map from a commercial service) can be a time-consuming process.

✔ **No advanced features:** Most topographic map Web sites don't have such advanced features as interfacing with a GPS receiver, the ability to change map datums or display terrain three-dimensionally, or options for customizing maps. These features are common in PC mapping programs.

A number of these limitations are addressed by commercial map Web sites that I describe later in the "Commercial topographic Web map sites" section.

Deciding between Web-based maps and mapping programs

Here are my recommendations as to whether you should use Web-based topographic maps or topographic mapping programs:

✔ **Infrequent use:** If you just want to print out a topographic map every now and then, a free Web-hosted map site probably meets your needs.

✔ **Frequent or sophisticated use:** If you use topographic maps often, want to create custom maps, or interface your GPS with a digital topographic map, you're better off with one of the map programs described in Chapter 13 or trying a commercial Web site that offers topographic maps.

✔ **Quickies:** Even if you regularly use PC mapping software, topographic map Web sites are great for quickly creating or viewing maps.

Reviewing Topographic Map Web Sites

Here are some of the Web sites that you can visit to access topographic maps of the United States. I cover both free and commercial sites and discuss some of their basic features. If you're near a computer with an Internet connection, you can follow along as I step through some examples on how to display and use topographic maps on several free Web sites.

Web sites come and go, and user interfaces and site features change.

Using Maptech MapServer

Maptech (`http://maptech.com`) is a map and navigation software company that produces topographic, nautical, and aviation mapping products. (I discuss its Terrain Navigator software in Chapter 13.)

To showcase its map technology and sell products, Maptech hosts *MapServer*, the free Web service database that contains maps and the names of cities, lakes, mountains, and other features. You can visit MapServer by pointing your Web browser to `http://mapserver.maptech.com`.

Displaying MapServer maps

MapServer can't read your mind to know what map you want to look at, so you first enter some search information in the upper-left corner of the MapServer Web page. For example, suppose you're interested in looking at a map of the city of Bar Harbor, Maine. (Try the lobster ice cream if you're ever in the neighborhood.) To display the map, follow these steps:

1. **Enter** Bar Harbor **in the Enter City or Place Name text box.**

   You can also enter the ZIP code of a location (and click its Go! button) or click the Advanced Search button to find a map by either its name or its latitude and longitude coordinates.

2. **Choose Maine from the Select State drop-down list box.**

3. **Click the Go! button.**

   A list of places matching the place that you entered is displayed. In this case, I get 24 matches for Bar Harbor (as shown in Figure 19-1). Click the first entry for a map of the city of Bar Harbor. You know that's the right one because it's identified as a *Populated Place* (under the Type heading).

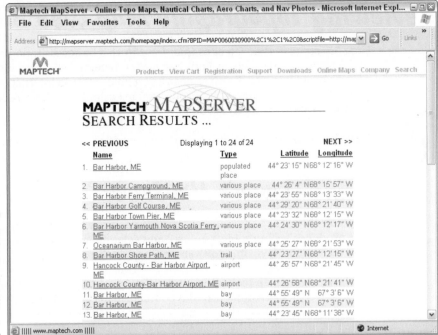

MAPTECH   Products View Cart Registration Support Downloads Online Maps Company Search

MAPTECH MAPSERVER
SEARCH RESULTS ...

<< PREVIOUS   Displaying 1 to 24 of 24   NEXT >>

Name	Type	Latitude	Longitude
1. Bar Harbor, ME	populated place	44° 23' 15" N	68° 12' 16" W
2. Bar Harbor Campground, ME	various place	44° 26' 4" N	68° 15' 57" W
3. Bar Harbor Ferry Terminal, ME	various place	44° 23' 55" N	68° 13' 33" W
4. Bar Harbor Golf Course, ME	various place	44° 29' 20" N	68° 21' 40" W
5. Bar Harbor Town Pier, ME	various place	44° 23' 32" N	68° 12' 15" W
6. Bar Harbor Yarmouth Nova Scotia Ferry, ME	various place	44° 24' 30" N	68° 12' 17" W
7. Oceanarium Bar Harbor, ME	various place	44° 25' 27" N	68° 21' 53" W
8. Bar Harbor Shore Path, ME	trail	44° 23' 27" N	68° 12' 15" W
9. Hancock County - Bar Harbor Airport, ME	airport	44° 26' 57" N	68° 21' 45" W
10. Hancock County-Bar Harbor Airport, ME	airport	44° 26' 58" N	68° 21' 41" W
11. Bar Harbor, ME	bay	44° 55' 49" N	67° 3' 6" W
12. Bar Harbor, ME	bay	44° 55' 49" N	67° 3' 6" W
13. Bar Harbor, ME	bay	44° 23' 45" N	68° 11' 38" W

www.maptech.com   Internet

Figure 19-1:
Search for places by name, state, ZIP, or coordinates in MapSearch.

MapServer provides you with a bonus: You can also view several other types of maps. These map types appear above the map as tabs, as shown in Figure 19-2, and include

- ✔ **Topo Map:** A United States Geological Survey (USGS) topographic map of the area

- ✔ **Nautical Chart:** A National Oceanic and Atmospheric Administration (NOAA) nautical chart of the area (if navigable waterways are nearby)

- ✔ **Aeronautical Chart:** A Federal Aviation Administration (FAA) aeronautical chart of the area for use by pilots

- ✔ **Nav Photo:** An aerial photo of the area

The topographic map is displayed by default; change the display to another type of map by clicking one of the tabs. If the Nautical Chart or Nav Photo tab items are dimmed, those types of charts aren't available for viewing.

You can print the currently displayed map by choosing Print MY MAPS from the FUN TOOLS drop-down list box (lower-left corner of the screen, under Coordinates).

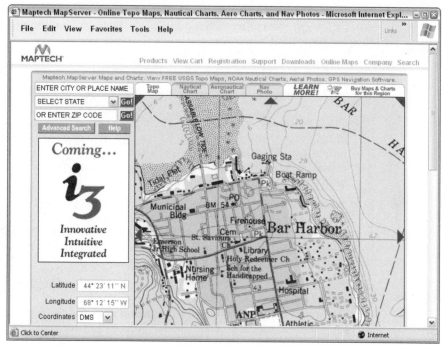

Figure 19-2:
MapServer offers topographic and other map options.

Moving around in a MapServer map

After a map is displayed, you can move around in it via

- ✔ **Direction arrows:** A series of eight red triangles surround the map. Click them to scroll the map in the direction they point.

- ✔ **Clicking:** Clicking inside the map centers the map on the location that you click.

Viewing coordinates in a MapServer map

As you move the cursor over the map, the coordinates of the location underneath the cursor appear to the left of the map, telling you exactly where you're located. This can be handy for finding the coordinates of a location to manually enter as a waypoint in your GPS receiver. From the menu of the Coordinates drop-down list box, you can display map coordinates in several different formats:

- ✔ **DMS/DM.MM/DD.DD:** Latitude and longitude (degrees, minutes, seconds, or degrees and decimal minutes or decimal degrees)

- ✔ **UTM:** Universal Transverse Mercator

For the lowdown on latitude, longitude, and UTM, see Chapter 2.

MapServer displays all map coordinates using the NAD 27 map datum. If you don't know (or remember) what datums are, head to Chapter 4 to read why they are important when you're using a GPS receiver.

Changing a MapServer map size

You can change the size and appearance of a MapServer map three ways:

- ✔ **Click To Zoom:** Underneath the map are a series of bars between icons of two magnifying glasses: one with a plus sign and the other with a minus sign. Click one of the bars to zoom in or out on the map. The bars closest to the plus magnifying glass zoom in, and the bars closest to the minus magnifying glass zoom out.

- ✔ **Scale:** The Scale drop-down list box allows you to change the scale of the map. For example, a topographic map can be viewed at 1:24,000, 1:50,000, 1:100,000, or 1:250,000 scale. The larger the number to the right of the colon, the less detail there is and the more area shown. A 1:100,000 scale map is shown in Figure 19-3.

- ✔ **Zoom:** Use the Zoom drop-down list box to change the size of the map, either showing it at 100% or reducing its size to 50% of normal. Select the size from the drop-down list box and click the Go! button. Figure 19-3 shows the same map at 50% as in Figure 19-2 at 100%.

Figure 19-3: Map of Bar Harbor shown at 1:100,000 scale with 50% zoom.

Using MyMaps

MapServer has a unique feature — MyMaps — that lets you create and save custom maps. After you create a map, you can refer to it for future reference, e-mail it to friends, or add a link to the map on a Web site.

The MapServer Web site has a comprehensive tutorial for using MyMaps, but read along as I show you quickly how to create a custom map. Display the map you want to customize and follow these steps:

1. **From the FUN TOOLS drop-down list box, choose Place an Icon.**

   This launches the MyMaps Wizard, which steps you through the process of building a custom map.

2. **When the map in the wizard is the one you want, click NEXT.**

3. **Click a point on the map that you want to label with an icon.**

   A blue arrow pointing to that location appears.

4. **Click NEXT.**

5. **Choose the type of symbol you want to associate with the location from the list of symbol categories; then click NEXT.**

   For example, if the location is for transportation, choose Transportation.

   A list of icons appears for the selected symbol type. If you choose Transportation, icons of cars, planes, and other vehicles are displayed.

6. **Click the icon you want to use and then click NEXT.**

7. **Enter a name to associate with the location; then click the Preview Name button to see the map. If you're satisfied, click NEXT.**

8. **Decide whether to associate a Web site with the location:**

   • If you want someone to click the map location to visit a specified Web site, enter a Web site address.

   • If you don't want a Web site link, click NEXT to continue.

9. **Click the SAVE TO MYMAPS button to save your map.**

A new drop-down list box named MYMAPS is added to the MapServer Web page below the search boxes in the upper-right corner of the window.

✔ A list of all the maps that you've created appears in the list box. Choosing a map and clicking the Go! button displays the map.

✔ A Manage MYMAPS item in the drop-down list lets you delete a map or change its name.

MyMaps stores information about the map you've created as a Web browser cookie. Whenever you visit the MapServer Web site, it checks for map cookies and then displays the titles of any maps you've created in the MYMAPS drop-down list. Cookies apply only to the computer you used to create the maps; if you access MapServer from another computer, your MyMaps won't appear. Maptech offers free registration on its Web site so you can log in to MapServer from any computer and have your MyMaps available.

Using GPS Visualizer

GPS Visualizer is a slick, easy-to-use Web-based mapping program, written by Adam Schneider, that allows you to upload GPS waypoints and track files to a Web site and then overlay them on topographic and other types maps.

GPS Visualizer relies on online sources that provide free topographic maps, aerial photos, satellite images, and street maps. Unlike many other sites that are limited to making maps of the United States, GPS Visualizer can create maps of Canada, Europe, and other places in the world.

GPS Visualizer has a number of powerful options for creating customized maps. In this section, I describe how to make a map using some of the Web site's basic features. After you master the general procedure, you can experiment on your own with some of the other advanced options.

If you'd like to follow my examples, point your Web browser to `www.gpsvisualizer.com`. GPS Visualizer is free, but if you find it useful, the author requests a small PayPal donation as a way of saying thanks.

Before you can use GPS Visualizer to display maps, you need to install the free Adobe SVG Viewer plug-in to work with your Web browser. If you don't already have the plug-in, you can download the viewer at `www.adobe.com/svg/viewer/install`.

Downloading sample GPS Visualizer data

To demonstrate how GPS Visualizer works, I use sample GPS data available from the GPS Visualizer Web site — in this case, a GPS record of a drive down the California coast through the scenic artichoke fields. To download the data, follow these steps:

1. **Click the <u>Draw a map</u> link on the GPS Visualizer home page.**

2. **Right-click and choose Save As (or Save Target As, depending on your Web browser). Click the <u>GPX file from California</u> link to save the** `sample_calif.gpx` **file to your hard drive.**

You can input a number of different GPS data formats into GPS Visualizer, including *GPX* (a standardized format for inputting and outputting GPS data) and OziExplorer waypoint and track files, Geocaching.com LOC files, and tab-delimited text files. (Read about OziExplorer in Chapter 15; read about the sport of geocaching in Chapter 7.)

Displaying a GPS Visualizer map

After you have some sample GPS data to use, create a map with it. The GPS Visualizer map input form page, as shown in Figure 19-4, might seem a little intimidating with all its different options. To get started making maps, you can leave most of the default settings as they are. (If you're feeling a bit overwhelmed, click the simple version of the map form link to display just the basic input options.)

Each option has a question mark button to the right of it that you can click to display a window with more information about that option and how to use it.

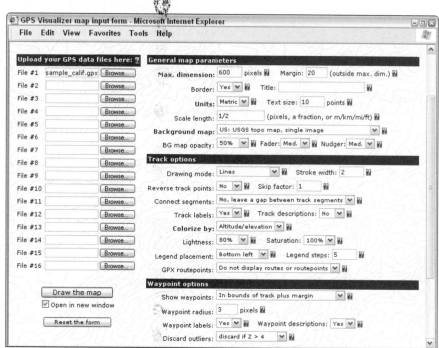

Figure 19-4:
GPS
Visualizer
map input
form page.

To display a map, you tell GPS Visualizer what GPS data you plan on using:

1. **Click the Browse button next to the File #1 text box and choose the location of the** `sample_calif.gpx` **file.**

   See preceding step list.

2. **From the Background map drop-down list box, choose US: USGS Topo Map, Single Image.**

   While you're there, check out the other background map options.

3. **Select the Open in New Window check box (lower left of the screen).**

4. **Click the Draw the Map button (lower left of the screen).**

   A new window shows a map with the GPS data overlaid on it (as shown in Figure 19-5). Some of the features displayed on the map include

   - *Waypoints:* Any GPS waypoints that were included with the uploaded data are plotted on the map, identified by a circle and the waypoint name. When you move the cursor over a waypoint label, the waypoint name changes color so it's easier to see. You can also click and drag a waypoint label to move it. When you do, a line is drawn from the waypoint label to actual waypoint location. This is useful if the waypoint label obscures something you want to see on the map.

   - *Tracks:* The GPS track data showing the travel route is drawn on the map. By default, GPS Visualizer shows the elevation for different segments of the track path in different colors; note the legend at the bottom of the map with what the different colors mean. When you create a map, you can have other data (such as speed, heading, or slope) displayed in color on the track path.

   - *Background opacity:* At the bottom of the map is a series of small rectangles that let you fade the background map image. Click one of the rectangles to set how faded you want the background map to appear. The rectangle on the far right displays the map in full color. The rectangle on the far left fades the map completely to white (so it isn't visible). Fade the background map to better see the colors of your track log and waypoints.

GPS Visualizer can show an *elevation profile* based on track data. Click the <u>Draw a profile</u> link at the top of the Web page to use this feature.

TerraSever-USA

TerraServer-USA is a popular Web site that provides free USGS topographic maps and aerial photos of the United States. (Chapter 20 contains an extensive description of the site and detailed instructions to display aerial photos.) Nearly all the commands used for viewing aerial photos also apply to displaying topographic maps. Visit the Web site `www.terraserver-usa.com`.

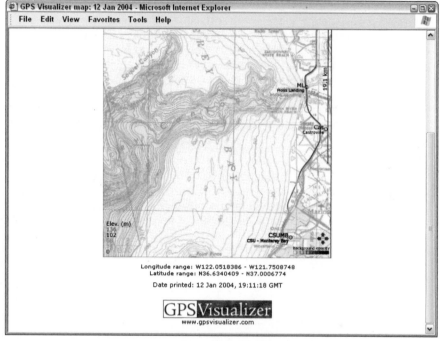

Figure 19-5:
A GPS
Visualizer
map display
with over-
laid GPS
data.

Commercial topographic Web map sites

Several commercial Web sites sell digital topographic maps as well as allow potential customers to view some of their maps for free (to get a hint of what their for-fee services are like). All these sites tend to have a similar business model, offering

✔ **Printed maps:** You can buy printed copies of maps you view online.

✔ **Subscriptions:** On some sites, you can view only certain types of free maps; to access other maps, you pay a subscription fee. Additionally, some sites offer different levels of services. For example, for an extra fee, you might get premium services, such as

- Downloading maps you can use with PC map programs
- Creating custom maps
- Uploading GPS data to use with Web-based maps

The cost of subscription services tends to be comparable or less than the prices of commercial mapping programs that you run on your PC.

When it comes to commercial topographic map Web sites, you're paying for convenience in accessing and using the maps online as well as having a number of different types of maps available in a single place. Although some of the same services are available for free elsewhere on the Internet, commercial map Web sites are priced reasonably enough that you can try them to see whether they meet your needs.

These popular commercial map sites, along with some screenshots, give you an idea of what it's like to use the online maps with your browser.

TopoZone

TopoZone, the first interactive Web mapping site on the Internet, provides a comprehensive collection of digital topographic maps and aerial photos for the United States. Any Internet user can freely search for and view USGS topographic maps; a screenshot of accessing a map with TopoZone is shown in Figure 19-6. For a yearly subscription fee of under $50, the TopoZone Pro service offers access to aerial photos, street maps, downloading USGS Digital Raster Graphics map, and other enhanced features. To read more about TopoZone, go to www.topozone.com.

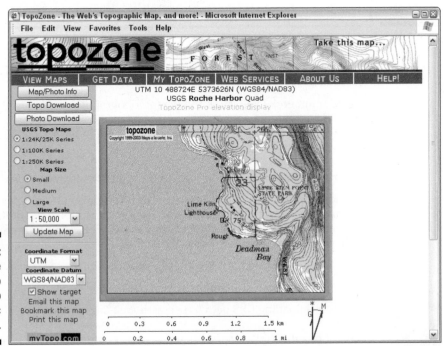

Figure 19-6:
Use TopoZone to view a Web topographic map.

MapCard

MapCard is a commercial Web map site oriented toward outdoor recreation users; the site was named the best new product of 2003 by *Backpacker Magazine.* The Web site offers topographic maps, aerial photos, lake depth charts for fishing, and tools for creating custom maps; Figure 19-7 shows a screenshot of a map displayed with MapCard. Although MapCard doesn't directly offer free online maps (a yearly subscription is under $30), the site does have a free "test drive" with which you can download maps and try out the subscription services for a single day. You can visit MapCard at www. mapcard.com.

MyTopo

MyTopo is a commercial Web site for creating custom USGS topographic maps or aerial photos; a screenshot of using the site is shown in Figure 19-8. You select a location you want to view (either by place name or coordinates), and MyTopo displays the map or photo. You customize the map by setting its size, selecting a portion of the map to display, and naming the map. A preview copy of the map as it will be printed is displayed. You can then order a copy of the map in several different sizes on waterproof or glossy paper.

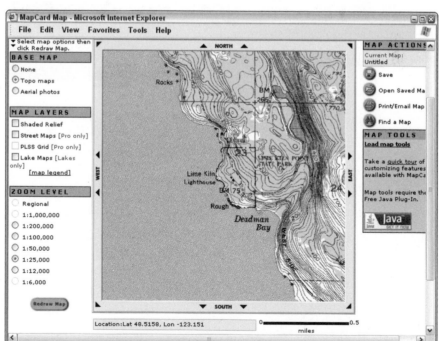

Figure 19-7: Access an online map with MapCard.

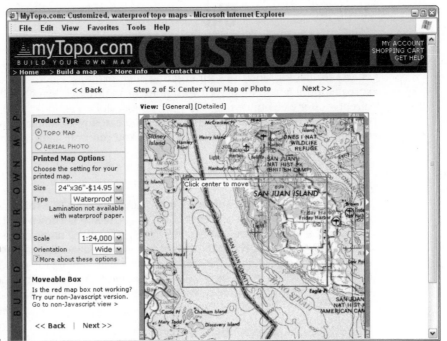

Figure 19-8:
Use MyTopo
to create a
topographic
map.

Chapter 20

Overhead Image Web Sites

· ·

· ·

Although many Internet users know about street mapping Web sites like MapQuest (see Chapter 18), fewer people are aware of Web sites that provide free *aerial* photos (taken from aircraft) and satellite data. These images complement traditional maps, displaying features that don't show up on topographic or street maps, such as vegetation and unmarked roads or trails. In addition, aerial photos and satellite images are often more up-to-date than topographic maps and provide more timely and accurate information.

In this chapter, I present several popular Web sites that you can visit to view aerial photos and satellite images; I also describe the basics of using three of my favorite aerial photo and satellite services.

I treat both aerial photos and satellite images as simply graphics images in this chapter because that's how you view them on the Web. Unless there's a need to specifically differentiate between an aerial photo and a satellite image, the word *image* in this chapter refers to both.

Using Web Aerial and Satellite Images

One of the biggest advantages to using an image captured from an airplane or satellite is that it shows reality — not a cartographer's representation drawn on a map. You can use aerial and satellite images to

✔ **Complement a topographic map to help determine your current location.**

✔ **Find roads and trails not shown on maps.**

✔ **Better understand how thick tree and brush cover will be in an area you plan to visit.**

Don't rely solely on these images for navigation. Aerial and satellite images typically don't have natural or man-made features labeled or show elevation contours.

✔ **View neighborhoods in urban areas.**

✔ **Augment marketing endeavors, Web sites, or presentations.** Aerial photos are always attention-getters.

The two types of aerial photos and satellite images available on the Web are

✔ **Government:** Governments use aircraft and satellites to map land for administrative and research purposes. Some maps are for intelligence gathering, but these images usually aren't available to the public. Most government-produced images are usually free on the Internet. Keep in mind that many governments aren't as liberal as the United States in distributing images because of national security reasons.

✔ **Commercial:** A number of businesses specialize in taking aerial photographs or reselling photos and satellite images from other vendors. Some of these companies let users browse their Web sites freely for reduced-scale or *watermarked* images (images with an overlaid logo or text that might obscure detail), selling printed, full-size, unwatermarked versions of these images.

You can download free or commercial aerial photos for mapping programs (such as some of the programs I discuss in Chapter 14), but Web-hosted aerial and satellite image services work well for a quick look at an area you're interested in. Some advantages to using Web-hosted image services include

✔ **No need to have special software installed on a PC to view the images. (All you need is a Web browser.)**

Some Web sites might require you to use a specific Web browser. For example, to access GlobeXplorer images, you need to use Internet Explorer.

✔ **Access of images from any computer connected to the Internet.**

✔ **Simplified user interfaces of the Web pages that make viewing the images easy.**

To save and edit free aerial and satellite images displayed on Web sites, use the techniques that I discuss in Chapter 17. However, purchasing a downloaded image from a commercial site might be quicker and easier.

Airplane or satellite?

You might think that the photos displayed on TerraServer-USA and other Web-hosted mapping sites come from satellites, but these photos are actually taken from airplanes flying at precise altitudes (up to 25,000 feet) with specially mounted cameras. Images that come from satellites (or the Space Shuttle) *can* be photos, but they can also be composite images put together from data that comes from sensors that detect differences in moisture, vegetation, or terrain. In general, satellite images don't show as much detail as aerial photos. That's changing; commercial services (such as DigitalGlobe's QuickBird satellite) can produce high-resolution, color photos on demand for anywhere in the world. (See www.digitalglobe.com for some amazing examples of high-resolution satellite images.) In general, if you see images labeled Landsat, SPOT, SPIN-2, or QuickBird, they came from satellites. Most other images are photos taken from airplanes.

Don't expect real-time, spy-satellite accuracy from free Web images. These images can be over five years old and not show current roads or other features. (Image accuracy is better in wilderness, rural, or urban areas that haven't experienced a lot of natural or man-made change.)

Reviewing Aerial and Satellite Image Web Sites

Most aerial and satellite image Web sites like these have similar features and user interfaces, so when you figure out how to use one, using another site is easy. To give you a better idea of image resolution and how the sites work, I use a series of screenshots from each of these three Web sites to shows aerial photos of downtown Seattle, Washington. (If you look really, really, close, you can probably find a Starbuck's or two.) I personally like these Web sites because they offer a variety of free or reasonably priced images.

The data on each of these Web sites has strengths and weaknesses. Some display free, high-resolution color images with corporate watermarks as well as lower-resolution color images with no watermarks. When I'm looking for aerial or satellite images, I generally visit all three to find an image that meets my needs and budget.

The availability of aerial and satellite images on the Web can change. For example, MapQuest (the popular street map Web site) used to display street maps and aerial photos provided by GlobeXplorer, but the aerial photo service was discontinued in December 2003. Microsoft's TerraServer project stopped offering satellite imagery for locations all over the globe in 2000. Serving up images on the Web costs for bandwidth and storage; what's free today — particularly from commercial sites — might not be around tomorrow.

TerraServer-USA

In 1998, Microsoft, Compaq, the USGS, and several other partners launched the TerraServer Web site. The site was a technology demonstration for Microsoft software and Digital (which had recently been purchased by Compaq) hardware and was dubbed "the world's largest online database." TerraServer had a collection of compressed aerial photos and satellite images that took up over a terabyte (TB) of space. (A terabyte, which is 1,024GB, was a lot of disk space back then.) Anyone with an Internet connection could freely browse through the database of images.

Now renamed *TerraServer-USA* (www.terraserver-usa.com), this site provides aerial photos and topographic maps supplied by the USGS for just about anywhere in the United States. Although most of the aerial photos that TerraServer-USA provides are black-and-white, TerraServer-USA is adding USGS Urban Areas aerial photography collections of mapping major metropolitan areas with high-resolution, color aerial photos.

Displaying TerraServer-USA aerial photos

To display an aerial photo from TerraServer-USA, you first enter some search criteria. You can search for aerial photos three different ways.

Zoom-in searches

When you visit the main page of the TerraServer-USA site at www.terraserver-usa.com, you're greeted with a map of the world. Areas displayed in green contain map data. Move the cursor to a location that you want to view and click. Keep clicking and zooming in until the aerial photo you're interested is displayed.

General searches

Search for a TerraServer-USA aerial photo of a city or well-known location from the Search TerraServer text box. When you click the Go button, a list of the aerial photos that match the text is displayed. Click the text that describes the image you're interested in to display it.

You can make your search more specific by entering a city name followed by a comma, a space, and the standard two-letter postal abbreviation of the state.

For practice, try searching for a well-known landmark, such as the Space Needle in Seattle, Washington. If you enter **Space Needle**, you get the aerial photo of downtown Seattle as shown in Figure 20-1. There's not much detail, but you can find out how to increase the resolution in the section titled "Changing image resolution in TerraServer-USA."

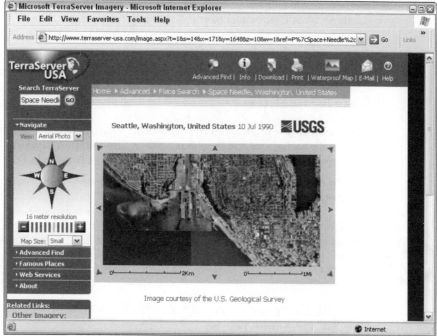

Figure 20-1:
A Terra-
ServerUSA
aerial
photo of
downtown
Seattle,
Washington.

Specific searches

The most accurate way to search TerraServer-USA for aerial photos is to use
the Advanced Find options:

- ✔ **Address:** Enter a street address for the location that you'd like to view.
  The City, State, and ZIP Code fields are optional, but using them helps
  narrow down the search.

- ✔ **Geographic:** Enter the latitude and longitude coordinates, either in decimal degrees or degrees, minutes, and seconds.

- ✔ **Place:** Enter a place name and the state (and optionally the country).
  You can enter a partial place name; for example, entering **San** with
  California as the state displays all the locations with names beginning
  with *San,* such as San Diego, San Francisco, and even Santa Clara.

  After you enter your search criteria, click the Go button, and the aerial
  photo is displayed. If several images match your selection criteria, you
  can choose the exact photo you're interested in from a list.

Moving in a TerraServer-USA photo

When you view an aerial map in TerraServer-USA, a frame with arrows surrounds the image (refer to Figure 20-1). Click one of the arrows to pan the
map in that direction. There's also a compass rose to the left of the image

that works the same way. Click a compass direction to scroll the map; for example, click E (for east) to scroll the map to the right.

Displaying a TerraServer-USA topographic map

In addition to displaying aerial photos, TerraServer-USA also can show a USGS topographic map of the same area that the aerial photo displays. (See Figure 20-2 for a topographic map of the area around the Space Needle.)

- ✔ **To display a map:** From the View drop-down list (to the left of the aerial photo and above the compass), select Topo Map. A topographic map in roughly the same scale as the aerial photo is displayed.

- ✔ **To display an aerial photo:** To return to the aerial photo image, select Aerial Photo from the View drop-down list.

TerraServer-USA is starting to provide high-resolution, color aerial photos of certain large metropolitan areas in the United States. If these images are available for the area you're viewing, *Urban Areas* will appear in the View drop-down list. Select Urban Areas in the list to display a color photo.

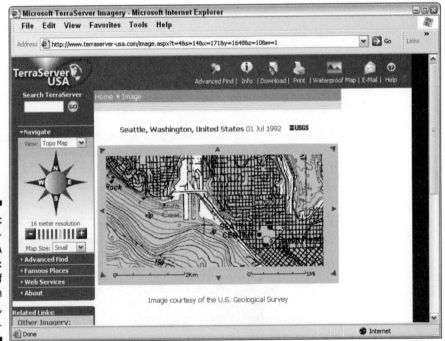

Figure 20-2: A Terra-Server-USA topographic map of downtown Seattle, Washington.

Changing image resolution in TerraServer-USA

After you display an aerial photo or a map, you can change the resolution. Resolution, especially when dealing with aerial photos, is expressed in *meters* (about a yard for nonmetric types). An aerial photo with 1-meter resolution means that you can see an object on the ground that's one square meter in size. The smaller the resolution number, the more detail the image shows. For example, Figure 20-3 shows the Space Needle viewed at 1-meter resolution.

Topographic maps can be displayed from 2 to 512 meters in resolution, and aerial photos can be shown from 1 to 512 meters. If there's data for an urban area with high-resolution, color photos, you can go from .25 to 64 meters; .25 meters is enough detail to start seeing people on the street, as shown in Figure 20-4.

A resolution scale is shown immediately below the compass, to the left of the map or aerial photo. To change the image resolution, you can either

- ✔ **Click one of the bars between the plus and minus buttons.** The farthest bar on the left provides the least amount of detail and largest area, and the bar on the extreme right shows the greatest amount of detail and the smallest area.

- ✔ **Click the minus button or the plus button.** This decreases or increases resolution one step at a time, respectively.

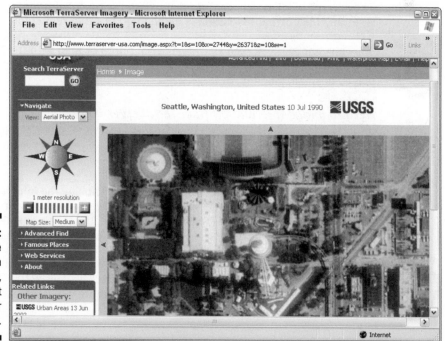

Figure 20-3: The Space Needle, in the center, viewed at 1-meter resolution.

Figure 20.4:
The Space
Needle
viewed at
.25-meter
resolution.

The current resolution is displayed above the scale. In addition, the bar representing the current resolution is highlighted in a different color.

You can change the screen size of an aerial photo or map with the Map Size drop-down list that's shown under the resolution scale. Images can be displayed in small, medium, or large sizes.

Getting image information from TerraServer-USA

When you use aerial photos, it's always important to know when the photo was taken so you can know how current it is. TerraServer-USA displays the date the photo was snapped (or the date the map was made) above the image.

You can get more detailed image information by clicking the Info item above the displayed image. For an aerial photo, the Image Info window provides additional details such as the image size in pixels, the map projection, and a grid overlaid on the image showing latitude and longitude coordinates.

Another excellent source of free USGS aerial photos is The National Map Web: http://nationalmap.usgs.gov. This online map displays aerial images and other U.S. government maps and is discussed in more detail in Chapter 21.

TerraServer.com

TerraServer.com (not to be confused with TerraServer-USA) is an offshoot of the original Microsoft TerraServer research project. When the original TerraServer was launched in 1998, the site offered SPIN-2 satellite imagery that covered Europe, Asia, and other areas outside the United States. The satellite data was leased for 18 months; in 2000, Aerial Images (the company that owned the leased data) decided to launch its own Web site, TerraServer.com (www.terraserver.com).

TerraServer.com sells aerial photos and satellite images from a number of different image providers. Currently, this site does not offer topographical maps, although that service is supposed to be on the way. You can freely view images that have a maximum 8-meter resolution. (An example image of downtown Seattle in this resolution is shown in Figure 20-5.) With 8-meter resolution, you can easily see large buildings, but the detail isn't as great as the 1-meter (or lower) resolution USGS aerial photos that TerraServer-USA provides. TerraServer.com does make higher-resolution images available; you just need to subscribe to the service to be able to view them. (Subscription fees range from $6.95 for a day's use to $99.95 for a year.) There are additional charges for downloading the images or ordering printed copies of them; depending on the size of the option and whether you want a digital or printed copy, expect to pay between $5–$80 per image.

Homeland insecurity

In December 2003, some aerial photos of Washington DC — long available from various Web sites — changed. Photos of such buildings as the White House, the Vice President's residence, and the Capitol were altered so only blurred pixels appeared instead of sharp detail. (You can view some of the before and after photos at http://cryptome.org/seatsuneyeball.htm.)

The changes were made by EarthData International, a company that the United States Geological Survey (USGS) contracts to take aerial photos. (The USGS then sells the images to companies for commercial use.) When EarthData went to the U.S. Secret Service to get permission to fly over airspace that's been restricted since the September 11, 2001, terrorist attacks, the Secret Service requested that the images of certain buildings be degraded.

The Federal government isn't alone in limiting Internet access to aerial photos. The New York state GIS (Geographic Information System) Clearinghouse (www.nysgis.state.ny.us) offers high-resolution aerial photos of the entire state but also restricts Web access to photos with areas that are deemed sensitive.

Just how much additional security is provided from censoring publicly available aerial photos is debatable. Images of the same government buildings and critical infrastructure facilities can be downloaded and viewed from other sources. And blacking out or reducing the detail of critical facilities might just end up drawing a terrorist's attention to someplace that domestic authorities have identified as a possible target. Sigh. Welcome to the brave new world of post-9/11.

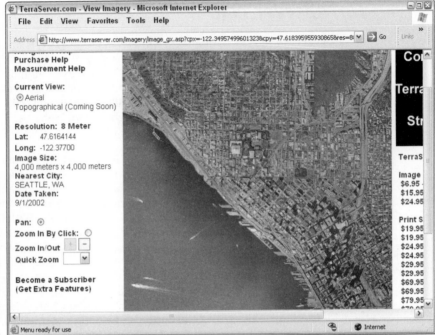

Figure 20-5:
A Terra
Server.com
8-meter
resolution
image of
downtown
Seattle,
Washington.

TerraServer.com has satellite images and color aerial photos available for many urban areas in and outside the United States that aren't available on TerraServer-USA. If you don't need high-resolution images, the free color images might meet your needs. Otherwise, you'll need to subscribe to the TerraServer.com service and order the images or generate screenshots of the images you're interested in.

Displaying a TerraServer.com image

To find an image, move your cursor over the Search item in the Web site's menu bar. Click one of the following menu items to see whether the TerraServer.com database has an image of the area you're interested in:

- ✔ **Coordinates:** You can search for an image by latitude and longitude coordinates, either in decimal degrees or degrees, minutes, and seconds.

- ✔ **City (United States):** Enter a city in the United States (and optionally, its state).

- ✔ **City (International):** TerraServer.com has a collection of international city images. Enter the city you're interested in viewing and its country.

- ✔ **Zip Code:** Enter a ZIP code to display the center point of the ZIP code area. (This applies only to the U.S.)

✔ **County:** Enter a county in the United States (and optionally, its state). An image with the center of the county will be displayed.

✔ **Address:** Enter a street address (United States) and the city and state (or ZIP code).

After you enter your search criteria and click Search, TerraServer.com queries its database for matches. The three possible search outcomes are

✔ **Bupkis:** No images in the TerraServer.com database meet your criteria.

Check your spelling or change your search criteria before you give up.

✔ **Multiple matches:** A appears with the matching images; you select the one you want. For example, if you search for a city named *Bend* but don't specify the state, you get a list of cities in Oregon, Montana, California, Texas, and other states.

✔ **Perfect match:** TerraServer.com found a single match in its database. Pay dirt! From the list of available image types (with the supplier, date, and resolution), click the image you'd like to view.

TerraServer.com has many international images, but don't expect photos of every place on Earth. The international images are mostly large urban areas and aren't available for all metropolitan areas outside the United States.

Moving in a TerraServer.com image

After you display an image, you can change the image's location by panning and its resolution by zooming in and out.

✔ **Panning:** *Panning* simply means moving the image to view an unseen area. It's like scrolling without the scroll bars. To pan the image

    1. Make sure that the Pan radio button to the left of the image is selected.

    2. Hold down the left mouse button on the image and drag the direction you want to move the image.

    For example, to see more area to the north of the image, drag down toward the bottom of the screen.

    3. Release the mouse button.

    After a moment, the new image is displayed.

✔ **Zooming:** TerraServer.com has a plus and minus button to the left of the image (refer to Figure 20-5) to control zooming in and out. (There's also a Zoom In by Click radio button that you can select so that when you click the image, you automatically zoom in.)

Unless you've subscribed to the TerraServer.com service, you can't zoom in on an image beyond 8-meter resolution. However, you can zoom out to view a larger area with less detail.

When you move the cursor over an image, the latitude and longitude coordinates of the location under the cursor are displayed to the left of the image. This is helpful for identifying specific locations.

GlobeXplorer

GlobeXplorer (www.globexplorer.com) specializes in selling online aerial photos, satellite images, and maps of the United States. You can browse through the GlobeXplorer's database of images for free, but all images are marked with a series of GlobeXplorer watermarks. If you subscribe to the GlobeXplorer service for a fee ($29.95 a month), you can view images without watermarks.

The watermarks aren't small and subtle. If you want to use the images for something other than personal reference, you'll need to subscribe to the service or buy a copy of the image without the watermarks. However, you can increase the resolution of images to 1-meter or less for a considerable amount of detail. GlobeXplorer also has a very large database of color images.

Displaying a GlobeXplorer image

GlobeXplorer uses the ImageAtlas Web-based tool to search through the company's database of aerial images. You start ImageAtlas from GlobeXplorer's main Web page.

After ImageAtlas is running, you can search for images three different ways:

- ✔ **Map:** ImageAtlas starts up with a satellite image, basemap of the United States. Click an area to zoom in, and keep clicking until the location you're interested in appears. The map to the left of the image shows such features as cities and roads to help you figure out where you are.

- ✔ **Address:** Enter the street address of the place you want to see in the text boxes next to the left of the image. At the minimum, you need to fill in a city and state or a ZIP code.

- ✔ **Latitude and longitude:** If you know the latitude and longitude of the location, you can use it to display the image. Enter the coordinates in decimal degrees in the text boxes to the left of the image.

After you enter the address or coordinates, click the Find Image button, and the aerial photo is displayed.

GlobeXplorer works only with Microsoft's Internet Explorer Web browser. If you're using Netscape, Mozilla, Opera, or another browser, you need to use Internet Explorer to access the Web site.

Zooming in on a GlobeXplorer image

After an image is displayed at GlobeXplorer.com, you can zoom in to see more detail. Underneath the image is a zoom scale, represented by a series of dots.

- Clicking the dot to the farthest left displays the largest area of coverage at the least amount of resolution. The dots on the extreme left display satellite images of the area.

- Clicking the dot on the farthest right displays the smallest area of coverage with the greatest amount of detail. The dots on the right display aerial photos of the area.

A zoom box lets you draw a rectangle over the part of the photo where you want to see more detail. Follow these steps:

1. **Select the Drag a Box to Zoom In radio button.**

2. **Move the cursor over the area you want to zoom in on.**

3. **Hold down the left mouse button and draw a rectangle over the area.**

   When you release the mouse button, the image zooms in to the area that you defined with the rectangle. An example of a zoomed in image at maximum resolution is shown in Figure 20-6.

Black-and-white or color?

Ever wonder why some images are shown in black-and-white while others are displayed in color? The short answer is that black-and-white film was used to create most of the USGS aerial photo data for the United States — and black-and-white film, processing, and photographic paper are cost-effective and stable. Color film, processing, and photographic paper are expensive, and color exposures (positives, negatives, and prints) can lose tonal quality over time. Commercial companies that produce custom aerial photos and images for resale tend to use color film for enhanced resolution and viewing. Most of the large urban areas in the U.S. have color images available because there is a greater opportunity for a commercial aerial photo company to sell the data, thus recouping the costs of taking the aerial photos and making a profit. Sometime in the future, high-resolution color images of the entire U.S. will be available, but for now, if the area you're interested is far away from a major city, you'll just have to settle for black-and-white.

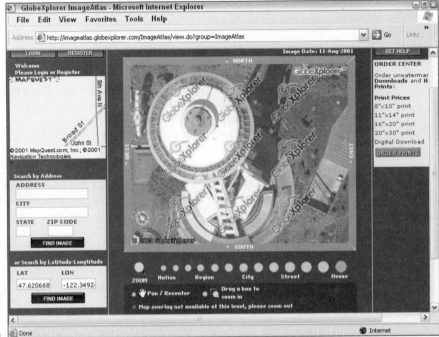

Figure 20-6:
ImageAtlas
display of
the Space
Needle,
zoomed in at
maximum
resolution.

Moving around in a GlobeXplorer image

After you display an image, you can move to a new location to focus on the area you want to view.

✔ A frame with compass directions surrounds the photo. Click the compass direction to scroll the image. For example, if you click NORTH, the image scrolls up to the north.

✔ Select the Pan/Recenter radio button beneath the zoom scale. When you click the image, the photo is reorientated so wherever you clicked appears in the center. You can also move the image by holding down the left mouse button while the cursor is over the photo and then dragging. When you release the mouse button, a new location is shown.

Overlaying a street map in GlobeXplorer

GlobeXplorer has a slick feature with which you can overlay a MapQuest street map over a portion of the image. (An example is shown in Figure 20-7.) Because an aerial photo isn't labeled with streets, this option can help you quickly orient yourself. To overlay a street map

1. **Select the Map & Aerial Overlay Toggle radio button beneath the zoom scale so that (Aerial On) is displayed**

2. **Move the cursor over the image.**

   As you move the cursor, a semitransparent image of a street map is overlaid on the image.

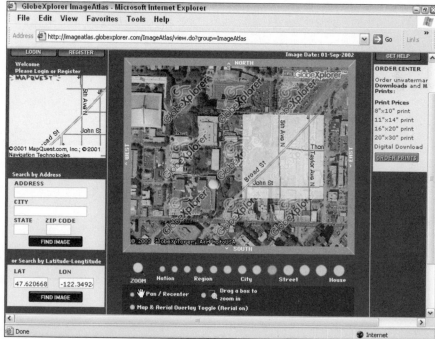

Figure 20-7: A street map overlaid on an aerial photo of downtown Seattle, Washington.

Part V
The Part of Tens

The 5th Wave — By Rich Tennant

So which is latitude and which is longitude again?

In this part . . .

All Dummies books have a part called The Part of Tens, and this one is no exception. This is a rather eclectic collection of GPS and map-related information. Stuff so intriguing and thought provoking that it deserved a part of its own (or something like that).

Chapter 21

Ten Great GPS and Map Web Sites

The Internet has a tremendous number of GPS and map resources. This chapter contains what I consider the ten best (actually, there's more than ten, but who's counting?) Web sites about GPS and digital mapping. Listed Web sites have product reviews, in-depth technical information, friendly people to ask questions, and many sources for free maps to download.

Comprehensive GPS Information

When I'm asked for an Internet GPS resource, I suggest these two Web sites:

✔ www.gpsinformation.net: Since 1997, Joe Mehaffey, Jack Yeazel, and Dale DePriest have compiled information about GPS, including receivers, software, and antennas. Their comprehensive and frequently updated Web site is packed with technical information, reviews, and common sense advice for novice to experienced GPS users. This site is a must for anyone who owns or is considering owning a GPS receiver. You'll discover something here, however much experience you have.

✔ http://vancouver-webpages.com/peter/index.html: Peter Bennett's GPS site was one of the first Internet sites devoted to the topic of GPS. The site contains links and information resources for different brands of GPS receivers. If you're writing your own program to interface with a GPS receiver, this is the place to find out about National Marine Electronics Association (NMEA) and other manufacturer communication protocols.

Current GPS News and Helpful Advice

The `sci.geo.satellite-nav` newsgroup is one of the best Internet resources for current GPS-related news. The newsgroup also features a cadre of frequent contributors who provide answers to all types of questions about GPS.

Before you post a question to the newsgroup, such as *What's the best GPS receiver?*, search through old posts with Google for previous discussion threads about your question. GPS newsgroup gurus are generally patient, but they do expect you to do a little homework first. If you can't find any archived information that helps, post a question (and provide as much detailed information as possible). If you're asking which GPS receiver might be the best, provide as much detailed information about your needs as you can.

If you don't have USENET newsgroup reading software or your ISP doesn't carry the `sci.geo.satellite-nav` news feed, you can view and post group messages with a Web browser at Google's cache of this newsgroup:

```
groups.google.com/groups?hl=en&lr=&ie=UTF-8&group=sci.geo.satellite-nav
```

Geocaching.com's discussion forums are an excellent source of news and advice. Because GPS receivers are integral to the sport of geocaching (read about this in Chapter 7), check out the GPS Units and Software forum where geocachers share their experience and wisdom with others. You'll find lots of timely news and reviews. Geocachers are some of the most serious civilian users of GPS, so there's excellent real-world information. The forums are located at `forums.groundspeak.com/GC`.

If you own a popular Magellan Meridian GPS receiver, one of the best sources of information on the receiver is the Magellan Meridian Yahoo! Group at `http://groups.yahoo.com/group/Magellan_Meridian`.

Technical GPS Information

If you're interested in technical, nitty-gritty details of GPS, check Sam Wormley's GPS Resources Web site. It's a collection of links to sites that get into the science of GPS and other resources that are more suited to the average consumer GPS user. Go to `www.edu-observatory.org/gps/gps.html`.

Free Maps

Yes, one of the joys of the Internet is that you can download all sorts of free digital maps. Most of the map data has been created by various government agencies and is made freely available to the public. In most cases, you'll need mapping programs to view the maps (described in different chapters of the book), but some of the maps can be opened with graphics programs to print and use. The biggest challenge in downloading free maps is finding them. Here are some Web sites that you should find helpful in your search:

✔ www.doylesdartden.com/gis: David Doyle is an environmental geologist (and dart frog aficionado) who maintains an extensive list of U.S. digital map resources. His list at this site is organized by state. You'll find hundreds of links for aerial photographs, topographic maps, geological maps, and many other different types of digital maps.

✔ www.macgpspro.com/html/newhtml/maplibrary.html: James Associates makes *MacGPS Pro,* a product for interfacing GPS receivers. The company hosts a list of United States and international free map sources.

✔ www.lib.berkeley.edu/EART: Unlike the United States (where digital maps are readily available), in other parts of the world, accurate maps are considered essential to national security and can be difficult to obtain. One of my favorite sources for international maps is the University of California Berkeley's online Earth Sciences & Map Library, where you can download topographic maps for many countries.

✔ www.lib.utexas.edu/maps: My other favorite academic map site is the University of Texas at Austin's Perry-Castañeda Library Map Collection. This site has an extensive collection of online maps (as well as links to sites that host maps) for countries and places all over the world.

✔ oddens.geog.uu.nl/index.html: The most comprehensive collection of map links on the Internet is Odden's Bookmarks. This European Web site has over 20,000 links to maps and map sites all over the world. You can spend hours browsing through links to international map sources.

Expert Desktop Mapping Guidance

Paul Pingrey is a longtime forester who recognized the importance of digital mapping for land management purposes and decided to spread the word. His Digital Grove Web site is a collection of mapping programs, map data sources, and information on how to create 2-D and 3-D maps. Pingrey focuses on free and low-cost programs, proving that you don't need to spend thousands of dollars on Geographic Information System (GIS) software or be a GIS professional to produce high-quality maps. Pingrey frequently updates his easy-to-navigate and well-designed site with new tools and information. If you're interested in desktop mapping (and you don't need to be land manager or forester), check it out at www.digitalgrove.net.

Definitive Terrain Modeling Information

This book really only scratches the surface of some of the cool things you can do with 3-D mapping. The most definitive Internet resource on the subject is John Childs' *Digital Terrain Modeling Journal.* Childs' Web site presents practical how-to tutorials, data sources, and news for creating 3-D maps. Even if you aren't interested in making your own 3-D maps, you should visit this site just to see some of the stunning images that are possible to create by using free and low-cost software. Childs' site is at www.terrainmap.com.

Chapter 22

Ten Map Printing Tips

*I*f you're using a digital map, odds are that sooner or later you're going to want to print it. Paper maps don't run out of batteries, and they're pretty easy to carry wherever you go. You can just use the Print command to transform the bits into ink, but some other techniques make using a paper map easier.

Make Your Paper Count

The more map and information you can get on a sheet of paper, the better. Most home and business printers are usually fed a diet of 8.5 x 11-inch paper . . . but 8.5 x 14-inch, legal size paper exists, too. One legal size sheet gives you 119 square inches of print area; an 8.5 x 11-inch sheet has only 93.5 square inches of print area.

Some mapping programs can reduce the map scale to get more data on a page. For example, more of the map appears when you print at 75 percent of the original instead of 100 percent. Remember, though, that the detail on the map becomes smaller and more difficult to read when you reduce the scale.

Just remember when you reduce the size of a map that displays a printed scale, such as 1:24,000 or one-inch-equals-a-mile, that the scale will no longer be accurate on the reduced map.

Print in Color

Maps are usually printed in color because it's easier for the brain to recognize and process colors than plain black-and-white. For example, on a United States Geological Survey (USGS) topographic map, you can tell at a glance that lightly shaded green areas are forested and that a solid red line is a major highway. Although navigating with a black-and-white map is certainly possible, using a map that's printed in color is quite a bit easier.

Print the Scale

A map without a scale is like a recipe with only the ingredients listed — not the quantities. You can guess that you add a tablespoon of salt instead of a cup, but the dish tastes a whole lot better if you know the proper amounts. The same is true with a map. If the scale is printed on a map (especially with distance rulers), you can easily judge how far features are from each other.

Print UTM Grids

Most mapping software that supports topographic maps can overlay Universal Transverse Mercator (UTM) coordinate system grids on the map. If you're using a GPS receiver with your map, UTM grids make it extremely easy to figure out where you are on the map. Just look at the GPS coordinates of your position, and then count the Northing and Easting tick marks on the map to find your location. (Chapter 2 shows you how to use UTM coordinates to plot locations.)

Use Waterproof Paper

If you plan to use your map outdoors, consider printing it on waterproof paper. Waterproof paper for common inkjet printers uses a vinyl material to produce waterproof, durable, and tear-resistant maps. The paper is a little thicker than regular paper, but you can still fold it. There is also special waterproof paper for copiers and laser printers that serves a similar function.

Waterproof paper is a little pricey — about a dollar a sheet. To prevent yourself from wasting expensive paper from printing blunders, first print the map on normal paper to make sure that it looks right.

Never use waterproof inkjet paper in copiers or laser printers. The heat of their printing processes can melt waterproof inkjet paper and wreck the printer.

Here are three sources of waterproof paper for your maps:

- **Latitude 26:** This company sells waterproof inkjet paper in a number of sizes, including rolls. Its Web site has information on paper specifications and pricing: www.lat26inc.com.

- **National Geographic:** National Geographic sells waterproof Adventure Paper for inkjet printers. You can order it from this Web site: http://maps.nationalgeographic.com/topo/adventure.cfm.

- **Rite in the Rain:** Rite in the Rain is a popular supplier of waterproof field notebooks and paper. If you want to print maps on laser printers or copy machines, Rite in the Rain makes the right kind of paper for you. This Web site has a list of various waterproof paper products: www.riteintherain.com.

If you're not venturing into the weather, consider using digital photography paper if you have an inkjet printer. The quality and detail is much better than plain paper for topographic maps.

Waterproof Your Plain Paper

If you must use plain-paper maps outdoors, here are some ways to avoid a runny, pulpy mess:

- **Carry your maps in a watertight map case or a resealable food storage bag.**

- **Create waterproof maps with these options:**

  - *Sealers* coat a piece of paper in clear plastic. One of my favorite commercial sealers is *Map Seal*. A 4-ounce bottle coats approximately 8–10 square feet of paper and costs around $7. You can find this at www.aquaseal.com/map-seal.html.

  - *Contact paper* is transparent plastic with a sticky back. You can sandwich a piece of paper between two sheets to waterproof the map. Contact paper, which is cheap, comes in rolls so you can cut it to size. Just remember that contact paper doesn't hold up over the long haul.

- *Lamination* involves placing the paper between sheets of a special plastic that seals (when heated) around the paper. Copy centers charge a few dollars to laminate a letter-size piece of paper.

Maps laminated with thick plastic can't be folded. Lighter laminates can be folded.

If you're on a budget, put two maps together back to back and then laminate them. If you're laminating many maps, the savings add up.

Print More Map Area

If you're planning on visiting a specific place, add a little more area to your map than you think you need. It's tempting just to print a map that shows exactly where you're going — and nothing more. But what if you decide to take a side trip to someplace just off your route that isn't on the map? What if you're interested in a feature you see in the distance? From my years of search and rescue and outdoor recreation experience, I've discovered that you should always have more map than you think you'll need.

Put North at the Top

Most maps are orientated with north at the top. When you print a map, follow the same convention. If the map doesn't have a compass rose that indicates directions, you'll know that

✔ North is at the top of the map.

✔ East is to the right.

✔ South is at the bottom.

✔ West is to the left.

If you're using a graphics program to edit a digital map, consider adding a north-pointing arrow in case the map doesn't have one. It's a reassuring reminder that north is indeed the direction you think it is.

Use the Best Page Orientation

Before you print your map, decide which page orientation will work best. In your software's Page Setup dialog box, select the orientation.

✔ *Portrait* prints the map lengthwise. This is the default for most printers.

✔ *Landscape* prints the map widthwise.

Use the Print Preview command (if the software supports it) to see what the printed map will look like. If the orientation doesn't display as much of the map as you want, change the orientation to the other format.

Beware of False Economy

I can remember when gas stations gave away road maps for free. (I sometimes catch myself saying, "Back in the days when maps were free . . . " when I'm reminiscing.)

It's easy to think that the days of free gas station maps are back. You can download free maps from the Internet or use inexpensive mapping software. Get a digital map, fire up the color printer, and you've got a map! (Just remember the cost of the paper, ink cartridges, printer wear and tear, and the time involved in printing a map.)

Here's an expensive example. An entire USGS 7.5 minute topographic map takes either nine sheets of 8.5 x 11-inch paper or six sheets of 8.5 x 14-inch legal size paper if you're printing at 1:24,000 scale. The costs add up when you're using special paper and lots of color, which empties your ink cartridges. Compare this with shelling out six dollars for an official copy of the USGS map.

Sometimes paper maps for a few dollars can't be beat.

Chapter 23

Ten Tips for Athletes

1 do a lot of running and biking, every now and then entering some pretty crazy endurance events like ultramarathons, Ironman triathlons, and adventure races. A GPS receiver can make a pretty good training partner: You can use it for lots of things besides helping you avoid getting lost. This chapter is for athletes who exercise outside in the fresh air (sorry, no gym tips) and want to know how to incorporate GPS receivers into their workouts. Observant readers will notice more than ten tips in this chapter. It's your bonus for getting to the end of the book (and paying attention).

General GPS Tips for Athletes

GPS tips in this chapter apply to a number of different sports:

✔ Different uses for GPS when exercising

✔ GPS limitations while training

✔ Carrying a GPS receiver

Using a GPS receiver for training

A GPS receiver not only helps you successfully get between Point A and Point B but is also handy for staying found. These tips apply to almost any sport:

✔ **Measure distances over known courses:** Instead of guessing the course or route length, you can use a GPS receiver to measure the distance with a fair amount of accuracy.

✔ **Better understand the elevation of courses:** Elevation data can give you a more accurate sense of how flat or hilly a course really is. Even if your GPS receiver doesn't have a barometric altimeter (which is required for more precise altitude measurement), the elevation data associated with recorded tracks gives you a ballpark idea of how steep a course is.

✔ **Better understand speed:** Your GPS receiver has a trip computer that provides information about your maximum, minimum, and average speed. By analyzing track data, you can measure your speed over individual sections of a course.

✔ **Discover new courses:** Uploading recorded tracks to an aerial photo or topographic map shows you where you've been and can also reveal nearby roads or trails that you didn't know about.

Your GPS receiver can play a few roles as an electronic training partner:

✔ **Data logger:** In this mode, the GPS receiver records data that you process when you get back home. You download the data to your PC and a program that analyzes the track log. While you're working out, you never really look at the GPS receiver (unless you get lost, of course).

You can use any general purpose GPS receiver as a data logger. I like the Garmin Geko series because they're small, lightweight, inexpensive (the 201 model is under $140) and easy to carry. (Avoid the Geko 101 because it can't interface to a computer, which means you can't analyze track logs.)

When you're logging data, follow these rules:

• *Lock sufficient satellites:* Always make sure your GPS receiver has a lock on at least four satellites (the minimum you need for a good 3-D fix) before you start your workout.

• *Start clean:* Before you start, clear the active track log. When you're finished working out, immediately turn off the GPS receiver.

Always download the active log to your computer first before saving it in the GPS receiver. Some GPS receivers remove the track date and time data or compress the number of tracks when you save a track log.

✔ **Coach:** In this mode, you use the GPS receiver to give you immediate feedback while you're working out. It's still logging track data, but you're looking at the screen, checking your speed, distance, and time. Several GPS receivers on the market are specifically designed to perform as a workout coach; I discuss these models in this chapter.

Don't use your GPS receiver's battery saver mode if you're using your GPS receiver to record tracks while you're working out. The accuracy of your tracks will be diminished because satellite data is received less often. Use rechargeable batteries instead.

Aside from a GPS receiver and a cable to download the collected data to a computer (see Chapter 9 to read how), you also need software so you can analyze your performance based on the tracks that have been recorded. Some possibilities include

- ✔ **Endless Pursuit** (www.endlesspursuit.com)**:** This Web-hosted, work-out-logging product is designed specifically for athletes. I review this in the section, "Endless Pursuit."

- ✔ **TopoFusion** (www.topofusion.com)**:** Although this mapping program wasn't designed primarily to log workouts, its authors include features so an athlete better understands his or her performance over a set course by analyzing track data, including moving, stopped, uphill, down-hill, and flat time; up/down/flat distance; average uphill/downhill grade; and maximum speed. A recent beta version of the program included an athlete's logbook and difficulty-and-effort indices for record tracks. This program, reasonably priced at $40, is turning into one of my favorite log-ging tools.

- ✔ **GPS utility programs:** Two shareware programs — GPS Utility (www.gpsu.co.uk) and GARtrip (www.gartrip.de) — are general-purpose GPS tools but have features for analyzing track logs. Both programs have features that examine distance, speed, and time data. Registered ver-sions are available for under $50.

- ✔ **Spreadsheets:** Because track data can be exported into comma- or tab-delimited text files (see Chapter 9 for a list of GPS conversion utilities, with some tips on using them), if you know your way around a spread-sheet program such as Microsoft Excel, it's pretty easy to write your own formulas and macros to analyze the data that you collect.

GPS receiver limitations for training

Before you start training with a GPS receiver, don't expect precise accuracy of the receiver all the time. Speed and distance measurements are based on exact position data; if the location coordinates the GPS receiver is reporting aren't accurate, the speed and distance data isn't accurate, either.

The main cause of inaccurate GPS data is poor satellite signal reception. When you train under heavy tree canopies, in canyons (whether natural or the urban type from tall buildings), or anywhere satellite signals are obstructed, your speed and distance data isn't going as accurate as if you had a clear sky.

To me, this isn't critical. The data from my GPS receiver is far more accurate than guessing how far and how fast I've gone. I treat a GPS receiver as simply another tool that gives me training data to process so I can fine-tune my workouts and performance, just like using a watch or a heart-rate monitor.

Here are a few ways to address GPS accuracy issues for training:

- **Repeat and average:** If you're measuring a specific running or biking course, do it several times and average the results to compensate for any GPS inaccuracies.

- **Watch for breaks:** Watch for any possible breaks in satellite coverage on the course that might affect accuracy. This is usually easy to spot because track points displayed on a map will suddenly be off-course and are easily distinguished by jagged lines.

How to carry your GPS receiver on foot

If you use a GPS receiver for your outdoor workouts, one of your biggest decisions will be how to carry the GPS receiver. The simplest way is just to hold it in your hand, if it's free. Of the number of other different ways to carry a GPS receiver (which I discuss next), the best carry methods will

- **Provide optimal GPS satellite signal reception:** Where you work out might dictate how you carry your GPS receiver. If you live on the plains (flat) without any trees and have excellent satellite reception, you have more options than in the Pacific Northwest (heavy tree canopies).

- **Be comfortable:** Carrying a GPS receiver should not distract you from your workout. However you carry it, it should be comfortable, and you really shouldn't notice carrying or wearing it.

Here are some different ways to carry a GPS receiver while working out. How you carry a GPS receiver usually ends up being a personal preference. Try a few of these methods to see which one works best for you.

Armbands

Armbands, especially with smaller, lightweight GPS receivers, are one of my favorite forms of no-hands carry. An *armband* is simply a GPS receiver case mounted to an adjustable elastic band.

When worn on the upper arm, the GPS receiver isn't blocked by your body as much as wearing the receiver at your waist, which means better satellite signal reception. In areas without many sky obstructions, armbands can also be worn on your forearm, so you can look at the screen while you exercise.

I use an armband with a plastic case that's produced by Endless Pursuit (www.endlesspursuit.com). The case fits a Garmin Geko like a glove. After you adjust the elastic band, it's hard to tell you're wearing it. (See Figure 23-1 for an illustration of the armband.)

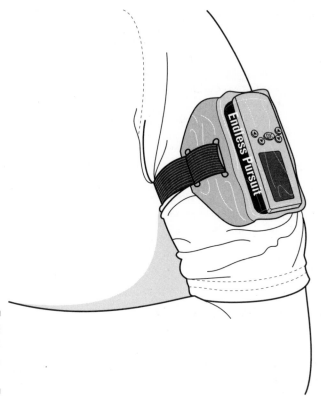

Figure 23-1:
Carry a GPS
receiver in
an armband.

Not many armbands are built for small and mid-sized GPS receivers. Look for armbands designed for Family Radio Service (FRS) radios. If you're handy with a sewing machine (or know someone who is), it's relatively easy to make an armband out of nylon, elastic, and Velcro for your GPS receiver.

Cases, belts, pockets, and packs

Most GPS receiver cases have a loop on the back to hold the case on a belt.

If you're wearing shorts or tights and don't have a belt, waist packs for carrying a radio or a cassette/CD player are an option. These packs can accommodate larger GPS receivers. They're not very noticeable when you're working out because they're designed not to bounce much. Small fanny packs and waist packs that carry water bottles also carry a GPS receiver.

If the GPS receiver is small, try carrying it in your front pants pocket. I've carried a Garmin Geko while running and cross-country skiing in trail-running shorts and tights with zipper pockets. Although satellite reception is sometimes lost while under heavy tree cover, the GPS receiver records track data as long as I have a mostly clear view of the sky.

The main disadvantage to carrying your GPS receiver on or below your waist is that it's not the best place for satellite reception. There's a good chance that you'll lose the signal in areas with reduced satellite coverage.

If you use a hydration pack or a lightweight backpack, you can get your GPS higher for better satellite reception by mounting the case either on one of the front shoulder straps or putting the GPS receiver in the upper, top pocket of your backpack. (It isn't as accessible in the backpack pocket but should get good satellite reception.)

Water bottle hand straps

Many trail and ultramarathon runners run with water bottles in their hands, using special hand strap products that fit on a water bottle so you aren't always clutching the bottle and can relax your hands. (FastDraw by Ultimate Direction is one; see `www.ultimatedirection.com`.) I've seen trail runners with small GPS receiver cases mounted to these hand straps. Just add some Velcro to the GPS receiver case and the hand strap, and you're ready to go.

GPS Products for Athletes

Several GPS products on the market are specifically designed for athletes. These products offer athletes specialized features that normally aren't found in general purpose GPS hardware and software.

Endless Pursuit

Endless Pursuit is an Internet-based service that allows athletes to track their training on the Web. The service is based on using a Garmin or Magellan GPS receiver to collect data about your workout and then uploading the GPS data to a Web site through your browser. After the site collects waypoint and track data of a workout, it produces 40 statistics and 14 charts. (Sample results are shown in Figure 23-2.) You can review workout information such as

 ✔ Total time elapsed (at motion and at rest)

 ✔ Distance (uphill, downhill, and flat)

 ✔ Altitude

 ✔ Maximum and average speed (including uphill, downhill, and flat)

 ✔ Average pace

 ✔ Calories expended

 ✔ Power generated in watts

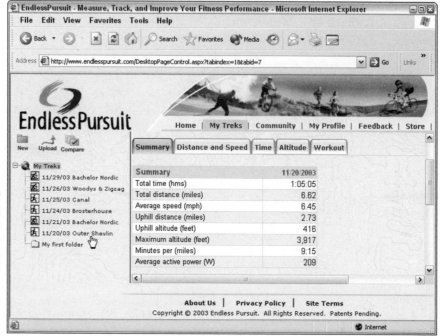

Figure 23-2:
The Endless
Pursuit Web
site bases
workout
information
on GPS
data.

The Web site also serves as cumulative training log for all your workouts. After
you sign in, a monthly calendar lists all your workouts by day, showing the
type of activity, what time of day you worked out, distance, and total elapsed
time (see Figure 23-3). Click a previous workout to display all the details about
the session, including aerial photographs and topographic maps of your route.
You can even compare workouts to see how you've improved.

Check the community section at the Web site where folks can post their
workout data for anyone who has Internet access. All the published workouts
(or *treks,* as Endless Pursuit calls them) are indexed. For example, you can do
a search for all the mountain bike rides in Central Oregon and get maps of
routes, trail reviews, and even download the waypoints and tracks associated
with the trek directly to your GPS receiver.

Endless Pursuit is easy to use and well designed. The data that it provides
goes far beyond the distance, speed, and time information from a normal GPS
receiver. (Note the add-on option to integrate heart-rate monitor data with
your GPS data.) Although just about any outdoor athlete can benefit from
Endless Pursuit, it's especially well suited for mountain and road bikers, runners, and triathletes.

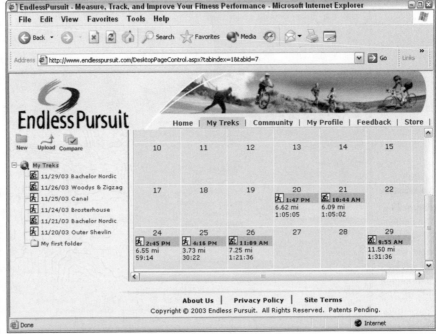

Figure 23-3:
Log your
workouts
with a
calendar
from
Endless
Pursuit.

To fully use the site, purchase a Performance Pass ($149), which allows you to store data for up to 150 workouts; you can delete old ones to free up space. Endless Pursuit also offers a bundled package priced at $299 that includes a Performance Pass, GPS receiver, cable, armband, and bike mount that provides everything you need to start logging GPS data.

You can register for a free trial of Endless Pursuit and read more about the service by visiting www.endlesspursuit.com.

Timex Speed + Distance/Bodylink

The Timex Speed + Distance system is a cigarette pack-size GPS receiver that straps on your arm and transmits data to a special wristwatch. You can look at your watch and see how far you've gone and how fast you're going.

Timex updated the system in 2003, adding more components and calling it *Bodylink*. In addition to the GPS receiver and watch, the Bodylink includes a heart-rate monitor (the GPS receiver, watch, and heart-rate monitor are shown in Figure 23-4) and a data recorder that collects data from both the GPS receiver and the heart-rate monitor. You can connect the data recorder to your personal computer to upload your workout data and analyze it with the included software.

Figure 23-4:
Timex
Bodylink
GPS
receiver,
heart-rate
monitor, and
watch.

This is pretty close to being the Holy Grail for athletes who want performance data. Time, speed, distance, and heart-rate data can be viewed with training software to understand your fitness and the effectiveness of your workouts.

You can't use Bodylink for navigation. Your current location doesn't appear on the watch, and the system doesn't support tracks and waypoints. (Timex might add navigation capabilities to future models.) To find different Bodylink models, which retail between $250 and $300, go to www.timex.com.

Garmin Forerunner 201

Garmin's *Forerunner 201* is a GPS receiver primarily for runners: The receiver looks like an oversized watch and is designed to wear on your wrist. (The Forerunner 201 is shown in Figure 23-5.) Some of its features include

- ✔ Time (overall and lap), speed (current and average), and distance display
- ✔ Waypoint and track log support
- ✔ Stored workout history
- ✔ Pace and calories-expended information
- ✔ Large, easy-to-read screen
- ✔ Fifteen-hour, rechargeable lithium ion (Li-Ion) battery
- ✔ PC interface and training log software

Unlike the Timex Bodylink system (which Garmin originally provided the technology for), the Forerunner's GPS receiver is built into the watch: It doesn't require a separate armband unit.

The Forerunner 201 doesn't support a heart-rate monitor, but I wouldn't be too surprised if future versions will incorporate heart-rate monitor technology.

Figure 23-5:
The Garmin
Forerunner
201 GPS
receiver.

I'm impressed with the Forerunner 201's performance, especially for a first generation entry in this market. The satellite reception has been good, and its data is useful for understanding biking, running, and skiing workouts. (Garmin recently released the Forerunner 101, a cheaper model that runs on AAA batteries. I'd avoid this product because it doesn't have a PC interface, which means that you can't download and analyze your track data nor upgrade the firmware.)

The Forerunner 201 has a suggested retail price of $160. To find out more about product specifications and to download the user manual, go to `www.garmin.com/products/forerunner201`. There's also a great e-mail list devoted to the product that can be accessed at `http://groups.yahoo.com/group/GarminF`.

GPS Tips for Specific Sports

You can use a GPS receiver for almost any type of outdoor sport where you're in motion. Here's how GPS fits into the context of several specific sports.

GPS for cyclists

If you're a road cyclist or mountain biker, a GPS receiver can replace your bike computer because it can display time, speed, and distance information. Most GPS receiver manufacturers make bike mounts for their handheld models; these mounts also fit on motorcycle and snowmobile handlebars.

The main advantages of using a GPS receiver for biking are that it

✔ Doesn't need calibrating

✔ Is easy to switch between different bikes

✔ Has navigation features including maps (if supported)

Compared with bike computers, GPS receivers have a few disadvantages:

✔ Shorter battery life

✔ Higher price

✔ Larger size

✔ Accuracy affected by tree cover

If you just want to use your GPS receiver for logging data, such as recording trail routes under heavy tree cover, try stowing your GPS receiver in a backpack and mounting an external antenna on the top of your bike helmet, threading the antenna cable out the back of the helmet and into the pack where it's plugged in to the GPS receiver. It might sound and look geeky, but a setup like this gives you optimum satellite reception. Just make sure that the antenna cable is tucked in and secured so it doesn't catch on a tree branch.

Some Garmin GPS receivers, notably the eTrex models when used with Garmin bike mounts, can intermittently shut down when biking on rough terrain. Your GPS receiver probably isn't defective. The battery compartment of the eTrex doesn't provide a snug fit for the batteries; vibration can jostle the batteries around, causing power loss. If this happens, tape the batteries together or use a small piece of cardboard as a shim to fill the extra space.

GPS for golfers

Because golf is all about distance and getting a ball from Point A to Point B in the least number of strokes, GPS offers some interesting possibilities.

The simplest way to use GPS in golf is to bring your GPS receiver with you the next time you play and mark the center of greens as waypoints. When you play the course again, you can select the waypoints for a pretty good idea of the distance to the next green and use that information when selecting an appropriate club. (GPS receivers and devices like laser range finders aren't allowed in tournament play — and some of your purist golf partners might not approve of electronics for casual play.)

Some golf courses are on the GPS bandwagon, offering cart-based computers that display color maps; the distance to the greens, holes, and hazards; pro tips; and other information. As an example, visit www.riteconcepts.com to see a demonstration of its OnCourse GPS product.

A number of personal GPS products are developed specifically for golfers:

- ✔ **Suunto G9:** Suunto makes an oversize watch that's a GPS receiver that measures your strokes and stores game statistics (www.suunto.com).
- ✔ **SkyGolf:** SkyGolf sells a standalone GPS golf computer, the SG2 Personal Digital Caddie (www.skygolfgps.com).
- ✔ **PDA software:** A number of popular golf software packages come bundled with a GPS receiver for Pocket PC and Palm PDAs, including
    - • StarCaddy: www.starcaddy.com
    - • GolfPS: www.golfps.com

GPS golf devices can slow down the game while players fiddle with their electronic gadgets. If you use a GPS golf device, remember to be courteous to other players and not get too engrossed with your nonregulation helper.

GPS for paddlers and rowers

For athletes who row or paddle for fitness or in competitions, a GPS receiver provides a quick and easy way to gauge distance and speed without installing a speedometer in your boat; they're also cheaper than venturi speedometers.

I've seen GPS receiver cases mounted to canoes, kayaks, and rowing shells using Velcro, duct tape, webbing, and custom-made fiberglass holders, all optimally placed to let the athlete read the screen and click buttons.

Obviously, make sure that your GPS receiver stays dry. Your GPS receiver should have an IPX 7 rating (submersible for 30 minutes in one meter of water). Regardless of the rating, I use a waterproof bag. Voyageur bags (one is shown in Figure 23-6), priced under $25, are durable, watertight, and buoyant; it's easy to see the screen and use the receiver while it's in the bag. You can get information on the Voyageur product line by visiting http://voyageur-gear.com.

Windsurfing and GPS

GPS receivers are popular in windsurfing. Windsurfers use GPS receivers in waterproof bags to measure maximum speed and record tracks. Dennis Cornhill wrote a nice Excel spreadsheet for analyzing windsurfing track logs: www.geocities.com/denniscornhill/SailTrack.html.

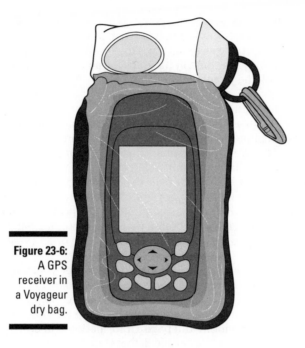

Figure 23-6:
A GPS
receiver in
a Voyageur
dry bag.

If you're using a GPS receiver in any type of watercraft, tether the GPS receiver (or its case or bag) to yourself or the boat. This is good insurance against your receiver swimming to the bottom.

GPS for race directors

If you're organizing and promoting a race with running, cycling, cross-country skiing, or just about any other activity that follows a set course, a GPS receiver can be a handy tool. With it you can

- ✔ Measure the course distance.
- ✔ Create a map of the course by overlaying tracks on an aerial photo or topographic map.
- ✔ Use waypoints to mark the precise locations of aid stations.
- ✔ Publish the course track log on the Internet for athletes with GPS receivers who want to train on the course before the race.

One of my favorite programs for race planning is TopoFusion (www.topofusion. com; read more about this in Chapter 14). It imports waypoints and tracks from GPS receivers and displays them on aerial photos and topographic maps downloaded from TerraServer-USA. (Read all about TerraServer-USA in Chapter 20.) Its PhotoFusion feature makes it excellent for promoting races on the Internet.

If you bring a digital camera while recording course information with your GPS receiver, you can take photos at key points (such as intersections, extreme terrain, aid stations, or scenic views). Afterwards, TopoFusion associates the time you took the photo with time data in the track log and gives you the coordinates where you took the picture.

TopoFusion can automatically generate a Web page that shows the recorded tracks overlaid on both an aerial photo and topographic map. Wherever you stopped and took a photo with your digital camera, TopoFusion places a camera icon at that location on the map. (Just make sure your digital camera clock is synced with the time on your GPS receiver.) When someone views the Web page and moves the cursor over the camera icon, a thumbnail image of the photo is displayed in the upper-right corner of the window. If a camera icon on the map is clicked, the full-sized photo is displayed. Because athletes like to have as much information about a race ahead of time, participants will love you if you add this to a Web site promoting a race or an event.

TopoFusion does all the HTML and JavaScript coding for you; you don't need to know anything about developing a Web page. Just upload all the digital photos and the files TopoFusion created to a Web server, and you've got an instant online information source and interactive map for your race. If you can code HTML, you can modify the page's information and appearance.

Index

FOR DUMMIES®

PERSONAL FINANCE

0-7645-5231-7

0-7645-2431-3

0-7645-5331-3

Also available:

Estate Planning For Dummies
(0-7645-5501-4)
401(k)s For Dummies
(0-7645-5468-9)
Frugal Living For Dummies
(0-7645-5403-4)
Microsoft Money "X" For Dummies
(0-7645-1689-2)
Mutual Funds For Dummies
(0-7645-5329-1)

Personal Bankruptcy For Dummies
(0-7645-5498-0)
Quicken "X" For Dummies
(0-7645-1666-3)
Stock Investing For Dummies
(0-7645-5411-5)
Taxes For Dummies 2003
(0-7645-5475-1)

BUSINESS & CAREERS

0-7645-5314-3

0-7645-5307-0

0-7645-5471-9

Also available:

Business Plans Kit For Dummies
(0-7645-5365-8)
Consulting For Dummies
(0-7645-5034-9)
Cool Careers For Dummies
(0-7645-5345-3)
Human Resources Kit For Dummies
(0-7645-5131-0)
Managing For Dummies
(1-5688-4858-7)

QuickBooks All-in-One Desk Reference For Dummies
(0-7645-1963-8)
Selling For Dummies
(0-7645-5363-1)
Small Business Kit For Dummies
(0-7645-5093-4)
Starting an eBay Business For Dummies
(0-7645-1547-0)

HEALTH, SPORTS & FITNESS

0-7645-5167-1

0-7645-5146-9

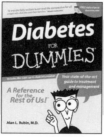

0-7645-5154-X

Also available:

Controlling Cholesterol For Dummies
(0-7645-5440-9)
Dieting For Dummies
(0-7645-5126-4)
High Blood Pressure For Dummies
(0-7645-5424-7)
Martial Arts For Dummies
(0-7645-5358-5)
Menopause For Dummies
(0-7645-5458-1)

Nutrition For Dummies
(0-7645-5180-9)
Power Yoga For Dummies
(0-7645-5342-9)
Thyroid For Dummies
(0-7645-5385-2)
Weight Training For Dummies
(0-7645-5168-X)
Yoga For Dummies
(0-7645-5117-5)

Available wherever books are sold.
Go to www.dummies.com or call 1-877-762-2974 to order direct.

FOR DUMMIES®

A world of resources to help you grow

HOME, GARDEN & HOBBIES

Feng Shui
0-7645-5295-3

Gardening
0-7645-5130-2

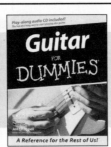

Guitar
0-7645-5106-X

FOOD & WINE

Cooking
0-7645-5250-3

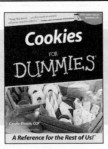

Cookies
0-7645-5390-9

Wine
0-7645-5114-0

TRAVEL

Italy
0-7645-5453-0

Hawaii
0-7645-5438-7

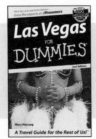

Las Vegas
0-7645-5448-4

Available wherever books are sold. Go to www.dummies.com or call 1-877-762-2974 to order direct.

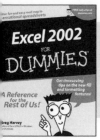

FOR DUMMIES

Helping you expand your horizons and realize your potential

INTERNET

The Internet FOR DUMMIES
0-7645-0894-6

The Internet ALL-IN-ONE DESK REFERENCE FOR DUMMIES
0-7645-1659-0

eBay FOR DUMMIES
0-7645-1642-6

Also available:

America Online 7.0 For Dummies
(0-7645-1624-8)

Genealogy Online For Dummies
(0-7645-0807-5)

The Internet All-in-One Desk Reference For Dummies
(0-7645-1659-0)

Internet Explorer 6 For Dummies
(0-7645-1344-3)

The Internet For Dummies Quick Reference
(0-7645-1645-0)

Internet Privacy For Dummies
(0-7645-0846-6)

Researching Online For Dummies
(0-7645-0546-7)

Starting an Online Business For Dummies
(0-7645-1655-8)

DIGITAL MEDIA

Digital Photography FOR DUMMIES
0-7645-1664-7

Photoshop Elements 2 FOR DUMMIES
0-7645-1675-2

Digital Video FOR DUMMIES
0-7645-0806-7

Also available:

CD and DVD Recording For Dummies
(0-7645-1627-2)

Digital Photography All-in-One Desk Reference For Dummies
(0-7645-1800-3)

Digital Photography For Dummies Quick Reference
(0-7645-0750-8)

Home Recording for Musicians For Dummies
(0-7645-1634-5)

MP3 For Dummies
(0-7645-0858-X)

Paint Shop Pro "X" For Dummies
(0-7645-2440-2)

Photo Retouching & Restoration For Dummies
(0-7645-1662-0)

Scanners For Dummies
(0-7645-0783-4)

GRAPHICS

PowerPoint 2002 FOR DUMMIES
0-7645-0817-2

Photoshop 7 FOR DUMMIES
0-7645-1651-5

Macromedia Flash MX FOR DUMMIES
0-7645-0895-4

Also available:

Adobe Acrobat 5 PDF For Dummies
(0-7645-1652-3)

Fireworks 4 For Dummies
(0-7645-0804-0)

Illustrator 10 For Dummies
(0-7645-3636-2)

QuarkXPress 5 For Dummies
(0-7645-0643-9)

Visio 2000 For Dummies
(0-7645-0635-8)

FOR DUMMIES®

The advice and explanations you need to succeed

ELF-HELP, SPIRITUALITY & RELIGION

0-7645-5302-X

0-7645-5418-2

0-7645-5264-3

Also available:

The Bible For Dummies
(0-7645-5296-1)

Buddhism For Dummies
(0-7645-5359-3)

Christian Prayer For Dummies
(0-7645-5500-6)

Dating For Dummies
(0-7645-5072-1)

Judaism For Dummies
(0-7645-5299-6)

Potty Training For Dummies
(0-7645-5417-4)

Pregnancy For Dummies
(0-7645-5074-8)

Rekindling Romance For Dummies
(0-7645-5303-8)

Spirituality For Dummies
(0-7645-5298-8)

Weddings For Dummies
(0-7645-5055-1)

TS

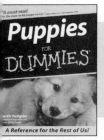

0-7645-5255-4

0-7645-5286-4

0-7645-5275-9

Also available:

Labrador Retrievers For Dummies
(0-7645-5281-3)

Aquariums For Dummies
(0-7645-5156-6)

Birds For Dummies
(0-7645-5139-6)

Dogs For Dummies
(0-7645-5274-0)

Ferrets For Dummies
(0-7645-5259-7)

German Shepherds For Dummies
(0-7645-5280-5)

Golden Retrievers For Dummies
(0-7645-5267-8)

Horses For Dummies
(0-7645-5138-8)

Jack Russell Terriers For Dummies
(0-7645-5268-6)

Puppies Raising & Training Diary For Dummies
(0-7645-0876-8)

UCATION & TEST PREPARATION

0-7645-5194-9

0-7645-5325-9

0-7645-5210-4

Also available:

Chemistry For Dummies
(0-7645-5430-1)

English Grammar For Dummies
(0-7645-5322-4)

French For Dummies
(0-7645-5193-0)

The GMAT For Dummies
(0-7645-5251-1)

Inglés Para Dummies
(0-7645-5427-1)

Italian For Dummies
(0-7645-5196-5)

Research Papers For Dummies
(0-7645-5426-3)

The SAT I For Dummies
(0-7645-5472-7)

U.S. History For Dummies
(0-7645-5249-X)

World History For Dummies
(0-7645-5242-2)

Available wherever books are sold. Go to www.dummies.com or call 1-877-762-2974 to order direct.